FICTIONS *of* GENDER

MCGILL-QUEEN'S AZRIELI INSTITUTE OF ISRAEL STUDIES SERIES

Books in the McGill-Queen's Azrieli Institute of Israel Studies Series reflect the disciplinary and methodological diversity that characterizes the field of Israel studies. Accordingly, the editorial board welcomes proposals for books that report on original research from all areas of scholarly inquiry related to the study of modern Israel, including fine arts, history, literature, translation studies, sociology, political science, law, religious studies, and beyond. The series, which is committed to academic excellence, encompasses comparative works that situate Israel in broader international and cross-national frameworks and works that apply a critical lens.

1 Fictions of Gender
   Women, Femininity,
   and the Zionist Imagination
   Orian Zakai

FICTIONS
of
GENDER

Women, Femininity, and
the Zionist Imagination

ORIAN ZAKAI

McGILL-QUEEN'S UNIVERSITY PRESS

Montreal & Kingston | London | Chicago

ISBN 978-0-2280-1705-9 (cloth)
ISBN 978-0-2280-1706-6 (paper)
ISBN 978-0-2280-1827-8 (ePDF)
ISBN 978-0-2280-1828-5 (ePUB)

Legal deposit second quarter 2023
Bibliothèque nationale du Québec

Printed in Canada on acid-free paper that is 100% ancient forest free
(100% post-consumer recycled), processed chlorine free

We acknowledge the support of the Canada Council for the Arts.
Nous remercions le Conseil des arts du Canada de son soutien.

LIBRARY AND ARCHIVES CANADA CATALOGUING IN PUBLICATION

Title: Fictions of gender : women, femininity, and the Zionist imagination /
    Orian Zakai.
Names: Zakai, Orian, 1974– author.
Description: Series statement: McGill-Queen's Azrieli Institute of Israel Studies
    series ; 1 | Includes bibliographical references and index.
Identifiers: Canadiana (print) 20230147674 | Canadiana (ebook) 20230147712
    ISBN 9780228017066 (paper) | ISBN 9780228017059 (cloth)
    ISBN 9780228018278 (ePDF) | ISBN 9780228018285 (ePUB)
Subjects: LCSH: Hebrew literature—Women authors—History and criticism.
    LCSH: Hebrew literature, Modern—19th century—History and criticism.
    LCSH: Hebrew literature, Modern—20th century—History and criticism.
    LCSH: Jewish women authors—19th century. | LCSH: Jewish women authors—
    20th century. | LCSH: Women in literature. | LCSH: Feminism in literature.
    LCSH: Feminism—Israel. | LCSH: Zionism.
Classification: LCC PJ5020 .Z35 2023 | DDC 892.409/3522—dc23

TO BRENDA

CONTENTS

Figures   ix

Acknowledgments   xi

INTRODUCTION
Reading from the Rift: Zionism,
Feminism, and Women's Writing   3

1

A TALE OF TWO SISTERS
Women, Femininity, and the National-Patriarchal Home   22

2

GENDERED PLOTS
Zionist Women Writers and the Space of the Indigenous Other   49

3

THE NATIONAL CAREGIVER
Gender and Ethnicity in Zionist Women's Writing   80

4

METAPHORS OF DIMINISHMENT
From Women's Writing to National Security   115

EPILOGUE
The Father, the Daughter, and the Question of the *Korban*   145

Notes   153

Index   187

FIGURES

0.1 Dora Pickman, Ramat Yohanan, 1944. Author's family photo. 13

0.2 Dora Pickman, celebration for the holiday of Shavu'ot, 1944. Author's family photo. 13

0.3 Kibbutz members working in the stone quarry of Kibbutz Ein Harod, 1941. Photograph by Zoltan Kluger. 14

4.1 Yemenite girl at the Ayanot Agricultural School from Ada Mimon (Fishman), *Hamishim shnot tnu'at ha-po'alot, 1904–1954* (Tel Aviv: Am Oved, 1958). 129

4.2 Still from Otto Preminger's *Exodus*, 1960. 135

ACKNOWLEDGMENTS

The writing of this book, which started as a dissertation at the University of Michigan, spanned over a decade of thinking, doubting, deliberating, drafting, and revising – processes that are often lonely experiences. As I conclude this project, however, it is comforting and humbling to recognize with gratitude how many others were in fact present for me all this time, and how much I owe to their generosity and grace.

I am immensely grateful to my dissertation advisor Carol Bardenstein for her patient and warm mentorship and her unwavering faith in my project. Carol's uncompromising critical insights have driven me to expand my analytical horizons, and to constantly strive for more rigorous, original, and precise thinking. I thank Ruth Tsoffar for inspiring conversations, for her attentive reading and perceptive commentary on my work, and, in particular, for being a guide and a model in the process of opening up texts and investigating the possibilities that they hold. I thank Shachar Pinsker for his advice and support, which were invaluable in initiating me as a scholar of Hebrew literature. I feel fortunate for having worked with such a kind and generous mentor. I would like to extend my deep gratitude to Anton Shammas, whose insightful remarks at the early stages of writing have shaped my overall approach to the politics and poetics of texts. I hope I have managed to follow Anton's advice and read the texts of the past with acute awareness of the present.

Several institutes, forums, and funds have supported this project financially and academically. I am grateful to the Frankel Institute for Advanced Judaic Studies at the University of Michigan for a yearlong post-doctoral fellowship, and fruitful discussions with the remarkable 2012–13 cohort of institute fellows led brilliantly by Jonathan Freedman and Deborah Dash-Moore. My gratitude also goes to the Hadassah Brandeis Institute for hosting me as a Helen Gartner Hammer scholar-in-residence and for a research award that allowed me to make significant progress in this study. I am thankful for research grants and awards from the University of Michigan, Middlebury College, and George Washington University that allowed me to conduct invaluable research in Israel. I am most grateful to McGill-Queen's University Press, especially to the acquisition editor Richard Ratzlaff, managing editor Kathleen Fraser, and copy editor Sara Penn for their professionalism and care in bringing this book to light. I also thank the two anonymous reviewers for their insightful remarks on my work. This book could not have been accomplished without the support of colleagues at the Department of Classical and Near Eastern Languages and Civilizations at George Washington University who are the best supportive and kind group of colleagues one can wish for, and who took great care to allow me time to research and write. My gratitude is especially extended to my generous and wise mentors Christopher Rollston and Eric Cline. I would also like to thank students in my course Gender and Sexuality in Israel for insightful conversations that have constantly prompted me to refresh and sharpen my thought process on the issues at stake in this book. I am grateful to the many dedicated archivists at the Central Zionist Archive in Jerusalem, the Gnazim Institute, Beit Ariela, and the Rishon Le-Zion Archive for their help in accessing essential research materials.

I would not have survived the long and lonely process of research and writing without friends and colleagues, who not only offered gracious and thoughtful commentary on chapters of this book, but also provided mental support in difficult moments of self-doubt and uncertainty. I am immensely indebted to Ilana Szobel for her generous mentorship, deep engagement with my work, and priceless words of encouragement. I am grateful to Adi Baruch for decades of true friendship and emotional nurturing, to Efrat Bloom for her sensitive remarks on my work, for her invaluable help with translations, and for her warmth and generosity, to Yanay Israeli for the depth of his thinking and the kindness of his soul, to Maayan Eitan for intellectually stimulating conversations and emotional space, and to Sara Feldman for her collegiality and support.

I am grateful to my parents Avi and Michal Zakai for their unwavering love, for their faith in me, and for their incredible patience. Finally, my wife and partner Brenda McLain not only endured me at moments of frustration and anxiety, as well as during long hours of presence-absence while I was occupied with writing, but she has also been an astute commentator on my work and a constant source of inspiration whose layered and nuanced thinking deeply affected my own. I cannot fathom the completion of this book without our sessions of reading the chapters out loud which made it possible for me to imagine my words finding a reader. I am grateful and fortunate to have such a beautiful, brilliant soul in my corner.

FICTIONS *of* GENDER

INTRODUCTION

READING FROM THE RIFT
Zionism, Feminism, and Women's Writing

———

When I began working on this project, I found myself, time and again, seated at the lunch table of the senior citizens – or, *vatikim* in Hebrew, meaning the veterans or the founders' generation – in the communal dining room of the kibbutz where my mother was born and raised. I did not come there to do research for my project. At the time, I did not really conceive of my own lineage as related to my study of Zionist women's writing. I was spending a year of "study abroad" at home. It was likely that this would be the last time I get to see my maternal grandmother, and so my mother and I travelled often during that year to visit with her in the Upper Galilee kibbutz. My grandmother was never a very talkative woman, and, now in her nineties, she has sunk into an almost permanent silence. However, her women friends, with whom she had shared meals for over seventy years, were excited about my project. They smiled with satisfied recognition when I mentioned a publication or a public figure they remembered from their youth. They told me of instances of sexual harassment in the Labor movement, of discrimination against women in the *Palmah*,[1] and of the feeling that their contributions as women were going unrecognized by the official history of Zionism. Their stories resonated with what I read in the scholarship at the time, stories of ideological commitment alongside gendered frustration and disappointment.

Yet, while the conversations with the veteran women "pioneers" attracted me,[2] I was already aware of the friction between the direction of my work and the nostalgic origin story I was recovering on these journeys back to the kibbutz. By now, I knew that the story of my grandparents and their friends who had removed basalt rocks from the territory at the foot of the

Golan Heights to prepare the grounds for what is now a flourishing kibbutz was part of a different history than the one I had learned in school. What I once learned in my youth to be a story of sacrifice and glory, I now thought of as one of colonization and the construction of Eurocentric hegemony in Palestine. The establishment of kibbutz Shamir in 1944 was part of the Zionist effort to claim the area called the "Finger of the Galilee" for the future Jewish state. The residents of the nearby villages of Al-Muftakhira, Al-Dawara, Al Hamra and Khiyam Al-Walid were displaced during the 1948 War, and like most of the Galilee's villagers, were not allowed to repatriate after the war.[3] The home itself, as Hagar Kotef writes in a recent volume, was a tool "of destruction and expulsion" inhabited by "lives and selves whose very being is a form of injury."[4]

By the time I was visiting my grandmother in the 2000s, the story of my grandparents was no longer a heroic story for me. Now, I thought of it as the story of a small elite group of settlers that needed to be critically revaluated in light of the disastrous implications it had for others who had been, and are, part of this space. As my feminist consciousness became more and more bound with the critique of nationalism, colonialism, and racism, the question of how to approach the stories of the women founders of the kibbutz, like the question of how to read the writings of early Zionist women from a feminist point of view, became tantamount to the question of who I am as a woman and as a feminist vis-à-vis the history of my family, my ethnic group, and my national belonging.

This book offers an updated feminist approach to Zionism through the lens of early Zionist women's writing; it asks not only how women positioned themselves within the androcentric Zionist space, as previous studies have done,[5] but also how their national self-making was imbricated into the larger systems of ethnocentric nationalism, settler-colonialism, and the constitution of Ashkenazi Jewish hegemony in Israel/Palestine. As such, this book is also a critical interrogation of what I see as the origin story of the Zionist and Israeli feminist consciousness, seeking to confront those who were dubbed "the mothers of Israeli feminism"[6] with the concerns of contemporary global feminism. While the main corpus of this book is the large but rarely studied body of early Zionist women's writing, the questions raised by the contemporary debate about the relationship between women, Zionism, and power are at the core of my investigation. Departing from scholarship that protagonizes the masculine subject in the Zionist narrative and casts women as the antagonists, I refract the Zionist imagination through the dialectic between women as national subjects and femininity as a national trope, as situated within the intersectional dynamics of gender, ethnicity, race, and national identity. In this light, far from being external or marginal to the Zionist project, the story of Zionist women, I argue, points toward depth structures of the early Zionist imagination that are still at play in the cultures and politics of contemporary Israel/Palestine.

Zionist Oedipus: Masculinity, Psychoanalysis, and the Symbolic Family

Gender has long been a productive field of inquiry of Zionist and Hebrew culture, enabling scholars to interrogate the junction between Zionism as a political project of settlement and state building and Zionism as a project of identity invested in forming a new Jewish self, countering what was conceived as a weak and feminized diasporic Jewish identity. Through the lens of gender, scholars have been able to articulate the construction of this new identity in terms of new relationships between the body, place, and culture. Evolving in the last few decades, the body of scholarship on gender and Zionism has predominantly focused on the transformation of Jewish masculinity – from the figure of the effeminate diasporic student of the Torah into the figure of the muscular worker and defender of the Land – postulating this narrative as a constitutive metonym of the Zionist master-narrative as a whole.[7]

While the study of Zionist masculinity has evolved as a vibrant field of inquiry as of the 1990s, the unacknowledged naissance of the research may be traced to two semi-academic essays by Jay Y. Gonen and Lesley Hazleton. Gonen's 1975 attempt at a psychoanalytic critique of Zionism maps the Zionist narrative of return onto the Oedipal drama, by conceptualizing the essential Zionist gesture as a breach of the command of the divine father through which the Zionist sons venture to conquer the body of the "mother-land."[8] Hazleton's 1977 pioneering study *Israeli Women* is considered the first critique of the doctrine of the "myth of equality," which prevailed both the Israeli consciousness and the international image of Israel up until the late 1970s and beyond.[9] According to this "myth," Israeli women enjoyed full gender equality, exemplified by the mandatory conscription of women to the Israeli army, as well as the fact that Israel had a female prime minister (Golda Meir from 1969 to 1974). Against the grain of this popular perception, Hazleton, an American journalist, furnished a critical account of the Israeli patriarchy, drawing on hundreds of interviews with Israeli women. Invoking Gonen's psychoanalytic model of the Zionist desire for the Land as an incestuous drive, she asks:

> But while Zion played Jocasta to the male pioneers' Oedipus, where was the Agamemnon for the women pioneers' Electra? What value could all this libidinous attraction have for them? What archetypical images could it arouse in a woman's mind? What role was there for women in this scenario of sons and fathers fertilizing the motherland?[10]

The centrality of psychoanalysis in this discourse is further underscored in Daniel Boyarin's seminal work on Zionism, psychoanalysis, and masculinity in which he discusses Zionism and psychoanalysis as complementary enterprises facilitating the invention of modern Jewish masculinity, which, against the grain of the older models, conforms Jewish identity to the norms of Western gender stereotypes.[11] In this context, psychoanalysis fleshes out the affinity between the gendered constellation of the heteronormative family and the formation of the nation. Along similar lines, Naomi Seidman decodes the emergence of Hebrew as the national language through what she describes as "the primal scene" in which patrilineal continuity from father to son is enabled through the suppression of the diasporic Yiddish-speaking mother.[12] As Hazleton has observed, women's "dilemmas of desire," to borrow David Biale's term, have little room in this Oedipal drama.[13]

Thus, within this framework, femininity became a category tantamount to Otherness in relation to Zionism, signifying the "negative" in a series of gendered binaries that had undergirded the early Zionist imagination, including land/diaspora, power/weakness, heroism/victimhood, independence/dependence, and so on. While this scholarship offers important insights into the inter-relations between gender, nationalism, and colonialism, I contend that the uniform identification of femininity and women as the Other of the nation has left crucial aspects of Zionist women's investment in Zionism in need of further interpretation. In turn, this scholarly gap funnels the discussion into an insular intra-Jewish-Ashkenazi framework in which Jewish Ashkenazi women are positioned against Jewish Ashkenazi men. Within this framework, the Mizrahi and Palestinian[14] Others of the Zionist project are rendered almost invisible. Consequently, I suggest, the gender-based study of Zionism remains detached from the contemporary sensibilities of global feminism regarding questions of intersectionality and the involvement of Western feminism in nationalism and colonialism.

The "Master Narrative" and the "Mother Narrative"[15]

In her groundbreaking study of the autobiographical writings by early Zionist "women pioneers," Tamar Hess theorizes that in the forgotten writings of these women, "the woman-reader may find … a kind of 'mother's bosom' … the pioneer story, which is the infrastructure of present Israeli identities, changes when it is written with a feminine pen and read by a conscious feminist mind that can draw on its renewed force."[16] Compounding this statement, the opening lines of the book furnish an intimate relationship between the researcher and the object of her study: "In Passover 2000, we drove, Ronnen, Rachel – still a fetus in my womb – and me to kibbutz Dgania, to the archive … we sat in the room, which Hayuta Bossel described as the room where she gave birth to her daughter Hadassah, eighty one years earlier."[17] This powerful point of departure – reading the memories of the woman-pioneer Hayuta Bossel about the birth of her daughter, while the scholar herself is pregnant with her own daughter – charts an emotional-intellectual landscape that, I would argue, is shared by other Israeli feminist scholars who have richly engaged with the creativity and experience of early Zionist women, or, as dubbed by Hess, "the mothers of Israeli feminism."[18] This landscape is perhaps best captured by the title of Hess' book, which cites a poem by the Hebrew poet Rachel Bluwstein, "The Mother's Bosom of Memories," and thus forms a metaphoric kinship between women writers, women scholars, and women readers, geared toward the recovery of a feminist matrilineal lineage as a source of empowerment against the grain of the androcentric Zionist space.

In the historiography of Hebrew women's literature, motherhood serves both as a metaphor and as an important thematic focus. Motherhood appears, for example, in the title of Miron's seminal study of the beginning of Hebrew women's poetry, *Founding Mothers, Stepsisters*.[19] Along the same lines, Pnina Shirav identifies the author Dvora Baron as the "mother of a new tradition in Hebrew literature" and asserts, "We should talk about the mothers of Modern Hebrew literature just as we talk about the fathers of Modern Hebrew literature."[20] Lily Rattok, in the afterward essay of her pioneering anthology of Hebrew women's prose, uses the term "double

birth" to describe the disjointed history of Hebrew women's fiction, marking
the woman author both as a daughter being born as a woman-author and as
a mother giving birth to women's literature.[21] Finally, Tamar Merin, in her
study of Israeli women's literature of the 1950s and 1960s, argues that the
lack of "literary mothers" causes the authors of the early days of the state to
turn to "literary fathers" as a model and source of influence.[22]

Merin's argument reflects a prevalent air of orphanhood hovering over
the history of Hebrew women's literature, despite the objective presence of
women writers in Modern Hebrew literature since its inception.[23] Dvora
Baron, the only woman-writer who was appreciated as part of the early literary cannon of the "revival era," remains "a disappointing mother" by dint
of her self-seclusion and withdrawal from the Zionist public sphere,[24] while
other early writers like Nehama Pohatchevsky and Hemda Ben-Yehuda
are forgotten and rejected as unworthy mothers by the later generations.[25]
Frustrating mother-daughter relations also appear as a prominent theme in
the study of Hebrew women's literature. For example, Rattok discusses what
she calls, "The hidden story: mother-daughter, daughter-mother" unfold-
ing throughout the evolution of Hebrew women's literature.[26] Hess devotes a
chapter in her book to "The mother, the daughter and the pioneering body"
in which she unpacks the fraught relationship of pioneer-culture with motherhood manifested in the renunciation of the private sphere endemic of this
culture and the constitution of children as a collective resource.[27] As Shirav
observes, the representation of mother-daughter relationships, in as much as
it is ripe with tropes of "absence, silence, repression and suppression," forms
a kind of shared poetic "code" of Hebrew women's literary imagination.[28]

While the investment in the recovery of the mother by feminist scholars
of Hebrew literature connects to general trends in French and American
feminist scholarship,[29] there is further significance to this recovery in the
context of Hebrew and Israeli culture, in light of the Zionist rejection of the
yiddishe momme, the Jewish East-European mother who was construed in
the Zionist imagination as the quintessential diasporic Other of the nation.[30]
In women's literature, this often translates into the story of the abandonment
of the mother as a constitutive move of the pioneering narrative, in which
the detachment from the diasporic home carries an ideological significance
as part of the Zionist rebirth.[31] It is in this context that the desire to recover
"feminist mothers" indeed acquires its subversive political significance.
What I call the Zionist "mother narrative" emerges from the scholarship on
Hebrew women's writing as a counter-narrative to what scholars of Zionist

masculinity have framed as the Zionist masculine "master narrative."[32] If the latter is a story of growth, progression, setting roots, and developing muscles, the "mother narrative" is a negative plot aimed backward toward everything that is marked as Other and abandoned through the Zionist ethos of the "negation of exile."[33] As such, this narrative is almost never told explicitly but instead needs to be extracted from women's expression of longing, guilt, and absence. In this light, we may understand how the mental content embedded in the study of early Zionist women often vacillates at the threshold between academic, political, and personal investments, which speaks to the difficulty of turning a critical eye to these women as an object of study. And yet, with all its immense insight on which I often draw, the intellectual project of recovering the Zionist "mother narrative" – in the broader sense of recovering forgotten women's experience and creative expression, and carving out matrilineal cultural lines of succession – often bolsters the interpretive boundaries of what I see as the solipsism of the gendered study of Zionism wherein we keep our questions and interrogations "within the family," so to speak. In the following section, I begin to chart some paths toward breaching this framework by juxtaposing "the mothers of Israeli feminism" with the critiques of contemporary global feminism.

The "Mothers of Israeli Feminism" and the Intersectional Gaze of Contemporary Feminists

The term "intersectionality" was first coined by legal scholar Kimberlé Crenshaw and was developed substantively within the field of African-American feminist studies to account for the ways in which gender intersects with other axes of power and identity, specifically race and class, in shaping the experience of multiple interlocking forms of oppression affecting African-American women and other women of colour.[34] Drawing on the analysis by Crenshaw and others of the way the racism, misogyny, and capitalism work as mutually constitutive systems,[35] the field of intersectional studies came to offer a comprehensive critique of the interlocking operation of apparatuses of power and injustice from the point of view of those who are most oppressed. As a field that is grounded not only in scholarly work but also in the activist sphere, intersectionality has thus prescribed a new framework for social activism and solidarity between differently disempowered groups. It is in this context that several controversies erupted in the last decade surrounding the inclusion of individuals and organizations identifying as

Zionists in US-based progressive settings.[36] This has culminated in January 2017 as the new global women's movement formed in the wake of Donald Trump's election to the US presidency adopted an international agenda of social justice, and asserted its commitment to the "decolonization of Palestine" and the dismantling of "prison walls to border walls, from Mexico to Palestine."[37] In response, Jewish American journalist Emily Shire published an opinion piece in the *New York Times* entitled "Does Feminism Have Room for Zionists?" that challenges the inclusion of the Palestinian struggle in the vision of the new women's movement:

> As a proud and outspoken feminist who champions reproductive rights, equal pay, increased female representation in all levels of government and policies to combat violence against women, I would like to feel there is a place for me in the strike. However, as someone who is also a Zionist, I am not certain there is ... For my part, I am troubled by the portion of the International Women's Strike platform that calls for a "decolonization of Palestine" as part of "the beating heart of this new feminist movement."[38]

One of the March's leaders, the Palestinian American activist Linda Sarsour, responded to Shire in an interview for *The Nation*, noting that "one cannot be a Zionist and a feminist" as the two positions are located on diametrically opposed sides of the global and intersectional struggle for social justice.[39] This, in turn, provoked a series of heated responses from American Jewish women and men, protesting what they saw as their exclusion from the movement. Here, I view Sarsour's statement not so much as an assertion about who is allowed in and who is excluded from the feminist movement, but rather as a critical question addressed to Zionist feminism charged by decades of feminist postcolonial and intersectional inquiry. It is, therefore, an important question to grapple with.

As a historical phenomenon, I argue, women like Hemda Ben-Yehuda, Nehama Pohatchevsky, Dvora Baron, Hannah Thon, and the other protagonists of this book were part of the history of Zionist feminism and proto-feminism. Most of these women not only participated in the struggles for women's rights in Zionist society,[40] but also furnished compelling critiques of Zionist patriarchy in their literary work. By articulating the emergence of a new kind of feminine subjectivity grounded in the nation, they may indeed be considered the "mothers of Israeli feminism." Yet, in order to understand their complex legacy for the cultures and politics of Israel/Palestine, it is necessary not only to recover their voices against the backdrop of a history of androcentric cultural repression, but also to critically examine their creative and political interventions in the context of the broader dynamics of power entailed by the Zionist project.

As of the 1990s, the scholarship emanating from third-wave feminism had deconstructed the ambiguous position of European women as both subjugated subjects and agents of power in national and colonial settings, and critically studied the complicity of Western feminism – often called "white feminism" – in systems of racial and colonial power.[41] In this context, I suggest that Zionist women writers are part of the history of Israeli feminism in the same way that Gayatri Chakravorty Spivak views Charlotte Brontë's *Jane Eyre* as part of the history of Western feminism, namely, as part of the constitution of a particular strata of women as subjects of individuality, rights, and power.[42] To a large extent, then, the story of early Zionist women that is depicted in this book is a story of Jewish Eastern-European women's entry into the history of "white feminism," namely, the transition of Jewish women from the intersectional position of the double marginalization as Jews and as women in Europe[43] to the position of the white/whitened Western women in the space of Ottoman and Mandatory Palestine. Several scholars have discussed the process by which Eastern-European Jews, who were themselves Orientalized and Othered by modern antisemitism (and, at times, by Western-European Jews), came to reconstitute themselves as Western subjects vis-à-vis the Palestinians and the Jews of Middle-Eastern and North-African descent, through what Aziza Khazoom calls the "great chain of Orientalism."[44] As it concerns women, I suggest, this story, had distinct characteristics and ramifications shaped by the mutually constitutive operation of gender, ethnicity, and nation in the Zionist space and imagination.

Thus, I ask in this book what it would mean to look back at the creative and political interventions of "the mothers of Israeli feminism" through the critical lens of intersectional and postcolonial feminism. For this purpose, I join the question of how Zionist women responded to their marginalization in the androcentric Zionist culture with the question of how they positioned themselves vis-à-vis the "other Others" of Zionism. By unpacking the ways in which Zionist women writers have articulated this junction of power and powerlessness, the following chapters seek to contribute to the understanding of their complex legacy. My point here is not to devalue their accomplishments as women in a patriarchal world, but rather to present them as historically situated subjects whose presence in pre-state Palestine had cultural and political ramifications that exceed the realm of gender alone.

Power, Powerlessness, and the Production of Femininity

The two pictures of my grandmother seemingly tell two different stories about Zionist femininity (figures 0.1, 0.2). The first features the body of a woman pioneer dressed in short khaki pants and a white blouse – an outfit almost identical to the one worn by a male pioneer – and a quasi-uniform of sorts that marks their bodies as "soldiers" in the enterprise of "working the Land." This image seemingly represents the erasure of gender difference, specifically femininity, in the construction of the ascetic Zionist body. Yet, as a way of probing the Zionist woman's position of power and powerlessness, it is productive to look at this image from two different, albeit not exactly opposite, perspectives. In a short essay published in the Israeli feminist blog *Politically Koreet*, Yael Avrahami reflects on a similar picture circulated widely online in which her own pioneer grandmother Aviva Alef appears wearing khaki shorts while pushing a cart of rocks at a strip mine (figure 0.3). Avrahami responds to the media's celebration of this picture as a symbol of gender equality and sexual freedom in early Zionist society. She writes:

> Let me tell you the real story of this picture. Lottie Parchek escaped Czechoslovakia at the age of 17 to go with the Youth Aliyah to kibbutz Beit Ha-shita. She thought she was going to an agricultural boarding school and that she would return home at the end of the war. Very naïve girl. When she got off the boat she was assigned the Hebrew name Aviva arbitrarily. This was how things were. In the kibbutz, they had to live "pioneer life." She once told me that they had to staff the guard-towers in the valley. The immigrant girls who were afraid to guard alone had to "kiss" male-pioneers so that they would come to guard with them at night. To "kiss," that's all she told me. I hope it was not more than that. In the Youth Aliyah, it was forbidden to speak in the language of home. Everyone had to speak only Hebrew. Aviva was caught speaking Czech with her friend and was expelled, at that point her parents and brothers were probably already in Theresienstadt … Aviva, my grandmother was sent to the strip mine

0.1 Dora Pickman, Ramat Yohanan, 1944.

0.2 Dora Pickman, celebration for the holiday of Shavu'ot, 1944.

as punishment. She did not push cart or blow-up rocks. She cooked and washed clothes for the male pioneers. When the photographer arrived, he staged the picture that you see, since he wanted girls' legs in the frame, and my grandmother's legs were famous.[45]

Upon reading Avrahami's description, I noticed that in pictures that feature both of my grandparents in khaki shorts and a white blouse, my grandfather's shorts are always longer, almost reaching the knees, whereas the shorts on my grandmother seem to be deliberately designed to flesh out her bare legs. What appears as an androgynous uniform that negates gender difference, in fact, carries different meaning when it is donned on differently gendered bodies.

A different outlook on a similar image is offered in Eyal Sivan's documentary, *Jaffa: The Orange Clockwork*, which critically interrogates Zionist aesthetics. In one instance, Palestinian author Elias Sanbar is

0.3 Kibbutz members working in the stone quarry of Kibbutz Ein Harod, 1941.

watching a clip from an old Zionist film in which a group of Zionist women and men are marching through a grove dressed mostly in the same outfit of khaki shorts and white shirts. Sanbar comments that the cinematic image of the marching settlers in uniform-like outfits seems to elude the intention of its creators to glorify the Zionist cause as it exposes the fact that "a highly militarist, warlike message is being drummed out."[46] The Palestinian gaze therefore views my grandmother's body in the khaki shorts as a symbol of the militarization of the Jewish body as it sets out on the settler-colonial conquest of indigenous lands. The image that signifies the objectification of women in Zionist culture for Avrahami denotes the body as means of violence from a Palestinian perspective.

At first glance, the second picture of my grandmother (figure 0.2) depicts dramatically different politics of the body than the first picture. If femininity is, at least on surface, negated in the first picture, it is emphasized and flaunted in the second. Here, my grandmother wears a white dress that she spreads wide as if to expand its scope. Indeed, the ubiquitous presence of the dress takes up the most space in the frame. Whereas in the first picture, she stands straight looking directly at the camera, in the second, her body is twisted as she turns her head back toward the camera, which creates a sensuous and seductive effect, while simultaneously holding on to the white dress, signifying purity, virginity, and innocence. The two pictures also feature two disparate relationships between the body and the space of the Land. In the first, her hand firmly grips a branch of a thorny plant; the barren landscape behind her seems to correspond with her ascetic body. In the second, the lushness of the banana grove coincides with the curving of her body. Her firm grip on the plant suggests ownership of the Land in the first picture, while in the second, she is integrated into the landscape more naturally and passively, in a way that reenacts the mythical scene of the "Daughters of Israel" dancing in the orchards wearing white, a story that was itself tied to sexual violence, since it commemorates an ancient ritual involving the kidnap and rape of the dancing girls. Here as well, femininity is a site of contradiction and violence.

Despite the apparent contrast, it is clear that the two images are two moments of the same aesthetic and ideological world. The asceticism of the first image is aligned with the vision of whiteness and purity emanating from the second image through what I call "metaphors of diminishment" in chapter 4, referring to the association of nationalized femininity with the reduction of excess, naturalness, and purity, in which the colour white is featured as a prominent feminine metonym. Moreover, the militaristic agenda embodied by the uniformed body coincides with the imposition of sexual purity on the female body, which is often loaded with implicit ideologies of racial and national purity.[47] The two images also intersect through the prevalence of sexual violence as an undercurrent of the national project. The elusive dualities that characterize the aesthetics and interrelation of both images are endemic to the complexity of the feminine as a national category – so often obscured in studies on masculinity. In contrast with others, I see Zionist women as actively involved in producing Zionist femininity as a site of national meaning. In the pictures of my grandmother, in this sense, I see not only an object of the Zionist male gaze, but also the evolution of an active agent of a national ideology that asserts her belonging to and ownership of the space around her, and therefore entangles herself in the intersectional landscape of racialized, national, and colonial power structures. Thus, in the following chapters, I probe the production of femininity by women writers as a process of meaning and identity construction in which multiple cultural categories and hierarchies of power intersect. Femininity itself, I postulate, is an inherently intersectional category.

As Hamutal Tsamir explains in the context of the gender dynamics of Modern Hebrew Literature:

> As we recall, women are the margins of the nation, they are at one and the same time inside and outside the nation: they are its most internal Other, through which the nation defines its uniform and coherent identity, but – or precisely because of that – they are excluded from accessing subjectivity and representativeness in the nation, namely, the apparatus of unification and repression ... [but] their bodies and identity are imbued with the national identity; they are the text upon which this identity is marked and carved, but in an inversed way, as they mark it from the margins, from inside and outside at once.[48]

Tsamir acknowledges the presence of femininity as an object of the nation – its innermost object – but for her, the metaphoric structure through which femininity is produced, and whose paradigmatic example is the land-as-woman metaphor, is precisely what precludes women from accessing national subjectivity. Thus, the 1960s women poets that she studies subvert this system by activating the "horizontal logic of the metonym, which places the subject and the object next to each other in a way that exposes identity (or subjectivity) as a series of performative practices of imitation and repetition."[49] The stakes are different, I argue, for the early Zionist women operating at the high time of Zionist ideology to which they were unequivocally committed no less than men were. For them, as I show throughout this book, producing femininity as a meaningful category of the nation is imbricated in the constitution of their own subjectivity; as such, it is part of their proto-feminist initiation. Thus, Zionist women's engagement with their own gender calls for analysis and deconstruction not only as a subversive performance, but also, by dint of its role in shaping distinctions and hierarchies between the self and Other in the Zionist space, and, ultimately, in shaping Zionist and Israeli subjectivities.

Femininity itself emerges as a precarious category in the history of gender and feminist studies. Indeed , early feminist theory considered femininity as merely the negation of masculinity, and thus constructed masculinity and femininity through a series of binaries – active/passive, strength/weakness, reason/emotion, spirit/matter, mind/body, subject/

object, self/Other – in which the second term always represents the absence of the first; for instance, passivity as the absence of activity, emotion as the absence of reason, objectivity as the absence of subjectivity, and so forth. By the 1970s, the evolution of cultural feminism alongside psychoanalytic and poststructuralist feminism was associated with a re-evaluation of "the feminine" as a cultural category with positive content, albeit one that is repressed by the dominant androcentric culture. American theorists such as Carol Gilligan and Nancy Chodorow, for example, discussed alternative "feminine" ethics and modes of identity formation grounded in the concepts of care and relationality, rather than in the process of egocentric individuation and the application of abstract morals.[50] Similarly, French poststructuralist feminists, including Luce Irigaray, Hélène Cixous, and Julia Kristeva, have theorized "the feminine" as Otherness that eludes or is repressed by the masculine symbolic order, but also as a subversive force that has the potential to undermine this order.[51] Despite the obvious discrepancies between their conceptual points of reference and theoretic language, poststructuralist and cultural feminisms shared the desire to upset the gender binary system by assigning meaning to the feminine difference in itself, not as the negation of the masculine.

From the point of view of third-wave feminism, these conceptualizations were critiqued for essentializing femininity as the attribute of white womanhood. In this sense, upholding "femininity" as a category that has its own innate content entails the erasure of differences of power and access to agency between women.[52] In the context of postcolonial theory, femininity is therefore interrogated as a constitutive category at play in the formation of intersecting racialized and colonial hierarchies. Thus, for example, Richard Dyer's important discussion of whiteness and femininity shows how the two are mutually constitutive in upholding values of racial purity.[53] Deconstructing the operation of colonial regimes in the intimate sphere, Ann Laura Stoler has shown how the presence of white women in the colonies entailed stricter racial segregation, as they were construed as potential victims of the indigenous Other deemed as a sexual threat.[54] Vron Ware has underscored how feminine vulnerability was weaponized in racist and colonial discourse as a metonym of the vulnerability of the colonizer vis-à-vis the indigenous subject as a potential aggressor.[55] From this point of view, the image of my beautiful grandmother in her white flowy dress seems to acquire additional, more sinister, meaning. Is her white dress a component in an aesthetics that is grounded as much in racialized premises as it is in sexualized binaries? Could the spreading of the dress also be read as a metonym of the endeavour that brought her there, expanding the Zionist space, while camouflaging the inherent violence entailed by this process through the quintessential image of white innocence?

The History of Women and the Genealogy of Gender

Applying a contemporary intersectional and postcolonial lens to the productive dialectic between the constitution of Zionist women as subjects of the nation and the production of Zionist femininity as an object of the nation is the central investigation of the following chapters. By tracing the contours and resonances of this dialectic, this book aims to contribute both to the study of the history of Zionist women and to the genealogy of Zionist gender dynamics, as well as intervene in the contemporary debates on Zionist feminism by shedding light on the long history of the fraught inter-relations between women, Zionism, and feminism.

Chapter 1 considers the emergence of women as Zionist subjects at the intersection of gender, modernity, nationalism and colonialism, against the backdrop of what I call the "national-patriarchal home." At the centre of this chapter stands the Ben-Yehuda family which was inscribed into the Zionist lore as "the first Hebrew family." Previous studies, focusing on the family's patriarch, the well-known lexicographer Eliezer Ben-Yehuda often celebrated as "the father of Modern Hebrew," employed the story of the family to illustrate the silencing of women as part of the emergence of Zionist culture.[56] By pivoting scholarly attention to Ben-Yehuda's first and second wives, the sisters Dvora and Hemda Ben-Yehuda (née Jonas), I examine the early encounter of women and Zionism as both destructive and productive. In what follows, I unpack the contrasting fates of the two sisters: Dvora, on the one hand, passed away from tuberculosis at an early age and was iconized as a feminine martyr at the altar of the nation; Hemda (née Paula), on the other hand, lived a long and productive life as a nationalist, and became the first Hebrew woman prose writer in Palestine. Taking this contrast as a point of departure, I read the story of the sisters in two ways: first, as emblematic of the dialectic between women as national subjects and femininity as a national trope; and, second, as a significant historical example that illustrates the stakes involved in the transition of Jewish women from the context of European modernity to the national settlement project. Based on extensive research into the writings of Hemda Ben-Yehuda, this chapter provides a historical and conceptual point of departure to the story of Zionist women, while also introducing many of the ethno-gendered dynamics that will be unpacked in the subsequent chapters.

Chapter 2 expands the outlook on the emergence of Zionist women's subjectivity in relation to the space of Palestine as an indigenous space. Reading fiction by three major early Zionist women prose-writers, Hemda Ben-Yehuda, Nehama Pohatchevsky, and Dvora Baron, I analyze the way they narrate instances of appropriation, expulsion, and colonization. While the dominant paradigm in the study of gender and Zionism associates the colonization project with the masculinization of Jewish identity, I read women's writing in light of the postcolonial feminist critique of Western women's investment in national and colonial systems. Drawing on this theoretical framework, I show how women writers ground Zionist feminist subjectivity in the settler-colonial imagination by tying questions about women's rights and equality to the assertion of Jewish nationalist agency and the appropriation of indigenous identities and spaces. In these stories, the constitution of women's agency is often bound with the assertion of domination over territory, which is sometimes manifested as the constitution of a "pure" Jewish space and imagined as analogous to the "pure" feminine body set up against the threat of contamination by the indigenous Other. Furthermore, the Zionist self itself is imagined in these fictions as quintessentially feminine, powerless, and victimized; consequently, the Zionist claim to the Land is imagined as analogous to women's claims for gender justice. The chapter concludes by asking whether Zionist feminism is in fact an example of the problematic entanglement of Western feminism, nationalism, and colonialism.

While chapter 2 focuses on women's position vis-à-vis the question of Palestine and the Palestinians, chapter 3 investigates their position in the intra-Jewish politics of ethnicity between Ashkenazim (European Jews) and Mizrahim (Jews of Middle-Eastern and North African descent). This chapter analyzes literary and biographic writings by Zionist women activists, who undertook the role of "national caregivers" – such as nurses, community volunteers, and social workers – in relation to the evolving ethnically marked social margins of the Zionist settlement, composed mostly of Mizrahi Jews, whose communities were largely impoverished and disempowered by their immigration to Palestine. Drawing on Mary Louise Pratt's term of the "contact zone"[57] as a space of cultural encounter within the context of asymmetrical colonial relations of power, I highlight the Zionist "contact zone of care" as a focal point of the ethnic hierarchy of power in the Zionist space. While the casting of European women in roles related to the colonial "civilizing mission" vis-à-vis racialized and colonized communities was a prevalent phenomenon in many contexts, I trace the particular infrastructures of the Zionist Mizrahi/Ashkenazi architecture of power through the writings of Zionist "caregivers." Reading fiction and memoirs by Zionist authors and activists Nehama Pohatchevsky, Shoshana Bluwstein, and Hannah Thon, I show how the "contact zone of care" reflects the evolution of ethnic hierarchies in three distinct Zionist settings: the bourgeois colony of the first Zionist immigration wave, the ideological "socialist" commune of the second Zionist immigration wave (the Second *Aliyah*), and the evolving Zionist urban space of the inter-war period. Together, these three case studies tell a complex story about the emergence of ethnic power structures in Israel/Palestine. The chapter concludes with a discussion of what I see as the culmination of Zionist women's politics of "national caregiving," namely, the 1950s affair of the disappearance of Mizrahi babies from the immigrant transit camps, in which Zionist women's organizations were reportedly heavily involved. In this light, I read the Mizrahi families' testimonies about the affair as directing an "oppositional gaze" toward the Zionist contact zone of care, exposing its intergenerational traumatic ramifications.[58]

Chapter 4 brings the book's trajectory to a close with a comprehensive discussion of femininity as a national category. Here, I trace the contours of the Zionist discourse on femininity through tropes of diminishment, asceticism, simplicity, and reduction of excess. Far from being a marginal category, femininity in fact forms a focal point of the Zionist imagination. Reading prose and poetry by canonical and non-canonical women authors including Rachel Bluwstein, Rachel Katzanelson, Rivka Alper, and Dvora Baron in relation to cinematic and musical representations of Zionist femininity, I trace the tropes of feminine diminishment in multiple arenas from the discourse on women's writing, to the Zionist feminine body, and the politics of ethnicity and national security. In this context, I show how Bluwstein's preference of simple and ascetic poetics, for example, coincides with the misogynistic discourse about women's bodies, which, in turn, connotes the construction of the Zionist feminine body as a "white," colourless body. I proceed to show how this racialized and gendered discourse of feminine diminishment connects to the image of the "empty land" as a major trope in the rationalization of the Zionist colonization of Palestine. Ultimately, this chapter tells a story about the illusiveness of "femininity" as a category of the Zionist imagination. If in regulating women's writing and bodies, constructions of femininity serve to limit women's cultural and physical presence in the space of the nation, in the geopolitical context, the expansive resonance of femininity as a category of the nation fleshes out the ways in which the politics of gender, in fact, permeates all politics.

1

A TALE OF TWO SISTERS
Women, Femininity, and the
National-Patriarchal Home

———

Ben-Yehuda had a wife, and her name was Dvora, and she died
on Ellul 22, 1891, and she was buried, and he was consoled, and he
took her sister instead of her ... all in accordance with the custom of
the land.[1]

In 1894, editor Yisrael-Dov Frumkin, an ally-turned-rival of the Ben-
Yehuda family,[2] published a sarcastic and furious essay about the latest
scandal associated with them – the arrest of lexicographer and journalist
Eliezer Ben-Yehuda and his father-in-law Shlomo Naftali-Hertz Jonas by
the Ottoman authorities on charges of incitement to violence.[3] Frumkin's
fury was triggered by a rumour spread by a Romanian Yiddish newspaper, which alleged that Ben-Yehuda's first wife Dvora died of grief
caused by the arrest, when, in fact, she had passed away two years earlier in 1891. Conceived by Frumkin as an attempt to defame the rabbis of
Jerusalem whose accusations brought about the arrest, this minor event
of "fake news" sparked a diatribe ripe with misogynistic rhetoric aimed
the at Ben-Yehuda's consecutive marriages to the two Jonas sisters: Dvora
(née Jonas, 1855–1891), with whom he came to Jerusalem in 1881, and
Hemda (née Paula Jonas, 1873–1951), Dvora's younger sister whom he
married in 1892, a few months after the death of Dvora from tuberculosis.
In the essay, Frumkin teases out the scandalous implications of the
rumour regarding Dvora's belated death: "Now Hebrew language has to say,
my writers now propose that the Sephardim will denounce bigamy, while
Yiddish writers are reviving the dead, giving two women for one man, *and
two sisters at that!*"[4]

Itamar Ben-Avi, Eliezer and Dvora's firstborn, describes in his memoir a scene where Nissim Bekhar,[5] Ben-Yehuda's friend and an important Sephardi public figure, urges him to avoid the second marriage, exclaiming, "Are you not afraid of what they will think of you in the city, in the *Yishuv*, and in the diaspora?"[6] Like Frumkin's mocking remarks, this story alludes to the social discontent surrounding Eliezer's marriages to the two sisters. Overtly, the social response to Ben-Yehuda's marriage concerned his tuberculosis and the risk of infecting the younger sister as he did the older. Invoking the issue of bigamy, however, Frumkin's diatribe loads the marriage with a deeper "embarrassment" by tying it to the ethnic and cultural tensions between Yiddish and Hebrew, Sephardim and Ashkenazim, and Judaism, nationalism, and modernity. In the following pages, I situate the story of the sisters against the backdrop of these interlacing tensions which are endemic of the complex moment in Jewish history, where within a period of ten years, both sisters travelled between two shifting landscapes: first, the rapidly changing Eastern European Jewish home shaped by the multiple transitions of the father from his orthodox roots, to Hasidism, Russian radicalism, *Haskalah*, and, finally, to nationalism, and second, the diverse and no less turbulent setting of nineteenth century Jerusalem, where complex dynamics of modernity, religion, gender and ethnicity were compounded by the inception of the Zionist settlement project. The sisters' experience of these multiple transitions was further complicated by changing gender norms and the emergence of new gender ideologies.

The family as a metaphor has long been considered a prominent emblem of the nation modeling the kind of "natural" sense of attachment and belonging that one is supposed to feel for the national collective.[7] In gendered terms, the family also serves as an organizing principle of the national division of labour, assigning women the role of biological and cultural reproduction of the collective, and men with the roles of leadership, defense, and production.[8] What I call "the national-patriarchal home" refers to the ways in which, both as a metaphor for the nation and as its basic unit, the family is instrumental in maintaining the mutually constitutive relationship between the national order and the patriarchal order.

In the context of Zionism, the Ben-Yehuda family was inscribed into the national lore as the first Hebrew family. The myth of the Ben-Yehudas often centres on the insistence of Eliezer, often called "the father of modern Hebrew,"[9] on raising his and Dvora's firstborn, Itamar Ben-Avi, "the first

Hebrew child," exclusively in Hebrew, a language that was hardly used as a spoken language in the 1880s. This story has acquired mythical stature in the Zionist collective memory as the origin story of Modern Hebrew.[10] Naomi Seidman's incisive analysis of this story in the context of the gendered and sexualized dynamics of the emergence of Modern Hebrew paved the way for an understanding of the Ben-Yehudas as a paradigmatic household, whose story points toward cultural and gendered depth structures of the national project.[11] For Seidman, this is a story about how the silencing of women, specifically mothers, is embedded into the of the national family drama.[12] Shifting the attention from the nuclear Oedipal triangle to the story of the sisters, however, I examine the constitution of the Zionist home as both a destructive and a productive site for women – a site in which while one sister is silenced and iconized as a sacrificial lamb at the altar of the nation, the other becomes a vocal agent of the nation.

By the time of the famous arrest of Eliezer and Jonas then, Eliezer's wife was no longer the deceased Dvora Ben-Yehuda, but rather Hemda, who, far from fainting and dying in face of the ordeal, demonstrated resourcefulness and confidence. Indeed, she organized a petition on behalf of her husband, bribed various officials to improve the conditions of his imprisonment, and supported him vigorously up to his final acquittal.[13] Thus, coinciding with the image of the victimized frail wife, we see here the emergence of a woman as an assertive political actor. The anecdote therefore draws attention to the contrast between the two sisters in terms of their life-trajectory and their legacy in Hebrew culture. Dvora lived a short and tragic life: she reportedly suffered greatly from the isolation imposed on her by her husband's linguistic purism and had a difficult time learning the language. Eventually, she passed away, exhausted and ill, ten years after arriving in Jerusalem. Attributes often attached to Dvora in various commemorative and biographic writings, include "soft," "weak," "suffering," "sacrificial lamb," "delicate," "martyr," "pure," and "good." Her sister, Hemda, on the other hand, lived a long and productive life. She served as the producer of Eliezer's *Dictionary of Old and New Hebrew*, for which she advocated, fundraised, and continued the work after his death.[14] Hemda published numerous essays and stories in the various venues established by the Ben-Yehuda family (*Ha-or, Ha-tzvi, Hashkafa*, and *Doar ha-yom*), and wrote what she referred to as her "trilogy" of the revival of Hebrew – the biographies of Eliezer, Dvora, and their son Itamar

Ben-Avi. While she was never accepted as an author into the cannon of Modern Hebrew Literature, and was undoubtedly overshadowed by the memory of her renowned husband, Hemda did end up developing a prolific nationalist voice, and, in recent decades, her status as one of the first Hebrew women writers gained her more recognition through the work of Israeli feminist scholars.[15]

While she herself was not included as a protagonist of the myth of the first Hebrew family – consisting of Eliezer as "the Father," Dvora as "the Mother," and Itamar as "the Son" – through her extensive biographical writings, Hemda was largely the one responsible for developing and maintaining the myth. Hemda's narration of her sister's life, I contend, sheds light on a story that not only speaks to the structural split between women as national subjects and femininity as an object of the national imagination, but also offers insight into the complex historical moment in which certain modern Jewish women came to be reinvented as agents of the nation.

In turn, this analysis employs the structural role of the sister as a way of breaching the framework of the nuclear family and the Oedipal triangle. The sister, I suggest, is a radical Other of the Oedipal system; she has no role in patriarchal lineage, apart from serving as an alternate and rival of her sister. Additionally, the sister may also be theorized as the "Other" of the nation. Unlike the brother, whose figure is constitutive of the national imagination through concepts such as fraternity and "brothers in arms,"[16] the sister has no such role in the context of the nation. Sisterhood, in contrast to brotherhood, is a concept associated with transcending the boundaries of the national collective, often functioning as a feminist metaphor that signifies women's affinity to each other as an ideal horizon of all-women's solidarity against the patriarchy. In the wake of postcolonial and intersectionality studies, however, sisterhood, as used in the context of Western feminism, became associated with universalist assumptions, shaping feminist politics in accordance with the interests and experience of white affluent Western women while obscuring inequalities between women and the systems of power in which Western feminism was implicated.[17] Against this theoretical backdrop, the story of the Jonas-Ben-Yehuda sisters would also emerge here as a story about the ramifications of women's fraught investment in the nation in terms the possibilities and impossibilities of women's bonding and solidarity.

The Substitution of Women

In her seminal work, "The Traffic in Women," Gayle Rubin synthesizes the theories of Marx, Freud (through Lacan), and Levy-Strauss, to demonstrate how the organization of kinship around the incest taboo, on the one hand, and castration anxiety, on the other, determines the gender/sex hierarchy by positioning men as givers or exchangers and women as signs or objects of exchange.[18] The exchange of women, according to Rubin, maintains a network of bonds between men that sustains the patriarchal system. What I refer to here "the substitution of women," is, I suggest, another facet of the gender/sex system as charted by Rubin, where women are both exchangeable and instrumental in the facilitation of men's bonding.

The early chapters of Hemda's unpublished biography of her sister, *Kokho shel goral* (power of fate),[19] offer insight into these dynamics in the context of the patriarchal Jewish home in the modern moment. Her account, needless to say, cannot be taken at face value as an objective depiction of Dvora's life; Hemda was only a child when Dvora left for Palestine and therefore had little contact with her growing up. The information about Dvora's early life was likely mediated to Hemda through the recollection of other members of the family, such as Eliezer and the sisters' father. Indeed, as I will show later, there is a different version of Dvora' early life written by her son Itamar Ben-Avi, which in many ways contrasts Hemda's version. Still, Hemda's biography about the life of young Dvora and the processes that led her to Palestine arguably conveys shared knowledge transferred through the generations. While the biography is often imbued with ideology and the language of national mythmaking, many of the details in its early chapters dovetail with scholarship on Jewish women's complex encounter with modernity and nationalism.[20] Hemda's assumptions about the life-trajectory of her sister are also undoubtedly informed by her own life-story. In this sense, the biography can indeed be read as an inter-subjective "tale of two sisters." As such, it is a story of overlapping and contradicting identifications, desires, and substitutions, which in turn sheds light on women's stakes in the nation.

In her introduction to a collection of women's Yiddish prose from the period, Nurit Orchan has commented that the tensions and contradictions in the world of young Jewish women in the late nineteenth century were often manifested through an internal rift between the daughter's gendered identification with her mother and her attraction to the father as a representative of modernity.[21] Along these lines, Dvora's biography starts with a gendered survey of the patriarchal and matriarchal lineages of the sisters. The mother Rivka-Leah Barabish came from a financially stable family that was well supported by the banking business of her father. Conversely, Shlomo Naftali-Hertz Jonas came from a family of merchants, "all vibrant, full of life, inventive, inventions caused them to lose the money they inherited or received through marriage, all of them lovers of nature, and aspiring for changes and the unknown."[22] The difference between the families translates into a gendered distinction between the attitudes of the husband and wife towards modernity. Like the other men in his family, Shlomo Naftali-Hertz is said to have been an imaginative man with a passion for innovation. He underwent the intellectual and ideological shifts typical of many Jewish men of his generation, from *Hasidut*, to Russian radicalism, to the *Haskalah* movement, and, finally, to the Zionist project. According to this account, Jonas, who was a beer merchant by profession, always regretted the fact that because of his *Hasidic* upbringing, he did not receive any general secular education, and thus could not acquire a profession that better suited his intellectual interests and abilities. In contrast with her husband, Rivka-Leah remained pious and traditional, and, unlike the father's turbulent intellectual life, she had "a world of her own, more normal, without fantasies and imagination."[23] This depiction of the Jonas home fits well with the dynamics discussed in Paula Hyman's seminal work on gender, Jewishness, and modernity; in the wake of the modernization of the Jewish family, women were assigned as keepers of tradition within the home in order to allow men to experience modernity and secularization in the public sphere. Through this process, Jewish women, who in the more traditional family structure served as breadwinners to allow their husbands to study the Torah, were pushed into the private sphere.[24] Yet, if the mother signifies tradition and immobility, the daughter seems to be a site of change and dynamicity. The Jonas family dynamics seem reminiscent of the dynamics Tova Cohen has mapped in her study of the *maskilot*,[25] where the father-daughter bond is central in ushering the daughter's entrance to modernity.[26] If boys who discovered Jewish enlightenment, like Eliezer Ben-Yehuda himself, often experienced rupture from their traditional family and community, girls' secular learning was often administered by their fathers and was in fact a vehicle of bonding between daughters and fathers.[27] According to Hemda's account, against the backdrop of the mother's "unimaginative" lack of modern sensibilities, Jonas has chosen his eldest daughter Dvora as a partner in his intellectual endeavours. The biography reads, "The other children did not interest him at all. Only Dvora was like a friend to the father, and he believed that she will continue his enterprises ... The father and the daughter ... developed hand in hand, side by side ... toward a different life."[28] Arguably, implicit in this description is the subjectivity of the sister-author who is envious of the father's "chosen" daughter; in this sense, the implied rivalry between the sisters mirrors the rivalry between the mother and the daughter in the narrated reality.

The text further describes how Jonas joined his daughters' French lessons with a tutor he had hired.[29] Later on, French becomes "the language spoken at the home, but this does not bother the mother who does not speak it."[30] The substitution of the mother by the daughter dovetails with the gendered division of temporalities vis-à-vis modernity, in which women signify the immutability of tradition vs men's progress. Here, modern temporality is defined by the split between mother and daughter, in which the mother is silenced and the daughter is ushered into new possibilities of agency through her association with the father. To return to Seidman's analysis of the Ben-Yehuda home, which illustrates how the silencing of the mother was "built in" into the revival of Hebrew,[31] we see here how a similar process occurs a phase earlier. What we also see is that while one woman is indeed silenced in this process, another is in fact finding her modern voice.

According to Iris Parush's study of Jewish women's reading culture, the exclusion of Jewish women from Jewish learning institutions in conjunction with the opening of non-Jewish educational frameworks for women in the late nineteenth century formed "a window of opportunities" for Jewish women in the form of access to secular education, thus making them important agents of modernity in the East-European Jewish society.[32] Along these lines, Hemda's narration of her sister's life prior to her immigration to Palestine illustrates how, while Dvora was ultimately cast as the frail mother-martyr of the national home, the context of the modernizing Jewish family opened avenues for her to transcend gender restrictions, as it did for Hemda herself, and for many young women of their time. Notably, both Dvora and Hemda enter the nationalist scene as the "New Jewish Women" pursuing further these paths of modernization.[33]

At the heart of the system of kinship, from a psychoanalytic point of view, is the incest taboo, which, as Shira Stav has theorized, underlies all heteronormative gender-relations.[34] Unlike other taboos, such as incest between siblings, Stav argues, "Incest between the father and his (unmarried) daughter does not undermine the authority of any man, since the daughter belongs to him alone … the transgression of this taboo does not damage the basic power structures of the family and society, but rather aligns with them and reinforces them."[35] As Stav shows, incest operates as a sublimated possibility embedded in the relationship of power between fathers and daughters; the daughter's value, as belonging to the father, is determined only as an object of exchange between men. It seems plausible in this light, that at points of cultural transition and instability in which the family is restructured, glimpses of its disavowed content come to light; in this case, the father and the daughter thus briefly appear as a couple. In this narrative, when the young Eliezer enters the household, an opportunity is opened for renormalization of the family, namely, for the daughter to finally unravel the Oedipal entanglement by replacing the father with a husband. Notably, Jonas grooms the young *maskil* to take his place as the daughter's partner. By taking Eliezer in after he was thrown out of his uncle's home, Jonas follows a common pattern of mentorship relations between a young *maskil* and an older one. Relationships such as these, in which a wealthy Jewish man with affinities to the *Haskalah* becomes the benefactor of a younger man with the same inclinations, were prevalent, and often served as an important lifeline for the young transgressors who were typically banished from their own families.[36] Ushering Eliezer's path to the world of secular learning was another context in which Dvora collaborated with her father. In order for the young Yiddish and Hebrew-speaking *yeshiva bocher*[37] to continue his studies in a secular high school, Dvora was tasked with teaching him French and Russian. It was in this tutoring setting that 18-year-old Dvora and 15-year-old Eliezer reportedly fell in love and decided to marry.[38]

Upon acquiring the basic vernacular knowledge, Eliezer, encouraged by Jonas, left for four years to study in the Dvinsk gymnasia. To comfort Dvora, according to the biography, Jonas promised her that "we will go as well"[39] referring to his intention to take Dvora on a trip to see the big cities of Yalta and St Petersburg. This plan did not materialize as Jonas ended up going by himself. However, a similar scene reoccurs, when Eliezer decides to leave for Paris upon finishing his high school education. Jonas once again is told to have consoled his daughter with promises of travel: "until you can go to Paris, we will go together both of us to Moscow."[40] The biography proceeds to describe the father and daughter's trip to Moscow and their ventures to the capital's intellectual circles, where "everybody notices Dvora's noble and delicate presence by her handsome father's side."[41] The modern desire for the urban space sustains a triangular relationship; here, the father and the future husband alternate and function as placeholders for each other.

Eve Kosofsky Sedgwick characterized the triangle as a structure, which is innately "a sensitive register precisely for delineating relationships of power and meaning, and for making graphically intelligible the play of desire and identification by which individuals negotiate with their societies for empowerment."[42] Through the gendered dynamics of mirroring and substitution in the Jonas-Ben-Yehuda households, we see the Jewish family at the intersection of Judaism, modernity, and nationalism as a constellation of crisscrossing triangles: father, mother, daughter; father, son-in-law, daughter; two sisters and a mother; two sisters and a father; two sisters and a husband; and, finally, mother, father, son – the first Hebrew family, the national-patriarchal home. Triangular relationships, according to Sedgwick, are depended upon the erasure of one side, and as such, tell a story about the making of Otherness. As shown in the following sections, while Dvora enters the realm of modernity and nationalism substituting the othered Jewish mother, ultimately, the triangular casting shifts again when she is written by her sister-substitute as the woman-Other of the nation.

From Dreaming of the "West" to Becoming Western in the "East": The New Jewish Woman on the Chessboard of Modernity and Nationalism

To her father she said: shall we play our farewell game of chess? … they were both good players, and after much deliberation, the father declared: checkmate! She smiled and said: "of course, since I am the winner in the game of love."[43]

According to an anecdote found in Eliezer's biography, Dvora, sitting in her wedding gown, played one last game of chess with her father before she joined Eliezer's journey from Vienna to Palestine. The image of Dvora as chess-player – essentially a strategic game of war – seems at odds with her typical representation as an innocent martyr swept up by the power of love and sacrificed at the altar of the nation. This evocative scene indeed closes the chapter of Dvora's life in which she functioned as her father's intellectual match, transposing her to the realm of the husband and the nation. Metaphorically, the game of chess denotes the real-life strategic "game" in which both sisters are involved, as they navigate the complicated intersection of modernity, gender, Judaism, and nationalism. Chess players seek to move forward and breach each other's terrain; yet, while a move forward on the board may advance one player toward to a triumphant endgame, it may also lead to the player's demise, since the meaning of each step is determined by an array of threats, restrictions, and opportunities; in this sense, the cultural-political field that the New Jewish Woman navigated at the threshold of modernity and nationalism was, I suggest, as complex as a game of chess.

In one chapter of Dvora's biography, evocatively entitled "Mothers," Hemda describes her sister's relationship with the three major cities in her life. "Mother Moscow," the text reads, "welcomed the Jewish refugee Dvora, but nonetheless, she felt herself a stranger to this country, its language, and its spirit, because she already contemplated a different life."[44] At this point, in a typical Zionist narrative, the reader might expect to find the emergence of Zionist conviction and desire for the Land, but Dvora's aspirations, according to this text, were directed elsewhere "to Paris, the mother of all humanity." Here, she hoped that "Eliezer Elianoff [Ben Yehuda] [would] be a great scholar,[45] teaching in the city of Paris, [where] she too will roam the circles of scholars, professors, artists and politicians and will observe their interesting lives, which will become her life as well."[46] Dvora's infatuation with Eliezer, like her relationship with her father, was intertwined with her desire to participate in modernity. Jonas himself reportedly imagined his daughter's future along the same lines: "one day Eliezer will be famous like Friedrich Schlegel, and Dvora by his side will be like Henrietta Hertz or Dorothea Mendelson, and she will live in Paris. It all fits."[47] The two women Jonas envisions as models for Dvora, Henrietta Hertz and Dorothea Mendelson (later Schlegel), both belonged to the circles of the emerging Jewish enlightenment movement in Berlin, and were pioneers of the Jewish salon culture (both notably ended up converting to Christianity). The eighteenth-century Jewish salonnières transcended social restrictions imposed on them by administering the salon as public space, which is an extension of the private sphere, where artists, intellectuals, and political actors would interact. As such, the salons were frontiers of modernization and assimilation where Jewish women could gain intellectual fulfillment and social influence, capacities that were otherwise unavailable to them.[48] Dvora's hope to roam the circles of the Parisian elite suggests a model of New Jewish womanhood, associated with the Western capitals, where both she and her father presumed her life as a young modern woman would lead her. While it is undoubtedly difficult to establish the accuracy of this account of Dvora's inner thoughts and aspirations, the alternative future that the biography charts for Dvora calls our attention to the stakes involved in her eventual move on the proverbial chessboard – from investment in European modernity to following Eliezer's national pursuits.

As part of the myth of the Ben-Yehuda Family, Dvora's choice of following Eliezer to Palestine is often rendered as a grand gesture of love and self-sacrifice. Yet, in many ways, it was a strategic move on the chessboard of modernity. Once the Jonases discovered Eliezer's plans to settle in Palestine (which he announced publicly in the *maskilic* newspaper *Ha-shachar* but did not share privately with Dvora), Jonas reportedly wrote to Eliezer to remind him of his promises to Dvora. Eliezer responded, perhaps diplomatically, that he did not dare to ask Dvora to join him on the journey to Jerusalem, given that he just found out that he is infected with tuberculosis. He writes, "After a week, a girl came into my room. It was she, Dvora."[49] It is worth noting that, at 27 years old, Dvora has waited for Eliezer for seven years, and has rejected other suitors. With Eliezer's change of plans, her dreams of Paris likely reached a dead end. Joining Eliezer on his journey to Palestine was a move forward in the sense that it was likely intertwined with the desire to participate in modernity. Nationalism, however, offered a very different kind of modern space than her dream of the Western capital.

In a brief memoir published in the revisionist newspaper *Ha-'am* in 1931, Hemda recounts the story of her own decision to marry Eliezer, and the dramatic break it required from her earlier plans.[50] Upon excelling in her studies in the local college for women,[51] her professor, "Was amazed by my announcement that I am leaving Russia not to attend a [West] European college, but to savage Asia."[52] As in Dvora's case, the professor's response attests to the fact that the aspirational horizons for a bright young Jewish woman wishing to transcend traditional gender norms was assumed to be in Western Europe. Later in the essay, Hemda recalls how in her last days in Moscow she visited the opera and a French exhibition in order to "bid farewell to the enlightened world that I will never again see."[53] Indeed, Hemda's dramatization of her own life trajectory parallels and may very well have informed her narration of her sister's life. This is especially evident in her narration of both sisters' decision to follow Eliezer to Palestine, which reoccurs several times in her biographic writings. The narrative of the Western woman breaking away from "civilization" and traveling to the "savage East" appears in these descriptions as an alternative to the narrative of regeneration and return that Eliezer is invested in:

> The two pioneers [Dvora and Eliezer] on board the ship are approaching their destination and they see the land. This moves one of them to the bottom of his heart, and to her it means nothing. Here is the shore: the ship anchors far, because of the rocks. Here is Jaffa: The East in all its wildness.[54]

> Ben-Yehuda was happy and cheerful to return to his land ... I [Hemda] was traveling to a foreign land, to the East, which attracted me and frightened me at once.[55]

For men of *maskilic* background, the idea of a "return" to the ancestral Land coincides with the romantic notion of European "regeneration" through the East[56], "a return ... directed toward the imagined East – the proverbial cradle of the (Judeo-Christian) civilization."[57] Standing alongside their husbands facing the shores of Jaffa, modern Jewish women like Hemda and Dvora Jonas had very different investment in the East. The story of return and regeneration, which was undergirded by Jewish knowledge developed in masculine settings, did not resonate with the modern future envisioned by the New Jewish Woman. Rather, the East is marked here as a space of irreducible Otherness against which the position of the Jewish woman as a Western woman is reinforced. In an unpublished manuscript, Hemda writes, "And all those veiled women of the Orient. And the Orient of which I have dreamt all my life, now that I belonged to it, scared me ... And it seemed to me that not many days shall pass before I myself will become one of these veiled women, and the whole world will remain behind the scarf."[58] The vision of the "veiled woman" as a dreaded final point of a woman's journey to the East evokes the gendered figuration of the East itself within the Orientalist imagination, in which the "veiled woman" is metonymic of the entire space of the Orient as a mysterious sensual space that the male Orientalist strives to penetrate.[59] In the gendered Orientalist fantasy, the Oedipal desire to return to the point of origin coincides with the desire to conquer the feminine space. The Zionist desire for the Land maps well onto this economy of Orientalist desire: here, the Zionist man seeks both to return to the motherland and to own her as a bride.[60] As women, Hemda and Dvora did not have the same access to the

Oedipal-Orientalist drama of return and conquest. The scarf of the Other woman thus becomes a metaphor of what is conceived as irresolvable rift between the world of European modernity left behind and the space of the Orient ahead. Casting herself and her sister in the drama of the Western woman entering the Orient, Hemda cements their position as Western subjects against the image of the Other woman.

It is worth noting here that Hemda misinterprets the vision of the veiled women in Jaffa. While she views the veil as a generalized metonym of the Orient, the veil has a more complex meaning in the context of Palestine, as it was mostly worn by urban women of the elite. Rural women, on the other hand, generally did not wear the veil.[61] While she sees in the veil a future of disappearing into primitive patriarchal society, the women Hemda saw in the streets of Jaffa were likely mothers and grandmothers of the urban women who would eventually establish the Palestinian women's movement and find voice and agency through the national project, much like Hemda herself.[62] In reality, Hemda was far from "disappearing" into the Orient; rather, the national project opened multiple avenues for her to participate in Western modernity. Indeed, instead of being completely detached from her beloved European culture, she would end up frequently travelling from Palestine to Europe as part of her advocacy and fundraising efforts for Eliezer's linguistic projects. In this context, she arguably gained more access to European modernity through nationalism than she would have had she stayed in Russia. The threshold marked by the veil in this sense is in fact the threshold between two shifting sites of modernity. Arguably, encoded into Hemda's vision of disappearance may be the memory of her sister, who indeed never reached Paris, and whose death in Palestine may be read as representing the disappearance of the New Jewish woman – the young educated modern woman who had dreamt of life in the capitals of modernity – within the national space.

Revisiting the scene that Seidman has insightfully interpreted as the "primal scene" of Hebrew's revival may further illustrate this. As the story goes, Itamar did not speak until the age of three, a state that the social circles surrounding the family largely blamed on his father's risky experiment of raising the child in Hebrew. Thus, with the encouragement of a family friend, Dvora took advantage of Eliezer's absence while he was abroad and begun singing Russian lullabies to the child. However, returning home earlier than expected, Eliezer caught the young mother in the transgressive act and became enraged with her for what he saw as a grave betrayal. Witnessing his father's rage and his mother weeping with alarm, Itamar then uttered his first Hebrew word "*aba*", meaning "father." Here, Seidman claims, "The mother's silence, self-sacrifice, and absence ... are built in into the mythical structure" of the nation.[63] While I concur with Seidman's analysis, there is one detail that may complicate this understanding. Seidman posits Dvora as representative of the traditional Yiddish speaking mother – Zionism's quintessential feminine Other. Yet, it is worth noting that Dvora did not sing to Itamar in Yiddish. Rather, she sang to him a song by the nineteenth-century Russian poet Mikhail Lermontov.[64] Silenced in this scene then is not the language of the Yiddish speaking mother, but rather the language of the modern "New Jewish Woman," notably the same language that Dvora herself taught to Eliezer at the beginning of their relationship.[65] In this sense, the lullaby scene could be read as emblematic not only of the silencing of the diasporic mother, but also of the closure of what Iris Parush called Jewish women's "window of opportunities."[66]

Could the Other Sister Speak?

Like my dear mother whom I hope at some point to bring to Jerusalem, I was a faithful daughter to my people, and my only dream was to marry a man who will possess the spirit of the ancient heroes of Israel. From childhood days, I loved the stories of the Maccabees, and of Hannah and her seven sons ... and then my father announced one time ... that he is going to bring a Hebrew teacher for his sons, a young man named Eliezer Elianoff. My brothers and sisters received the news with mockery, because they had no interest in learning Hebrew, this "dead language" which is of no use to anyone. Only I was happy about it ... and the next day I received the first lesson in Hebrew literature from him – reading the *Love of Zion* by Mapu.[67]

The quotation above taken from the autobiography of Itamar Ben-Avi tells a story about Dvora's relationship with the national project that utterly contrasts the story of Dvora's early life as told by Hemda. While according to Hemda's account Dvora was invested in modernity and completely alienated from the national project and the Hebrew language, Itamar attributes to his mother a deeply seated national sentiment that she had supposedly inherited from her pious mother. While Hemda emphasizes the evolving bond between Dvora and her father surrounding modernity, here the passage from tradition and religion to nationalism is naturalized through the mother-daughter lineage. There is reason to consider Itamar's version as having some truth in it. Indeed, as suggested earlier, Hemda heard the story about Dvora's meeting with Eliezer second hand and her narration is undoubtedly influenced by her own life story; Itamar, conversely, claims that Dvora told him her life story directly, when he was eight, as a way of consoling him after yet another vigorous clash with his father. In the context of Itamar and Eliezer's bitter Oedipal conflict, the constitution of a maternal lineage of "natural" nationalism deriving from primordial religious sentiments is conducive of Itamar's own self constitution as a nationalist vis-à-vis the figure of the dominant father. At stake here, is not only the biographical truth, but also conflicting formulations of the relationship between tradition, modernity, and nationalism as registered in the biography of the "First Hebrew Mother."

In this context, the question of Dvora's relationship with Hebrew emerges as a particularly crucial point of contention. Itamar claims that Eliezer was hired by Jonas to teach his children Hebrew, whereas in Hemda's version, which dovetails with Eliezer's own account,[68] it was Dvora who taught Eliezer European vernaculars in order to prepare him to pursue secular studies. Further, if Itamar maintains that Dvora was the only one of Jonas' children who was passionate about Hebrew, according to Hemda, Dvora could not understand "the devotion of her father and Eliezer for the dead holy language."[69] Moreover, the sisters' relationship with the Hebrew language emerges from the bulk of the accounts as one of the starkest points of contrast between the two sisters. While Dvora is told to have "learned Hebrew slowly, if at all,"[70] Hemda, by her own account, learned the language within six months of her arrival to Jerusalem.[71] This contrast appears as metonymic of the sisters' overall success or failure as national subjects. Indeed, in the myth of the "first Hebrew family," Dvora's difficulties with the language foreshadow her overall difficulties in the Land and even her death, while Hemda's relative ease in acquiring the language sets her up to become a nationalist writer and cultural agent. Be that as it may Dvora's relationship with Hebrew as emerging from the conflicting narratives was apparently more complex than is commonly thought. This relationship, as I elucidate in the following sections, points toward the intricate dynamics of the relations between Modern Hebrew, women as practitioners of the language, and femininity as a category of the national imagination.

The Feminization of Language and the National-Patriarchal Home

Itamar's autobiography refers to an incident that occurred a few days after his birth in which the Rabbi of the Ashkenazi community in Jerusalem met with Eliezer to urge him "to stop his preaching of making Hebrew into an everyday spoken language."[72] The timing of the meeting in the wake of the birth of the "first Hebrew child" is not accidental. Ben-Yehuda's well-known plan of raising the child in Hebrew fleshed out one of the most threatening aspects of the vernacularization of Hebrew for the Jewish traditional gender order – the prospect of mothers, and women in general, speaking the language. There is an important, but often overlooked, gendered fault-line between the use of written Hebrew for secular literature and journalism, which was already in practice from the time of the *Haskalah* and was fairly acceptable even in the context of Jerusalem (as evident by the existence of Frumkin's Hassidic Hebrew newspaper), and the idea of Hebrew as a spoken language in the private sphere.[73] While literary uses of the language had apparatuses that could limit, if at all allow, women's use of the language, the project of having Hebrew spoken within the home was predicated upon women's massive participation in a setting where their speech could not be monitored.

In her discussion of women's access to Hebrew, Parush mentions how Mendele Moycher Sfoyrim, the prominent Hebrew and Yiddish writer, "did not like Hebrew speech, and especially disliked hearing women speak Hebrew."[74] She further cites an incident told by the *maskilic* writer and translator David Frishman in which he recounts an encounter with a Hebrew-speaking woman, remarking, "I will always remember that this woman disgusted me."[75] As Parush makes clear, Frishman's strong emotional response is related to his understanding of women's Hebrew speech in terms of gender transgression, as he indeed asserts: "The Hebrew Tongue – I have always said – is male apparel; and male apparel must not on a woman be."[76] The *maskilim*, Parush explains, found it hard to forego the traditional gender division of power in which Hebrew, the language of sacred texts and thus a locus of cultural capital, was exclusively male terrain. The question of Hebrew speech was tied with the overall *maskilic* ambivalence regarding women and femininity. While the *maskilim* advanced secularization and modernization of the norms surrounding marriage, family, and gender relations, as David Biale has asserted, they "envisioned a family in which the position of women was at once better and worse than in the traditional family."[77] The ideal Jewish woman was imagined by *maskilic* culture as a delicate "angel of the home" according to West European bourgeois standards, as opposed to the image of the strong homemaker and provider that is common in representations of traditional Jewish households.[78] In this context, the "New Woman," namely, the educated woman involved in the public sphere, was a no less intimidating figure,[79] threatening the already fragile *maskilic* masculine sense of the self. Hebrew-speaking women initially seemed to have struck the same sensitive chord with men like Mendele or Frieshman, conceived as an unwanted by-product of modernization at odds with the desire to normalize Jewish gender relations. Yet in the last three decades of the nineteenth century, Parush notes, *maskilic* attitudes toward women's use of Hebrew transformed from deeply seated disdain to recognition of the importance of women's roles for the advancement of Hebrew, first, as readers of the emerging body of literature, and, later, as mothers who would teach the language to their children.[80] This tradition, however, required recalibration of the relations between Hebrew and femininity.

Parush cites Frishman's articulation of his change of heart concerning women's use of Hebrew:

> I was wrong! ... Let our sisters come and study ... for what are we yet lacking in our literature if not the slender and delicate hands of women who are able to tutor our sons? What do we demand, if not that gentle mothers shall with their soft fingers plant in our sons' hearts the love for our language and for the heritage of our nation? ... in the soft hearts of boys, resourcefulness shall be formed only by merciful women. On the padding of the soft cradle the child lays and his ear hears a pleasant tune sung in a divine voice which he will never afterward forget; those pleasant sounds are forever etched on his heart. In hands is a child borne, on knees is he trained, and his ear is touched with the lyrical poem, which his Hebrew mother sings to him in her language.[81]

The ubiquity of "feminine" attributes, such as "slender," "delicate," "soft," in this passage, and, of course, the elevation of the maternal context for Hebrew speech, all attest to the effort to resolve the *maskilic* dilemma vis-à-vis women and Hebrew by "feminizing" the language itself in a way that bolsters rather than undermines the *maskilic* vision of gender difference.

If earlier positions charged Hebrew-speaking women with coquetry and with using the language as "merely one more ... ornament,"[82] later on women's speech was conceived as freeing the language from the *melitzot*, the flowery idiomatic language that characterized *maskilic* literature, and therefore as a means to simplify the language and make it more natural. As *maskilic* poet Yehuda Leib Gordon writes, since women were not immersed in "a long tradition of Talmudic sophistry" they were capable of endowing the language with "a simple style that guilelessly follows the language's spirit with none of those excessive rhetorical flourishes that jar on the refined soul, of the likes of which it is said 'with neither adornment nor cosmetics.'"[83] The idea of refined simplicity and lack of excess was another attribute of the *maskilic* feminine ideal that was often presented against an image of a ridiculed verbose woman whose education was likened to excessive adornment and coquetry.[84] In this light, the attempt to transform Hebrew from a strictly liturgical language to an everyday spoken language was mediated by a negotiation of the categories defining proper femininity.

Eliezer himself advocated for women's use of the language along the same lines as the other *maskilim*: "the necessity of the hour is that the women must penetrate Hebrew literature; only she can bring warmth, softness, flexibility, and subtle, delicate and shifting hues in the dead, forgotten, old, dry and hard Hebrew language. Simplicity and exactitude in the place of unbounded ornateness."[85] Like YaLag and Frishman, Eliezer significantly envisions the private sphere as the quintessential space in which the feminine quality of the language may materialize: "Only the woman chatting with her child of joy or whispering love to her mate – only she will give speech the soul, the sublime spirituality, the pure scent of perfume, which will spread through the air as the scent of heaven and will fill the soul with supernatural divine feeling. This subtlety, this softness, this spirituality will be given to the language only by the woman by the power of her femininity."[86]

Notably, the Hebrew word that Eliezer uses for "femininity" is not the contemporary word *nashiyut*, but rather, *ishut*, a word traditionally used to refer to Jewish laws relating to marriage and intimate relations. In his dictionary, Ben-Yehuda includes the old meaning of the word in the definition but explains that "the new writers use it to refer to a woman's nature. E.g., the *ishut* of women; this woman has no *ishut*."[87] This definition discloses the emergence of "femininity" in the Modern Hebrew cultural space as a quality that is separate from women as beings in the world. Through the usage examples of the new term, the definition also reveals the double-edged implications of this construct, as it, on the one hand, allowed for the alarming possibility of the woman "who has no *ishut*," and, on the other hand, gave rise to the possibility of instilling femininity in the language itself. In the discourse on women's participation in the revival of Hebrew then, "femininity" is not Other of the language, but rather, signifies what the language and the nation at large should be – a natural living entity whose locus is everyday life, not the strictly masculine cerebral setting in which it has been situated by both traditional Jewish learning and *maskilic* culture. In the present context, it is worth noting how the invention of femininity as a concept is bound with the idea of a national language spoken at the national home in the national homeland, and thus, coincides with the transformation of Jewish nationalism from a cultural project grounded in European modernity to a settlement project based in Palestine. In this sense, the recovery of the "naturally nationalist" mother in Itamar's biographical account of Dvora, is, in fact, in line with the legacy of the father, a legacy which assigns the "feminine" with the role of embodying the naturalness of the nation and language.

Intersectional Encounters: Dvora and the Sephardim[88]

Whatever the truth about Dvora's initial relationship with the Hebrew language may be, it seems that she did eventually become proficient in the language. In fact, in 1887, five years after her arrival at Jerusalem, she was apparently fluent enough to begin teaching Hebrew at the Evelina de Rothschild School for girls in Jerusalem. This endeavour not only sheds another light on Dvora's access to Hebrew but also draws attention to a relatively unfamiliar aspect of Ben-Yehuda's Modern Hebrew project, namely, the relations of the Ben-Yehudas with the Sephardi community in Jerusalem. The Evelina de Rothschild school enrolled mostly Sephardi girls at the time, and was run by Fortuna Bekhar, sister of Nissim Bekhar.[89] In the late nineteenth century, the Sephardim comprised more than half of the Jewish community in Palestine. From the perspective of East-European Zionists, the Sephardim were perceived as part of the "East," toward which they bore an ambivalent attitude, in which, on the one hand, they sought to distinguish themselves as Europeans, and, on the other hand, they desired to reinvent themselves as natives through a fantasy Jewish-Arab synthesis.[90] It is in this context that Eliezer Ben-Yehuda's cultural investment in the

Sephardim may be understood as manifested, for example, by his choice of
the Sephardi pronunciation of Hebrew, which he, like others, found to be
more "authentic" than the Yiddish influenced Ashkenazi pronunciation.[91]
This symbolic attachment to *Sephardiness* as a cultural category coincided
with the social context in which the Sephardi community was also more
hospitable to the Modern Hebrew project. As Jack Fellman explains, the
Sephardim were a more stable, organic community that was more liberal on
religious matters than the Ashkenazim, and could thus afford to be much
more accepting of cultural innovators like Ben-Yehuda.[92] Moreover, while
the Ashkenazim of the "old *yishuv*"[93] all shared Yiddish as a spoken language,
interactions between Sephardi Jews of different origins, speaking different
dialects of Arabic or Ladino, like interactions between Ashkenazim and
Sephardim, were regularly conducted in Hebrew.[94] Thus, Eliezer is known
to have had significant relationships with members of the Sephardi elite,
including Nissim Bekhar, the scholar Yosef Meyuhas, and other Sephardi
intellectuals connected to the *maskilic* circle of the "Jerusalem group."[95]

Eliezer's symbolic attachment to the Sephardim also informed his
decision in the early days in Jerusalem that he and Dvora would wear
traditional Sephardi outfits: "Dvora covered her golden hair, and Ben-
Yehuda grew his beard ... with broken heart the Parisian college student
covered his European cloths with Sephardi *Jovia* and wore a red *tarbush*
on his head. Out of the two ugly traditional outfits, the *Ashkenazi* and
the *Sephardi*, Ben-Yehuda chose the *Sephardi* one, because he found in it
more style and easterness [*mizrahiyut*]."[96] The change of clothes enforce a
different social meaning on the gendered bodies of husband and wife. While
connecting the masculine body to men's dominant spiritual and public
roles, it imposes norms of modesty of the feminine body marked as a site of
seduction.[97] Yet, for Dvora, the Sephardi costume was also instrumental in
forming a connection with a community of Sephardi women in a way that
ultimately, I suggest, set her on another path to modernity.

In Eliezer's biography, Hemda describes how after the birth of Itamar,
three of Dvora's friends, two Ashkenazi women, and one Sephardi woman named Simha, performed a fertility ritual that involved barren women
stuffing the newborn under their blouse and pushing it out in an attempt
to mimic birth. According to this custom, women had to say, "I am not
alone anymore! I have a son!", but since the Ashkenazi women did not know
Hebrew, they were forbidden to speak in front of the newborn and had to
perform the ritual in silence. According to Seidman, this incident serves

as another example of the silencing of women's speech in the setting of the revival of Hebrew. Yet, from the present perspective, the presence of the Hebrew-speaking Sephardi woman performing the ritual in full is significant. While this seems like a minute detail, the intimate nature of the ritual where women's bodies are linked to each other in an act of mirroring that expresses deep affinity charts a possibility of Dvora's corporeal immersion into the indigenous space.

In 1887, while Eliezer set out on a long trip to Europe in order to raise funds for his newspapers and dictionary project, Dvora reportedly moved with the children to a Sephardi courtyard, "in the hopes that they would be more tolerant in their religious customs,"[98] and because she felt better among the Sephardi women "who were very kind to her, especially when she was wearing the velvet ribbon on her forehead, and Sephardi style head-cover."[99] While Hemda titles the chapter describing Dvora in the Sephardi courtyard "Lonely Dvora," the details of the story disclose the development of a new network of mentorship and support found among the Sephardi women, from whom she learned "to live on a small budget and use olive oil as the basis for the family's diet" as well as "to make a living out of embroidery and knitting, crafts which she knew well" having learned them from "her childhood tutor, a Polish woman, who taught her French and embroidery."[100] Notably, the crafts learned along with the European vernaculars as part of the initiation of the young woman to the role of the leisurely bourgeois "angel of the home," were now relearned from Sephardi women as a means of providing for the family, making Dvora into a breadwinning working woman for the first time in her life. While there is no way of knowing in which language the women communicated, and while there was undoubtedly a lot of non-verbal communication involved, Ashkenazi and Sephardi Jews in Jerusalem typically communicated in Hebrew. Furthermore, while Sephardi women were less likely to know Hebrew than Sephardi men, the presence of the Hebrew-speaking Simha at Dvora's delivery bed opens the possibility that some interactions between Dvora and her Sephardi woman neighbours did take place in Hebrew. This was perhaps a site in which she could practice Hebrew with interlocutors who were possibly more fluent than Eliezer in the vocabulary of everyday experience and the private sphere.[101] It is during the same period while Eliezer was abroad that Dvora reportedly decided "on her own" and without consulting Eliezer[102] to accept Nissim Bekhar's invitation to take a position as a Hebrew teacher at Evelina de Rothschild. It is tempting to think how the context of her relationship with the Sephardi neighbours may have had empowered Dvora to become an employed woman for the first time in her life. In this light, Dvora's path as a new woman, once initiated through a bond with her dominant father and the marriage to the nationalist patriarch, reaches its culmination through friendship and professional collaboration with Jerusalemite Sephardi women.

Yet, while Dvora's work at Evelina de Rothschild is seemingly a result of non-hierarchical collaboration with Sephardi agents of modernity such as Fortuna and Nissim Bekhar, it also places her in a different and more problematic history, that of Zionist Ashkenazi women's participation in the so-called "civilizing mission" toward Sephardi and Mizrahi communities in Palestine (and later in Israel). As discussed in chapter 3, Zionist women, like Western women in other colonial contexts, often took upon themselves the role of "national caregivers," as teachers, philanthropists, medical professionals and social workers, as a way of asserting their own position in the Zionist public sphere.[103] Dvora's involvement in this phenomenon is illustrated in one of the only remaining pieces of Hebrew writing attributed to her – the short essay titled "*takanat bnot yerushalayim*" (the improvement/repair of the daughters of Jerusalem) depicting her work as a teacher:

> The truth should be told that most of these girls, with all due respect, were uneducated even about the customs of *derekh eretz* [polite behavior], not to mention that they were completely devoid of learning and knowledge. How happy I am when I see them now, clean and tidy (and without any jewellery), sitting quietly and politely. This vision would fill with joy the heart of every *hovev tsyon* [man lover of Zion], and even more, the heart of *hovevet tsyon* [woman lover of Zion], and they also advanced in their study of Hebrew, Arabic and French, as well as needlework and crafts.[104]

The remark in parenthesis, "without any jewellery," points to the politics of ethnicity in shaping the Zionist feminine body (discussed further in chapter 4) that revolves around the desire to strip the "Oriental" feminine body of its excesses and ornamentation and to reshape it according to the Zionist-European aesthetics of simplicity, respectability, and asceticism.[105] At Evelina de Rothschild the removal of the girls' jewellery was part of the school's emphasis on "cleanliness and order .... [as] formative elements in feminine character,"[106] which was part of the larger mission "to cleanse the corrupted Judaism of the Jews in Islamic countries and, above all, to cleanse the women."[107] Through this lens, Dvora's employment at Evelina de Rothschild allows her to inhabit the coveted position of the Western European woman – if not as a Parisian salonnière, then as a Western woman "civilizing" the "Orient."[108]

Between the horizontal intimate space of the women's courtyard and the hierarchical institutional setting of the school, the meaning of Dvora's relationship with Sephardi women and girls oscillates between the politics of the colonial "civilizing mission" and the possibility of an embodied non-colonizing encounter between women. The scandal that erupted surrounding Dvora's burial could be understood as the closure of this possibility. Since the Ashkenazi rabbis initially refused to bury Dvora because of the ban on the Ben-Yehuda family, Eliezer threatened to have her buried in the Sephardi portion of the cemetery instead. The threat proved to be effective; the Ashkenazi rabbis yielded and she was buried in the Ashkenazi section on the Olive Mount, albeit in a distant plot, far from where the family burial site would later be set.[109] If Dvora's life had moments of blurring the ethnic boundary-lines, the husband's threat of placing her body across the racialized lines of division ends up reinforcing these lines. Furthermore, after the marriage of Eliezer and Hemda, the family moved to a new home in Jaffa street, which "Hemda decorated according to her European-Aristocratic taste."[110] She also reportedly took Itamar out of Nissim Bekhar's school and dressed the children in European clothes. In this sense, Dvora's death and the subsequent "substitution of women" closed another "window of opportunities," and cemented the position of the Ben-Yehudas as agents of the West in Palestine.

Checkmate: Death of a Modern Woman and the Scene of Sacrifice

With Dvora we should not be so strict and we should forgive her a lot. A few times during her illness, she spoke very harshly to me, which I really do not deserve, and nonetheless I keep suffering silently, although all this is certainly very difficult for me, and I almost broke down already.[111]

On Wednesday, a letter came from you that you cannot get a visa and so the mother-in-law cannot leave Moscow. I was not home and Dvora apparently fainted, and came under great danger out of grief ... I hope you will forgive her because one does not catch a person at their words in a time of grief. *I could not be angry with her, so I admitted her to the hospital*, and I will pay for everything even if it is ten ruble a week.[112]

I thought you could understand my harsh words that derive from my deteriorating health, but *you think I have become so wild* that I do not know how to behave toward my parents anymore.[113]

The heartbreaking correspondence between the Ben-Yehudas and Jonases in the months preceding Dvora's death conjure up an unusual image of the first Hebrew mother. Rather than a pure, delicate, and frail martyr, the letters present an angry woman, one that her father may view as *"so wild"* and one that her husband could not handle, so he has her hospitalized. Why was Dvora so angry? The letters imply that both Eliezer and Dvora were pleading with the Jonases to come to Jerusalem to help care for and finance their dying daughter and her children. In one letter, Eliezer requests that Hemda, in particular, would come to "help her sister" take care of the children, and thus sets the stage for the substitution of the dying woman by her sister. Indeed, what Hemda describes romantically as a young woman sacrificing herself for the charismatic patriarch and the nation was very much prescribed by Eliezer's need to sustain the patriarchal order by having the younger sister fulfill the feminine roles that the older sister could no longer perform. The tensions between the two families seems to have risen because of the Jonases' hesitations in conceding to these pleas. Elsewhere, Eliezer crudely dismisses Jonas' claim that they cannot arrange for visas: "Will you really not take pity on us, your children...? The visa issue is a laughing matter. Dozens of families arrive every day, and only you cannot get a visa?"[114] While these are the concrete circumstances surrounding Dvora's anger, it is difficult not to interpret this anger against the backdrop of the patriarchal system that has, by and large, made her deathbed. Here, the desire for her parents to come to Palestine may be understood as the desire to reverse the operation of the patriarchal exchange system, and restore the position of the *maskil's* daughter and the "window of opportunities" that was closed with her marriage and immigration.[115]

Eliezer's remark, "I could not be angry with her, so I admitted her to the hospital,"[116] situates Dvora in another modern context, namely, the *fin-de-siècle* discourse on women's mental health. Eliezer's depiction discloses that it was Dvora's emotional breakdown, not her physical illness, that led to her hospitalization. As Ellaine Showalter has shown, the description of women's angry or rebellious speech as wild or hysterical was a ubiquitous mode of disarming and silencing women's protest against the patriarchy, by rendering their speech as irrational.[117] Eliezer's recurrent pleas with Jonas to forgive Dvora seem to have had a similar effect in terms of marking her words as illegible "hysteric" feminine speech. From a contemporary feminist lens, Dvora on her deathbed may be understood as a modern woman reclaiming her voice against the national-patriarchal home that has become her tomb.

In Hemda's descriptions of her sister on her deathbed, anger is, expectedly, completely absent. Instead, Hemda stages a scene in which Dvora consoles Eliezer and absolves him of all guilt: "It seems to her [Dvora] that he [Eliezer] is tortured by the thought that he had sacrificed her and her children to the *molekh* ... and she wishes to console him, that this was a necessary sacrifice at the altar of the nation and the revival of the People, and that if she dies prematurely, it is evidence that the offering was received, that the scent of the incense reached high above and was accepted."[118] In describing her own first day in Jerusalem, Hemda shares a transformative and emotional scene at the site of Dvora's grave – culminating in another vision of a sacrificial ritual:

> My heart wrenched remembering the beloved sister, the goddess of the family, that out of her own good will sacrificed her young life for her People ... Ben-Yehuda seemed to me like the *molekh* in Gehenna, where mothers would sacrifice their babies out of religions ecstasy. For Ben-Yehuda, young women are sacrificed. I reached out my hands to him. And at that moment, I realized I do not belong to myself anymore and that he will do whatever he wants with me, and lead me wherever he will. Where? It was not clear to me.[119]

If earlier she described herself as standing on the ship feeling indifferent towards the sight of the Land, the fantasy of the pagan sacrifice seems to function in Hemda's own self-mythologizing as the moment in which she emerges as a nationalist. Through this scene, the substitution of women is framed by a ritual of virgin sacrifice. Hamutal Tsamir's analysis of the significance of the sacrifice ritual as a trope of the nation may help to elucidate the ramifications of Hemda's rhetoric here.[120] Drawing on the work of anthropologist Nancy Jay, Tsamir argues that, like the sacrificial ritual to the gods in tribal societies, the Zionist ethos of sacrifice sustains the organization of social relations as system of bonds between men undergirding the patriarchal control over women and territory. Yet, Tsamir argues, it is through the prestigious position of the sacrificed, which inherently includes qualities of vulnerability and passivity that are culturally associated with femininity, that women poets in particular were able to inscribe themselves into Zionist culture. Hemda's imagined entry to the nation through the scene of sacrifice exemplifies the implications of this analysis beyond the poetic sphere. Notably, she splits the gender dialectic of sacrifice by casting Eliezer as both performer of the ritual and the *Molekh* himself, while she and her sister are casted as sacrificial offerings. In authoring this mythical scene, however, Hemda insinuates herself into a very different position than that her sister. If Dvora's angry and distraught voice is silenced by the myth, Hemda is born as a nationalist author through it.

The ubiquitous presence of the trope of sacrifice attached to Dvora's memory invites a broader cultural reading of the Jonas' family eventual immigration to Jerusalem alongside Hemda as Eliezer's new bride, after formerly refusing to do so in response to Dvora's pleas on her deathbed. While the family's immigration derived from concrete circumstances, including not only the marriage of Hemda and Eliezer but also the tragic death of three of Dvora's children from diphtheria shortly after her own death, and the expiration of the family's permission to reside in Moscow, symbolically, Dvora is situated through this development in the position of the scapegoat, whose sacrifice predicates the assembly of the community as a cohesive collective.[121] Indeed, in this light, Hemda's "success" in the national sphere vs Dvora's "failure" may be understood not as a function of Hemda's superior qualities as a nationalist vs Dvora's supposed fragility and weakness, but rather as a result of the familial and material support that Hemda, in contrast to Dvora, was fortunate to have.

To conclude, I'd like to return now to the "famous affair" that landed Eliezer Ben-Yehuda and his father-in-law Jonas in the Ottoman jail. The incident was sparked by an article that Jonas published in Eliezer's newspaper *Ha-tzvi* in November 1893.[122] The article, titled "Mitsvot she-tsrikhot kavana" (commands in need of intention), called for a celebration of the holiday of Hanukkah with emphasis on the nationalistic significance of the story of the Makabim as a story of the struggle for Jewish sovereignty in the national territory. Citing this article, the rabbis of

Jerusalem turned Jonas and Ben-Yehuda over to the Ottoman authorities, alleging that the essay encourages the Jews to take arms against the government. In a recent study of the history of the relationship between the Mizrahim and the Palestinians, Hillel Cohen addresses the affair, highlighting the collaboration of the Ashkenazi and Sephardi rabbis against Ben-Yehuda and Jonas. The seemingly extreme act of turning in a fellow Jew to the authorities, Cohen shows, was motivated by the rabbis' perception of Eliezer's nationalism as a threat to the delicate balance that characterized the relations between the different indigenous ethnic groups in Palestine. Cohen further argues that the rabbis' anxiety was not unfounded, since Eliezer "indeed believed that the Jews should take over the Land," as evident from in his 1882 letter to Peretz Smolenskin, where he unfolds a plan to secretly and gradually purchase more and more territory and ultimately transfer the ownership of the entire Land from non-Jewish to Jewish hands.[123] According to Eliezer's biographer Joseph Lang, however, the arrest ended up vitalizing public support for Ben-Yehuda, who was subsequently "forgiven all his previous provocations," even by his rivals as he was now "perceived as a sacrifice on the altar of the national revival."[124] The fake story about Dvora's death cited at the opening of this chapter was obviously geared at augmenting this trend, shifting the public perception of the two patriarchs, Eliezer and Jonas, from belligerent intruders threatening the way of life of indigenous communities into helpless martyrs victimized by the rabbis. What begins then as an affair centring the masculine values of heroism and national strength ends up upholding the feminine position of victimhood and sacrifice. Indeed, it seems significant that Hemda's biographic writings about her sister often imply that her death was somehow caused by the rabbis' ban on Ben-Yehuda.[125] Casting Dvora as a martyr enables Hemda, like the Yiddish newspaper's fake news piece, not only to deflect a possible casting of Eliezer as responsible Dvora's tragic fate, but also to cast his antagonists, the ultraorthodox rabbis, as her victimizers. The "feminine" in this context may metonymically endow a collective – in this case, the Ben-Yehuda family as emblematic of the national collective – with the innocence and moral gravity of the victim position,[126] and, at times, as may arguably be the case here, it might help recast belligerent agents as the victims. As the following chapter shows, this political flexibility offered by femininity as a quality of the nation, serves as a valuable ideological and poetic asset for Zionist women authors as they venture to represent the relationship between Zionism and its indigenous antagonists.

GENDERED PLOTS
Zionist Women Writers and the Space
of the Indigenous Other

————

The Realm of Women

My fear dissipates, and I think, in this sense, women are better than men are. In the realm of women, the fist has less jurisdiction. I think that all women, of all races and nations, are somehow close to each other. And when I approach them, I have a feeling of "I dwell amongst my People."[1]

The year 1934 saw the publication of the inaugural issue of *Dvar ha-po'eelet* (the woman-worker's word), the monthly publication of the Zionist Women Workers' Movement, which would become a unique and consistent arena for Zionist women's public conversation.[2] This first issue opens with a short story entitled "On the Roads" (*ba-drakhim*) by an unknown writer named Tova Yaffe. The premise of the story, articulated in the quotation above, is the universal affinity between women in an imagined feminine space that is free from the politics of violence and power of the masculine "fist." It is not surprising to find this story placed so prominently in the newly founded venue of Zionist women's writing. Often coded through the metaphor of sisterhood, the idea of non-violent politics grounded in women's experience had a special hold on Western feminism as articulated for example by Virginia Woolf, a contemporary of *Dvar ha-po'eelet*, in *Three Guineas*:

For though many instincts are held more or less in common by both
sexes, to fight has always been the man's habit, not the woman's. Law
and practice have developed that difference, whether innate or accidental. Scarcely a human being in the course of history has fallen to
a woman's rifle; the vast majority of birds and beasts have been killed
by you, not by us; and it is difficult to judge what we do not share.[3]

Like Yaffe's assertion that the "fist" has less jurisdiction in the "realm of
women," Woolf's commentary here is not simply an essentialist platitude
about women's innate gentle disposition, but rather a phenomenological
impression of a social world in which women are less involved as aggres-
sors in physical violence. Yet, as many feminist postcolonial studies have
demonstrated, the fact that women are less active in executing concrete
acts of violence makes the study of their interventions a source of insight
into the systematic workings of violence and power in colonial and settler-colonial contexts.[4] Embedded in the colonial system of domination,
as Homi Bhabha has observed, is a split, but also an interdependence,
between the annunciation of Western enlightenment that the colonizer
presumes to benevolently instill in the colonized, and the violence entailed by the necessity of keeping the colonized subjugated.[5] In this way,
the non-violent and even anti-violent aspects of colonial culture, in fact,
always sustain and enable colonial violence. As Ilana Szobel and Shirly
Bahar have shown in an analysis of contemporary Israeli documentaries
about the Israeli occupation, the association of femininity with opposition
to violence allows the testimonies of Israeli female soldiers to "soften" the
militaristic "occupation machine," and thus contribute to the enduring
acceptability of the brutality of the occupation.[6] In this sense, women,
and femininity as a cultural category, facilitate the construction of the
colonizer as the subject of what Mary Louise Pratt has called the "anti-
conquest narrative," that is, "the strategies of representation whereby
European bourgeois subjects seek to secure their innocence in the same
moments as they assert European Hegemony."[7] Pratt's object of investigation, however, is European travel writing in colonial spaces which is
different in its circumstances and function from Zionist travel writing.
If European travel is an exploration of a foreign place encapsulated by
explorative "scientific journeys" that Pratt studies, the Zionist journey in
the Land is always construed as a part of a project of "homecoming," often articulated through mythical "re-mapping" that enforces the Land's

biblical past as a source of legitimacy of Jewish "nativeness" in the Land. Thus, the Zionist "anti-conquest" subject marks itself as such by dint of always already belonging to the Land.

In the story cited above, the narrator is a young woman walking back to her *kvutzah* (Zionist cooperative settlement) which she refers to as "my place" (*mekomi*).[8] Her narration is shaped by the ideological meaning that Zionist culture assigns to walking the Land as "means of maintaining and promoting emotional affinity and affiliation to the country as a 'place.'"[9] This becomes most evident as the narrator stop at the top of a hill to survey the space around her:

> I am thoroughly familiar with this road. I walk west. Horizons rise and fall before my eyes. Soon I will arrive to my favorite hilltop where the horizon widens, and I can almost see both where I came from and where I am going. On this hilltop, I pause for a short while as I always do to look at the mountains closing in on me with their strange forms and shades. Soon I will reach the valley. Near the valley, the shepherd is shepherding his herd of sheep. He has been sitting here from days immemorial, with his face rough and mute as a rock. I know him. He surely knows me as well.[10]

Standing on the highest hilltop, the walker's gaze is double; it spatially endows the narrator with *scopophilic* power over the entire space, and, at the same time, trans-historically construes the landscape as a mythical unchanging space. The narrator marks the Palestinian shepherd as part of the primordial landscape, alluding to the prevalent trope in Zionist rhetoric that construes the Palestinians as traces of the Land's biblical past, and thus paradoxically substantiate the Jewish claim to nativeness. The statement, "he has been sitting here from days immemorial, with his face rough and mute as stone," inscribes the shepherd into the static landscape which the narrator not only "knows well" because she has walked it numerous times but also claims to possess a deeper mythical knowledge of it.

There is, I would argue, a continuity between the narrator's mythifying gaze at the Land and her assertion of all women's universal affinity. As Chandra Talpade Mohanty elucidates, the universalizing assumptions of Western feminists often played into imperial and colonial politics by erasing the concrete contextualized experience of the Other woman.[11] Interestingly, the focal point of the story that describes the brief encounter between the

Zionist walker and a group of Arab women and girls unsettles the narrator's ahistorical and universal assumptions:

> I go down to the valley. The Arab women, two elderly women and a girl, sit by their jars, which they have just filled with water from the spring. They give me a dish and look at me puzzled. Their amazement is not clear to me. I approach them and ask for water. They show me a dint amidst the dirty valley where clean water springs. They speak among themselves: A woman? Yes, girl! When they first saw me, wrapped in my cape, with short hair, and with my head uncovered, they could not decide who I am and what I am, and only when the wind blew through my cape revealing my dress, they recognized me as a woman. The girl asks, "Are you not afraid walking by yourself?" And I answer, "No, is there fear? But all people are good." The girl does not agree, and is puzzled by my naiveté. She repeats my sentence with the irony of someone who knows the reality of life, "All people are good!?"[12]

While the narrator asserts women's universal affinity, the Arab women do not even recognize her as a woman at first; while she declares, "all people are good," the girl pushes back, and inverts the child-adult hierarchy by speaking ironically as "someone who knows the reality of life." The scene is presented as a pleasant, amicable encounter, but, curiously, it has an unsettling effect on the narrator's sense of space. As she continues her journey, she discloses: "Now the road is not very far anymore: one more slope, one more hill, one more slope and … I lose my count; and it is hard for me to calculate the number of hills and slopes awaiting me on the roads. These are the roads of the Land of Israel."[13] If at the beginning of the story, the walker's control over the space is manifested through concrete and mythical "knowledge" of "every hill and every slope," it seems that the actual encounter with the indigenous women disrupts her sense of control. While the story reclaims the ideological meaning of the space through the narrator's final statement: "These are the roads of the Land of Israel" – the narrator's disorientation undermines the story's premise. As a space of encounter with the Other woman, the "realm of women" cannot be located on the same plane as the mythical space of "the Land of Israel." Instead, it constitutes a disruptive and unsettling site of which the narrator's "knowledge" is contested.

In the December 1949 issue of *Dvar ha-po'eelet*, a few months after
the conclusion of the 1948 War which resulted in the establishment of
the State of Israel and the displacement of 700,000 Palestinians, Zionist
activist Dvora Dayan published a short account of her travels through the
Land, also entitled "On the Roads."[14] This piece opens with a description
of the changing landscape as a result of the war: "I pass through villages –
villages of new immigrants. 'Abandoned' they call them. In fact, they
were abandoned in the near past, and now – they are resettled and rebuilt.
The signs at the crossroads mostly show the old names. The new settlers
are giving their villages new Hebrew names."[15] Dayan's account reminds
us that what the Zionist subjectivity registers as "homecoming" is, in
terms of its objective effects on the Palestinian inhabitants of the Land, a
settler-colonial project whose completion Dayan observes as she describes
the process of rebuilding, resettling, and renaming the sites from which
the indigenous population had been displaced.[16] The villages are rebuilt,
resettled, and given new names, in a process that erases the memory of the
indigenous inhabitants both physically and symbolically.

Dayan continues: "There are two roads leading to the village: one,
temporary, hastily paved to bring building materials and supplies, and the
other, the older one – a path that the previous owners of the village had
used. I choose the older one. Through the stones rolling under my feet, the
solid rocks on which my foot slides, I feel the footsteps of our sons – the
conquerors of this place."[17] The last line emphasizes her strong identification
with the settler-colonial project as a mother. In choosing to walk the "older
road," she describes how the embodied interaction of the foot with the
rocks enables her to connect with the footsteps of conquerors, "the sons."
Thus, not only were "the previous owners of the village" displaced by "our
sons," now, even their road no longer bears their memory, but rather the
memory of "the conquerors." The fact that Dayan's youngest son Zohar
Dayan (Zorik) was killed in the war loads her account with the emotional
and political gravity of the grieving mother.[18] At the same time, the fact
that her oldest son Moshe Dayan became the general of the 1967 War, and
therefore responsible for the dramatic expansion of Israeli dominance,
situates her walk "on the roads" amidst the long history of Israeli conquest.
The remaining text focuses on Dayan's visits with the new women settlers,
most of whom Mizrahi immigrants deployed by the Zionist authorities
to populate the "abandoned" villages and cement the Israeli control over
the territory. The juxtaposition between Dayan's 1949 "roads" and Yaffe's

1934 "roads" underscores the link between symbolic superimposition of the Zionist space over the indigenous space and the political reality of expulsion and replacement.

While generally attuned to contemporary postcolonial and poststructuralist critiques, Hebrew literary criticism tends to construct a proverbial "realm of women" when analyzing women's literature, particularly women's writings from the pre-state period. By that, I do not mean to say that authors and literary works are not examined against their historical and cultural contexts, but rather that the discussion of women's writing indeed often postulates their detachment from "the fist" of masculinity. Much of the scholarly analysis of Hebrew women's writing from the early Zionist period is invested in tracing the ways in which these texts subvert the Zionist hegemonic narrative – disrupting its logic, revising it, offering alternative feminine narratives, and, ultimately, opening the Zionist imagination to "Otherness."[19] Indeed, as several scholars have highlighted through creative and sophisticated readings, the corpus of Hebrew women's writing from the high time of Zionist ideology features rich engagement by women writers with their own marginalization in the Zionist space.[20] Like most Zionist writing, women's writing focused on the crises and dilemmas of the Jewish national(ist) subjectivity, while generally obscuring or disregarding Palestinian presence in the Land. Still, I argue that the ways in which "the fist" of the settler-colonial project was inscribed into Hebrew women's writing are significant for the understanding not only of women's position in Zionism but also of the national project as a whole and its modes of self-representation in relation to the question of the indigenous Other. As I show in the following pages, when women authors did address the Zionist appropriation of the Palestinian space, they generally did not push against the politics of colonization or offer alternative women's politics. Rather, they constructed gendered plots that further substantiated and rationalized the project of colonizing indigenous lands and identities. In this chapter, I examine several of these narratives in the literary works of three major women prose writers of the pre-state period in the hopes of shedding light on the entanglement of Zionist women's imagination with the settler-colonial imagination, and, in turn, on the insight it provides into the depth-structures of Zionist culture.

Sexualized Settler-Colonialism and the
Phallic Gaze of Hemda Ben-Yehuda

And if perhaps Ben-Yehuda meditated in secret, who would the first
Hebrew mother be at the time of the revival and what name he will
give her, and if he thought that he will find in the Land of Israel a
daughter of a distinguished Sephardi family whose ancestors are
descendants of King David, and that he would not hesitate to sacrifice
her … here his hand was stopped: a lamb for a burnt-offering, at his
feet: Dvora, with her blue eyes.[21]

What do we need with these women activists [*askaniyot*], with their
psychology and their philosophy, who do not allow us to live a simple
life? Let us each take four Bedouin women, beautiful and healthy.
The Bedouin woman will bring him the horse and hand him the rifle
without asking "where are you going? And when will you be back?"
she is used to the climate of the Land and the work at home and in
the fields. She is not reading books, and her mind is not confused by
theories. She knows how to behave with her husband. Each of the
Bedouins will bear us four sons, and in one generation, we will have
a big and strong tribe.[22]

In his seminal discussion of settler-colonialism, Patrick Wolfe theorized
the ways that exogamy and miscegenation are built into the settler-
colonial framework.[23] In the metropole-colony system, Wolfe explains, the
colonizer's rape of indigenous women is a manifestation of his ownership
of their labour and bodies, and the offspring of the rape would not typically
be absorbed into white settler society; conversely, in the settler-colonial
system, miscegenation facilitates the reinvention of the settler collective
as a native collective by "breeding them [indigenous women] white."[24] The
two fragments of Zionist fantasy cited above resonate with the dynamics
described by Wolfe and the way they entangle gendered and racialized
politics. The first is a passage from Hemda Ben-Yehuda's biography of
Eliezer Ben-Yehuda. I noted in chapter 1 the importance of the virgin-
sacrifice trope for the lore of the first Hebrew family. Here the fantasy is
further complicated. By invoking the binding of Isaac scene,[25] "Blue eyed
Dvora" is imagined as an alternate to the more desired sacrificial offering:
the native Sephardi woman. The second quotation is attributed to Tzvi

Nadav, a member of the paramilitary Zionist organization *Ha-shomer*,[26] an organization whose culture was heavily invested in the image of the Bedouin horseman as a model of native virility. Both quotations juxtapose two crucial features of the Zionist sexualized and gendered fantasy world: on the one hand, the desire for a "strong tribe," in Nadav's words, derived from the coupling of the settler-patriarch and the native woman; and, on the other hand, the obsolete position of the New Jewish Woman vis-à-vis this fantasy world. Here, the narrative of the substitution of women is imbricated into the politics of the Zionist settler-colonial project.

Against this backdrop, I read two of Hemda Ben-Yehuda's most extensive works of fiction, "The Sin of Ephraim" (*Hataat Ephraim*) and "The Farm of the Rekhabites" (*Havat Bney Reikhav*), which together compose one narrative.[27] The gendered plot of these stories presents a settler named Ephraim who replaces his outspoken non-Zionist wife with a native "Hebrew-Bedouin" woman. Together the two stories may be read as an elaborate dramatization of Dvora's sacrifice scene in the quotation above. The native woman is posited as an offering to the patriarch to cure the crisis at the core of the settler identity. As Eliezer himself laments in his autobiography, "at some moments in life, when the memories of childhood overcome me ... I feel that I was not born in Eretz-Yisrael, and I would never be able to feel toward it the same deep affection that a person feels toward his place of birth and childhood."[28] The same crisis of an acute foreignness in the "Land" clashing with the emotional and intellectual investment in the idea of nativeness – seems to be the driving force of Hemda's protagonist in the stories under discussion here.

Published in several installments in Eliezer Ben-Yehuda's newspaper *Hashkafa* throughout 1902–03, the two stories narrate the adventures of Ephraim, whose wife is described in the first story as an opinionated non-Zionist woman holding political positions inspired by Tolstoian Russian radicalism – ideas to which Hemda herself was attracted before she was brought into the Zionist fold. At the opening of "The Sin of Ephraim," gender norms appear to be distorted. In the public sphere, Ephraim is a successful settler and an excellent ideological orator, but inside the home, he is silenced by the anti-nationalist arguments of his wife ("all people are one people"),[29] who eventually persuades him to leave Palestine for Australia. After spending some time abroad, however, he is overcome by his longing for the Land and resolves to return to Palestine leaving his wife behind in Australia.

Following the last installment of "The Sin of Ephraim" in the February 1902 issue of *Hashkafa*, editor Eliezer Ben-Yehuda hastens his wife to continue the story of Ephraim and provide the readers with a narrative of his successful return, noting, "we are all impatiently waiting to hear from the author ... what impression the state of the colonies made on him [Ephraim], and how he begins to cure the broken Yishuv."[30] Eliezer refers here to the real crisis of counter-immigration that took place in the Zionist colonies at the turn of the century with the transferal of the colonies' sponsorship from the Rothschilds to the Jewish Colonization Association (JCA), which imposed a harsher financial burden on the colonists.[31] However, in the sequel story, "The Farm of the Reikhabites," Hemda disobeys the prescription of the patriarch-editor, leading her protagonist away from the concrete historical context of the crisis in the colonies. Here, Ephraim decides to turn away from the colonies and go to the desert, as "It is not yet the time for me to go there [to the colonies] ... I have to walk, always walk, like the eternal Jew, to walk further, walk through the land, the length and breadth of it, until I find what I am looking for, until I reach my cause and find a solution to my dream."[32] The invocation of the diasporic image of the "the eternal Jew" carries two implications: first, that in a fundamental way Ephraim is still in exile, and second, that the true homecoming is to be sought not in the concrete political setting of the colonies but in the mythical terrain signified by the desert that is often coded in early Zionist culture as a space of myth and fantasy.[33]

As Yael Zerubavel notes, the figure of the Hebrew-Bedouin, the objective of Ephraim's quest, captured the early Zionist imagination as a response to the settlers' crisis of identity surrounding the ideal of nativeness.[34] This figure, rooted in a myth about Bedouin tribes which are descendants of the lost tribes of Israel, allowed the settlers to imagine the possibility of Jewish indigenousness in Palestine. Underlying this myth was a contradictory perception of the Bedouins as both quintessential natives connected with nature, passion, and sensuality and as nomadic people with no claims to the Land.[35] This dual mythification of the Bedouins created the cultural platform that would ultimately contribute to the displacement of the real Bedouin communities from their lands. Thus, the Hebrew-Bedouin fantasy is a paradigmatic example of the way the appropriation of native identity foreshadows and enables the appropriation of territory.[36]

The violence embedded in the mythification of the Bedouins is illustrated in the story through the figure of the settler Harbin, Ephraim's friend, role model, and leader of a Bedouin tribe, who is told to have escaped to the desert after killing a *fellah* (a Palestinian peasant), fleeing the colony for fear of punishment or revenge. The story thus displaces the actual violence of the settlers toward the natives to furnish instead the fantasy in which the Zionist settlers inhabit a native identity. As the following speech by Harbin shows, the substitution of history and politics for myth also intersects here with the substitution of women:

> As long as we do not dedicate ourselves to their national education, as long as they do not know Hebrew, ancient and new literature, what kind of emotions can we expect from them, what kind of education can they give our children?! We cannot deny that in our villages, we have left the women completely alone. Which of us has ever taught his wife anything or even read to her! Anyway, *today our women are in a position of ... Emotion, they lack emotion*! Look at my wife. She is a savage Bedouin, and before I came to the farm, she was hidden behind the curtain like all other women. She did not know anything about life, religion, moral obligation. But she is a descendent of a vibrant People and a natural being. She learned Hebrew, because she did not understand how she could be my wife, a mother of my children, and not know how to speak my language, the language of my People that soon became her people. She loves working the land simply because she has grown since childhood in the clear air, under the sky, and she loved spending nights outdoors with her brothers, guarding the herds, counting shooting stars.[37]

The breaking point of the speech marked by the ellipsis between the unfinished statement, "today our women are in a position of ..." and "emotion, they lack emotion" encapsulates the rift between the story of the national subjectivity of Zionist women and the Zionist-Orientalist fantasy of nativeness. The fact that a woman author is putting this speech in the mouth of a male settler – one who has notably left the colony and married a Bedouin woman – discloses the double voice that the Hebrew woman-author must adopt as she articulates her own interests within the national fantasy world. In Harbin's speech, the question of educating the women settlers is eventually abandoned in favour of a fantasy of a figure who needs no such education because she is a "natural being" whose immediate connection to the Land coincides with her "natural" subjugation to the

Zionist man. The coupling of the male settler with the native woman therefore emerges as a trope that illustrates the imbrication of the colonial, national, and patriarchal orders.

Harbin's story combines the exogamic plot with the colonial plot of "white men saving brown women from brown men," the phrase that Gayatri Chakravorty Spivak's coined as emblematic of colonial gender dynamics.[38] According to the story, he was awarded the Sheikh's daughter for curing her illness, and, in turn, replaced the Sheikh as a leader of the tribe after his death. As in the traditional exogamic system, the giving of the daughter creates a kinship between the two men and eventually culminates with the Sheikh bequeathing the leadership of the tribe to Harbin. This exogamic transaction thus supports a national-colonial fantasy that makes both Arab men and Jewish women obsolete and leaves Jewish European men to save Bedouin women. This story, of course, echoes early Zionist Orientalism wherein the Zionists are imagined as modernizers and civilizers of the Arabs. Here, Harbin teaches the tribe Hebrew, assigns them Hebrew names, and, importantly, "liberates" the women. In this way, the match between the Zionist settler and the native woman resolves some of the tensions surrounding gender and modernity. Zionist men can act as modernizers of the native woman, while also excluding the disruptive New Jewish woman from the national family.

Ephraim, however, rejects the option of living in Harbin's modernized Hebrew tribe and sets out instead to find the original Hebrew Bedouins. Just as with his initial move away from the colonies, Hemda pushes her protagonist further away from the realm of politics and into the realm of myth. The gendered implications of this move become most clear when Shlomit, Ephraim's Bedouin beloved, who was emancipated by Harbin in the modernized tribe, must return to live "behind the curtain" at the tribe of the "real" Reikhabites, where traditional gender norms still prevail.[39] The culmination of the masculine quest for nativeness thus coincides with the removal of women from the public sphere. While the story has been read as a call-in for women to come into the national fold,[40] it does in fact, stage an irreconcilable discord between women and the national fantasy of nativeness. "The Farm of the Reikhabites" therefore invites a double reading: on the one hand, it is a *tour-de-force* demonstrating the author's mastery over the early Zionist fantasy world; on the other hand, it is an announcement of the dissonance between the New Jewish Woman and the mythical core of the nation. For the Hebrew woman-author, it is thus a play of self-assertion and self-effacement that takes place in the space of the Other and is inscribed on the bodies of the native women.

Feminist readers of Edward Said have grappled with the meaning of women's gaze at the "Orient," given that the Occident/Orient distinction in itself is predicated on gender binarism, in which the "East" is associated with sensuous feminine sexuality awaiting the penetration of the masculine Western colonizer. Several scholars, including Reina Lewis, Lisa Lowe, Rana Kabbani, Billie Melman, and Maida Yeğenoğlu have interrogated European women's travel writing, both furthering and contesting the assumption that women's interventions in the colonized space are different from men's.[41] While, for some, women's representations of the "Orient" demonstrate the heterogeneity of the Orientalist framework and even undermine its rigid binaries,[42] others have argued that Western women's entry to the Orient merely supplements the male gaze allowing it to expand its scope of vision and control, but never offering an alternative to the Orientalist paradigm whose contradictory, heterogeneous, and flexible nature actually substantiates its efficacy.[43] Ultimately, according to Meyda Yeğenoğlu, the Western woman traveller constructs a "phallic" position for herself by occupying the position of the subject of the gaze vis-à-vis Orientalized bodies and spaces, and in this sense, her subjectivity is bound with the objectification of the "Oriental woman."[44] Likewise, I suggest, in furnishing a gendered settler-colonial plot in which native women are made available to Zionist men, Hemda Ben-Yehuda constitutes a phallic position for herself as an author by performing a kind of transaction, in which, while the European woman-settler is displaced from the myth, the European woman-author asserts her authorial agency by delivering the "native woman" as a panacea for the patriarch's crisis of identity.

It seems pertinent to conclude this discussion by invoking a contemporary novel that offers, to borrow bell hooks' term, an "oppositional gaze" at the sexualized colonial politics represented in "The Farm of the Reikhabites."[45] Palestinian author Adania Shibli's 2017 novel *Minor Detail* revolves around a true story of the rape and murder of a Bedouin woman by Israeli soldiers during the 1948 War.[46] While Shibli's novel is undoubtedly far removed from the fictions that we have been analyzing here, I argue that it is important to look back at these fictions in light of the violent horizon drawn by Shibli, which underscores the overlap between the conquest of Land and the conquest of women. Shibli's novel, like Ben-Yehuda's story, also takes place in the desert, but while Ben-Yehuda's

Zionist imagination assigns the desert symbolic meaning as a site of Jewish regeneration, the desert in *Minor Detail* is not a mythical space. Rather, it is a concrete territory that is strategically held by the soldiers during the final stages of the war. The novel begins by viscerally fleshing out the dissonance between the soldiers and the indigenous space. The platoon's commander is bitten by a spider in the very first scene, which causes him to experience shivers that are only subsided during the brutal rape "as the heat of her [the Bedouin woman's] body warmed him."[47] The scene lays bare the violent ramifications of rendering women's bodies as vehicles through which Zionist men resolve their own crisis vis-à-vis the Land. In Ben-Yehuda's story, the native woman is represented as a mute but passionate body who "could not articulate her feelings in beautiful words. But her love for me, the strong, wild, hot, love ... she was full of fire. No, not fire, flame, a limitless flame."[48] In the novel, the of the objectification and silencing of the indigenous woman are actualized through the commander's repeated physical gesture of covering the girl's mouth with his hand. In the context of the desert army base, this gesture is completely unnecessary given that the girl's cry for help would be futile. The visceral but meaningless gesture emerges as a trace of the early Zionist mythic code where the silencing and appropriation of the Other woman is placed at the heart of the settler-colonial project.

Foreign Hands: Nehama Pohatchevsky and the Pure Jewish Space

The author and social activist Nehama Pohatchevsky was born in 1869 in Belarus and immigrated to Palestine in 1889. She followed her husband Yhiel Michal Pohatchevsky, who was one of six men chosen by the Baron Rothschild to work as agricultural instructors in the Zionist colonies. The couple immigrated to Palestine and settled in one of the first Zionist settlements in Palestine, Rishon Le-Zion.[49] Pohatchevsky published short stories and essays in various Hebrew publications as of 1889. Her first collection of short fiction *Bi-Yehudah ha-ḥadashah* (In New Judea) came out in 1911,[50] and her second collection *Ba-kfar u-ba-ʿavodah* (In the Village and at Work) was published in 1930.[51] As a women's rights activist and as a founding member of several mutual aid associations,[52] Pohatchevsky was also known for being highly engaged in the social and political life of the colony and the *Yishuv*.

Like Hemda Ben-Yehuda, Pohatchevsky was never valued as part of the emerging Hebrew literary canon of the early twentieth century. Recent decades, however, saw renewed interest in her work in the context of the feminist explorations of early Zionist women's experience and creative work. Yaffah Berlovitz, for example, reads the themes of failure and melancholia prevalent in Pohatchevsky's oeuvre as a form of protest against the patriarchal Zionist system.[53] According to Berlovitz, Pohatchevsky's melancholic narratives form a critical position, "against the organization of the new society in Palestine as an unequal class-based system."[54] Orly Lubin also offers a rich close reading of Pohatchevsky's poetics, arguing that her writing subverts the dominant national culture by privileging concrete and contingent temporalities over the teleological determinism of the national narrative.[55] Recently, historian Moshe Behar recovered an unknown story by Pohatchevsky entitled "Flora Sporto" which was published under a pseudonym in the revisionist newspaper *Ha-herut*. Behar calls the story "the first Feminist-Mizrahi story written in Modern Hebrew in the Middle-East" and regards it as a point of departure for "a feminist-Mizrahi" alliance.[56] As powerful as these readings are in recovering the subversive potential of Pohatchevsky's stories, my readings in the following pages seek to unpack Pohatchevsky's vehement nationalism, and particularly her pronounced animosity toward the Palestinians, as a substantive dimension of her literary and public work. Against the prevalent understanding of Pohatchevsky's poetics as subversive, I interrogate the way she employs the category of "the feminine" as a vantage point for imagining a pure Jewish space that is predicated upon the operation of the disavowed "fist."

In the opening scene of Pohatchevsky's story "Bi-vdidut" (In Solitude), the depressed colonist Tzipora questions her mental health and contemplates ending her life: "Am I mentally ill? Why did the idea of suicide start occupying my mind?"[57] Soon afterward, it is revealed that Tzipora's distress has particular ideological origins. She is extremely troubled by her brother Amram's practice of employing Arab workers on the farm that they share:[58]

> Restrained hatred grows in me sometimes upon hearing such things, but later I regret my negative feelings towards my only brother to whom I devote my life. I repent and ask God to return the love to my heart. And, indeed, it gradually returns, but my peace of mind does not return, and I am tired of our farm, the work, and the entire existence of a forty-year-old maid. I decide that a Jewish farm created

in its entirety by *foreign hands*, is a *stain upon my world*, and I, who participated in building it in this way, carry the *sin* and therefore do not have a right to live in the world. Weakness overcomes me, and I see myself on the threshold of life with no light, with no faith, no need for my existence and no strength to stop it. Nothing is left for me but to let go of the paddle and let the waves carry my boat as they wish – it will sail to where the wind takes it, until it hits a rock and breaks into pieces.[59]

According to Wolfe, the elimination of the settler's dependency on indigenous labour is one of the core principles of the settler-colonial enterprise.[60] Through the language of "stain" and "sin" that permeates Tzipora's speech, Pohatchevsky transposes the issue of "Hebrew Labor" from the realm of politics and economics onto the ritualistic sphere of purity and contamination. In another speech, Tzipora uses the term "Avodah Zarah," the title of the Talmudic tractate on idolatry, to refer to Arab labour, employing the double meaning of the Hebrew word *Avoda* as both labour and worship. The term *Avodah Zarah* was fairly common in the discourse surrounding Hebrew vs Arab labour,[61] alluding to a particular vision of space and Jewish identity. Arnold Eisen explains that much of the Talmudic tractate of *Avodah Zarah* is an attempt to regulate Jewish life in a space where idolatry is pervasive.[62] As Eisen shows, after the destruction of the Temple, the Jews are left in a space without a public centre of worship, in which idolatry threatens to pollute not only the public space but also the private space and the body. Like the rabbinic tractate, Pohatchevsky's "Bi-vdidut" presents us with a Jewish self whose boundaries are deemed so porous that the very presence of foreigners in its vicinity threatens to annihilate it.

That this self is feminine does not seem coincidental. In Pohatchevsky's stories, devotion to the issue of Hebrew Labor is often attributed to women. In one particular story, a male protagonist who employs only Jewish workers is mocked by his fellow colonists for being sentimental "as a woman," implying the advocacy of Hebrew Labor constitutes feminine emotionality that goes against the masculine rationale of self-interested financial calculations.[63] In this context, the critic and editor Rachel Katzanelson,[64] a prominent leader of the Zionist Women Workers' Movement, comments in a commemorative essay about Pohatchevsky: "The surprising element in her nature was her pursuit of good deeds – 'the disaster of compassion' [*ason ha-hemla*] – and it seems that her charitable acts and her defense of Hebrew labor were carved of the same light – the light of, private and national, 'sick' conscience."[65] Notwithstanding Katzanelson's attempt to *other* the old colonist by tying her figure with the diasporic sensibilities of compassion and charity, she aptly notices here that Pohatchevsky's Zionist politics were marked by gender in a way that diverged from the dominant Zionist ethos. For Zionist pioneers, the meaning of "working the Land" was tied to masculine values of bodybuilding and productivity. Pohatchevsky, conversely, often associates it, on the one hand, with "feminine" ethics of hospitality and kindness toward the Jewish Other (the Jewish worker in this case), and, on the other hand, with a gendered sense of anxiety regarding the contamination of the Jewish space by the Arab Other, connoting the colonial anxiety surrounding the purity of the white feminine body.[66]

In the same essay, Katzaneleson also observes that "Bi-vdidut" revolves around the conflict between what she sees as "two races: She is the daughter of the north, weaving sequels to her beloved books in real life, and he is the native son of the Hebrew colony whose streets are full of Arabs."[67] Here, Katzanelson discerns how gender difference intersects with national divisions in Pohatchevsky's stories. While the women in her work are often depicted as more devoted Zionists than the men, the feminine nationalist devotion is bound with a sense of resentment vis-à-vis a perceived Arab and masculine dominance. In "Bi-vdidut," as Katzanelson implies, the female protagonist sees herself as opposing an "Arab-Masculine" alliance. At one point in the story, Tzipora witnesses an argument between a male colonist (employer of Arab workers) and his wife, who, like Tzipora, advocates for Jewish workers. In the heat of the argument, the wife sarcastically asks the husband: "Why don't Jewish men marry Arab women? – they have so many virtues: they work with clay and bricks, carry all kinds of heavy loads on their heads, and ride the donkey behind their husbands; and the children, the children that Arab women bear, they are skilled since birth in every kind of hard work – a real pleasure!"[68] Invoking the possibility of the substitution of women that served as the theme for Ben-Yehuda's Orientalist fantasy discussed here earlier, Pohatchevsky draws an analogy between marriage and labour, and thus assigns the employment of Arab labour the transgressive connotations of miscegenation. The wife's sarcasm illustrates the friction between the settler-colonial logic of "strengthening the tribe" and the national concern for racial purity.[69] If in Ben-Yehuda's story native women are sexualized, here too they are signified as strictly corporeal figures – labourers and child bearers. Notwithstanding the opposite attitudes toward the settler-native match in the two stories, I suggest that Zionist "gender troubles" are illustrated in both through the exchangeability between Jewish women construed as political subjects and Arab women construed as bodies available to Zionist men.

An earlier essay by Pohatchevsky may elucidate her gendered nationalist position further. The brief article titled "Memories of One of the Women-Farmers in Eretz-Yisrael," published in the Hebrew journal *Ha-Melitz* in 1893, situates the Jewish feminine subject in the context of the Zionist politics of colonization.[70] The essay is divided into two parts, with the first taking place in Europe and the second in Palestine. The thematic connection between the two parts is ostensibly loose, and, at first glance, seems to be based merely on the fact that both anecdotes take place by water (the first by a river in Russia and the second by the Mediterranean Sea). Yet, a careful reading reveals that the two parts also intersect through the double experience of ethnonational and feminine vulnerability. The first part depicts the young Pohatchevsky spending a day by the river with a group of Romanian nationalists: "Below the pure and calm water flow, and nature is peaceful ... we are peaceful and happy, we miss nothing. We talk fancifully and think of lofty ideas with great consequences in days to come."[71] Here, the flow of the river suggests a sense of harmonious and joyful closeness between the narrator, her companions, and the space around them: "I, as a persecuted Hebrew ... am still happy with my friends, the Romanians."[72] Yet, at one point, her sense of ease is upset: "the whisper of one of the young men reminds me who I am; 'look, Carl, how beautiful the eyes of that Jewess!' My heart pounds, I am angry."[73] As an object of sexualizing and racializing gaze, the narrator's sense of joy and belonging transforms into rage, estrangement, and vulnerability. A similar transition occurs in the second part of the essay, which finds the narrator participating in a political meeting in Jaffa, Palestine. Looking through the window in the room where the meeting is held, she first describes a feeling of harmony and joy that is connected with the view of the water, as in the first scene: "I looked at the sea, and how beautiful was the view in front of my eyes – a square of sand, a ship, and the roaring waves of the sea ... My eyes were drawn to this wonderful view. I forgot the whole world as if I was bound by a dream."[74] However, the joyful feeling changes into distress as her attention shifts from the sea to the land, which, she is reminded, is not owned by Jews:

Suddenly a pleasant voice came from one of the other viewers: "if this square was ours, we would have built a nice garden on it and planted trees in it." This excess was enough to arouse thousands of pleasant ideas within me, but – these ideas turned into bitter doubts – "if this was ours!" How far is it from being possible? I looked at the sea once again, and now the sun has sunk within its waves as if forever. My heart went to the far ends of the sea west and north, I remembered my brothers there, I remembered the plight of our great People, I remembered… "Why do you cry, sister Nehamah?" – said one of my [women] friends, but I did not answer, I left the banister and with a heart full of emotion. I entered the library and the spirit of the People of the Book with all its might and glory was revealed to me, and from the bottom of my heart, I heard a voice speaks to me: is it really that far from being possible?[75]

Notably, in both parts of the essay, there is a transition of the speaker's attention from the water – which signifies flow and harmony between the self and Other – to the land as a site of contention and rivalry. In this case, the intersectional injury of the Jewish woman in the diaspora emerges as parallel to the injury of the not-owned square that likewise acutely disrupts the self's relationship with her surroundings. The comparable structure of the two narratives thus creates an analogy between the pain inflicted on the subject through her objectification in the European antisemitic discourse and the pain of not owning the Palestinian space. In this way, endemic to Pohatchevsky's nationalist poetics, gendered grievances are conflated with national-colonial claims.

A similar episode appears in Pohatchevsky's essay, "A Journey in the Land" from 1908.[76] This travel journal describes a space that is almost completely devoid of Palestinian presence, and yet, it features similar frustrations with Arab ownership of the Land as in the 1893 essay. Here, the narrator's distress is triggered by the view of the Jezreel valley:

Midway through the [Tavor] mountain we stopped, because the wonderful valley was revealed to us, the Jezreel Valley with all its beauty and glory. Carpets, wonderful carpets spread out under the sky. All straight, green, beautiful. All sown, plowed, growing. The eye cannot be satiated with the beautiful views of all the delight of this piece of land, but the heart pounds forcefully with excitement and sorrow, that the wonderful valley is not ours, that others rule it. Our brothers did not redeem it soon enough, our People did not attempt to develop its tormented strength here, did not ask for space for Hebrew glory here, to heal it and resurrect it... we left the Jezreel Valley to others.[77]

The subsequent history of the Jezreel Valley or Marj Ibn 'Amer sheds ironic light on this passage. Between 1912 to 1925, the owners of the Valley, the Sursock family of Beirut, sold it to an organization named the American Zion Commonwealth with the intention of facilitating Jewish settlement.[78] The Palestinian sharecroppers were displaced and most ended up destitute in shanti towns at the outskirts of Jaffa and Haifa.[79] That is to say, the site of Pohatchevsky's grievance is soon to be a settler-colonial "success story." Interestingly, a distinctive feature of Pohatchevsky's representation of the Land is the absence of the Zionist trope of the "empty land" that often served to rationalize the colonization of Palestine. Pohatchevsky, instead, stands envious and frustrated facing the prosperous cultivated Palestinian lands. A similar description appears in one of Pohatchevsky's stories, where a young "pioneer" is travelling through the Land:

The orange orchards she passes through, the gardens, the wide fields, sowed with various crops, make her envious: here, the entire plain is sowed – the wheat, barley and lupine take up vast space from the road to the horizon, villages and cities spread up to the mountain range. All this extensive settlement is theirs. We own only a few spots, seen in the distance, and still they ceaselessly cry that we dispossess them from their land – all this richness, all this goodness, all this blessing, and we are pushed to the sands, the rocks, the swamps![80]

This sense of resentment concerning what the subject sees as an unjust division of land and power intersects the gendered and nationalist frustrations in Pohatchevsky's writing, where a sense of Jewish weakness and fragility vis-à-vis the Arab Other in Palestine often resonates with the gendered protest of many of her protagonists against masculine dominance. At one point in "Bi-vdidut," Tzipora complains: "My brother has the trait that is common to all Eretz-Yisraeli youth of speaking always of himself: 'My vineyard,' 'my house,' 'my orchard' etc. ... indeed my brother has more right to speak of it, and still when he speaks ... I feel a great insult like that of a person who is trampled by foot."[81] The distress of the feminine subject over gender inequality on matters of property ownership and inheritance is entangled with the distress of the Zionist settler over not owning the entire land. The common analogy between Jews and women, as the two parallel Others of modernity in Europe, is here transposed into the national arena of land conquest in Palestine creating a Zionist line of thought that appears distinctly at odds with the dominant Zionist narrative in terms of its gender politics. If the dominant narrative presents a heroic masculine subject conquering the virgin "empty land," here we find a vulnerable feminized subject protesting her exclusion from the wealth and prosperity of the land cultivated by indigenous people. Notably, Pohatchevsky's position as a nationalist woman author is opposed to that of Hemda Ben-Yehuda. While as seen earlier Ben-Yehuda occupies a phallic authorial position, Pohatchevsky, in contrast, writes from a position of a porous, feminine self that is faced with what she sees as an unjust division of land and power, between men and woman, *and* between Jews and Arabs.

The most pronounced articulation of Pohatchevsky's vehement nationalism is her intervention in the famous debate surrounding Itzhak Epstein's 1908 essay "Sheelah na'alamah" (Hidden Question), a debate that is considered the first public debate over the Arab question in Palestine. Epstein, a Hebrew teacher from the colony of Rosh Pina, wrote the article after having witnessed the expulsions of Palestinian sharecroppers from the lands intended for the northern colony of Metula. Distressed by the sight of the Palestinian *fellahin* losing their land, he calls in the article for greater consideration for the rights of the Arab sharecroppers in buying lands for Zionist settlement, and, more broadly, Zionist investment in Jewish-Arab cooperation in working the land.[82] While Epstein's concept of such cooperation was largely based on the Orientalist conception of the Zionists as modernizers and civilizing agents in Palestine, his ideas were considered radical at the time and provoked angry responses by fellow settlers. Several public figures, including the Zionist ideologue A.D. Gordon and the author Moshe Smilansky, wrote counter essays rejecting Epstein's "benevolent" concerns.[83] Pohatchevsky was notably the only woman who participated in the discussion. In her essay "Sheelot gluyot" ("Well Known Questions"), she writes:

> How badly the people of Israel wanted to be liked by the Russian people, to acquire their love? We gave the best of our sons for the freedom of the People of the Land ['*am ha-aretz* – the Russian people

in this case], and how did they repay us? ... We should leave this foolish road and go straight to our revival. We should start caring for ourselves, our existence and our happiness ... "What we can give to the Arabs they cannot receive from anyone else?" Our God in heavens! Why should we always give and give? To one – the spirit, to another – the body, and to the Arabs – the remainder of the hope to live as free People on our historic land?![84]

Pohatchevsky's cry, "why should we always give and give?" connects with the many self-sacrificing female characters in her stories who indeed "give and give" to the point of self-negation. Curiously, giving is ubiquitously marked in her stories as the quintessential feminine-nationalist trait. In chapter 3, I interrogate further the complexity surrounding the idea of giving in Pohatchevsky's writing and the way it connects with the gendered role of the national caregiver she often occupied. Here, however, I conclude the discussion of Pohatchevsky's politics by noting that the association of the nationalist desire to occupy the space of the Other with "feminine" sentiments of vulnerability demonstrates the heterogeneity of the Zionist gendered imagination, and thus disrupts the analytic framework that construes the appropriation of the space of the Other as exclusively bound with the "masculine" politics of the "fist." Instead, through the figure of the Zionist settler as a deprived feminine "giver," Pohatchevsky offers a gendered reinforcement of the morally privileged position of the victim as a vantage point for the colonization project.[85]

Dvora Baron and the Expulsion of the "Sister"

Dvora Baron (1887–1956) was a unique figure in the Hebrew literary land-scape as the only woman prose-writer whose work is considered part of the early twentieth-century Hebrew literary cannon alongside male authors such as Yosef Hayim Brenner and Shmuel Yosef Agnon. While her women contemporaries were denied access to classical Hebrew texts, Baron, the daughter of the town's rabbi, was allowed to listen in on the boys' lessons in the town's small *beit midrash* (Jewish schoolhouse) where he taught. Upon her 1910 immigration to Palestine, Baron was already known in the Hebrew literary community as a promising young author. There, she met Yosef Aharonowitz – a prominent figure in the Zionist workers' movement, *Ha-poel ha-tzair* – whom she married a year later. Baron and

Aharonowitz also collaborated professionally; she became editor of the literary section of the movement's publication of which he was the chief editor. This placed Baron at the very heart of the emerging Zionist literary elite in Palestine. In 1923, however, Baron and Aharonowitz startled the small Zionist community when they laconically announced their resignation. While Aharonowitz continued to hold public offices in the following years, Baron enclosed herself in her Tel Aviv apartment that she hardly left from 1923 to the time of her death in 1956. During this thirty-three-year period of seclusion, she wrote what is considered to be the more significant and evolved part of her literary work. [86]

While she was the only one of a generation of women writers who had been ushered into the centre of the Hebrew literary arena, as Sheila Jelen and Shachar Pinsker explain, the reception of Baron was often skewed by gendered attitudes. Early Zionist critics celebrated her singularity as a woman writer while also devaluing the "poetic significance" of her work, thereby construing her as a nostalgic and sentimental author whose stories furnish heartwarming visions of the East-European Jewish town (the *shtetl*).[87] By the early 2000s, however, feminist scholars such as Naomi Seidman, Orly Lubin, Wendy Zierler, Sheila Jelen, and Shachar Pinsker have begun to challenge the earlier readings of Baron. They emphasize, for example, the critical and subversive aspects of Baron's work, particularly her articulation of feminine protest against the patriarchal norms of traditional Jewish society as well as against the androcentrism of the Zionist project.[88] Baron's poetics are mostly understood as unsettling the linear and teleological temporality encapsulated by the Zionist ethos of the negation of exile. At the core of this ethos is a clear break from and erasure of diasporic Jewish existence in favour of the creation of the new Zionist identity and culture rooted in the Land. In the words of Amnon Raz-Krakotzkin, the Zionist settlement in Palestine is understood in this framework as "a normalization of Jewish existence ... the full materialization of Jewish history or, at least, its resolution."[89] Thus, life in the diaspora is considered as an inconsequential "intermediate period ... a state of deficient, abnormal existence in which the 'spirit of the nation' could not come to its full expression."[90] According to Raz-Krakotzkin, the negation of exile ethos coincided with the denial of the Palestinian history of Palestine; through this frame of thought, the non-Jewish history of the Land is erased, as the Land is construed as the empty territory awaiting to serve its role in Jewish history. In this sense, as Raz-Krakotzkin argues, it is essential to recover the diasporic, not as an aberration to be negated, but rather, as a generative locus of Jewish consciousness that may set the ground for "decolonization of the Jewish-Israeli entity."[91] As several scholars have theorized, the negation of exile ethos has significant gendered implications given that the diasporic Jewish existence was often marked as passive, weak, and thus effeminate, in contrast with the values of the strength and heroism associated with masculine national culture.[92] In this sense, that Baron is a woman writer who often writes about women's experience seems to coincide with her focus on the diasporic space. Theoretically, in this oft-cited paradigm, recognizing the feminized Jewish diasporic Other as part of Jewish history goes hand-in-hand with the recognition of the history and claims of the indigenous Other.[93]

Jelen and Pinsker note that not only is much of Baron's work set in the diasporic space, but even "in those instances in which Baron wrote about the move to Palestine, her representation was not much different from her literary depiction of the *shtetl*."[94] Wendy Zierler has likewise theorized that "by resisting the dominant trends of Hebrew fiction in her day, Baron effectively resisted 'literary immigration' into the realm of male Hebrew letters."[95] According to Zierler, Baron's exploration of women's experience entails her detachment from Zionist politics insofar as they are embodied in the act of immigration to the Land (*Aliyah*). "Baron's fiction (when it touches upon these topics)," Zierler continues, "typically depicts Zionist immigration either as a male phenomenon from which women are excluded or as a thoroughly futile exercise."[96] Thus, according to Zierler, Baron's stories constitute fictions of "female 'non-immigration.'"[97] Rather than narrate a clear rift between old diasporic Jewish life and the new Zionist life in the Land as prescribed by the negation of exile ethos, Baron, according to these readings, radically constructs a continuity between the old and the new, the diaspora and the Land, and thus opens a unique space of Otherness in Modern Hebrew literature.

Yet, while according to the logic undergirding this new valuation of Baron's work, recovery of the diasporic feminine Other should somehow set the stage for recognition of the Other history of Palestine, it is ostensibly clear that this subversive potential is far from being fulfilled in her stories. While this is by no means surprising in the context of the literature written in the highly ideological setting of pre-state Zionist society, I contend that against the backdrop of the multiple readings of Baron's poetics as subversive, it is important to also unpack and theorize the particular ways in which her writing reinforced the Zionist project of colonization albeit, like the other authors discussed here, she often articulated the project in different gendered terms. What scholars often saw in Baron's writing as the replication of the Jewish diasporic space in Palestine also coincided with the complete erasure of the Palestinian Other. This, again, is typical of the literature of the period, and yet, I suggest, it carries different significance when it is set within what is considered proto-feminist Hebrew writing.

The story "Metamorphoses" (*Gilgulim*) was beautifully read by Shachar Pinsker as offering "gender critique of the Zionist project of nation-building"[98] through sophisticated dialogue with "*talmudic* and *midrashic* literature."[99] As I show below, however, this story also imposes the mystically loaded Jewish space it creates onto the colonized space of Palestine in a way that erase the history of the Other. According to Pinsker's reading, Gittel, the female protagonist of the story, occupies a complex position through which the past, present, and future emerge as inextricably entangled. This position contrasts with the hegemonic teleological and linear narrative held by the male protagonists of the story. When Gittel first sees the plot of land that she and her husband are assigned in Palestine, she is reminded of an instance from the beginning of the story, where she and her friend set up an imaginary garden by their home in the *shtetl*. Inspired by their play garden, the girls go on to plant a real one, but, since they have no room in their yard, they do so "outside of the fence" on an uncultivated plot belonging to their gentile neighbour. Seeing the plot of land in Palestine, Gittel immediately "recognizes her old 'sandbox' that magically grew and expanded as she approached it."[100] The final scene of the story that depicts Gittel's father visiting her garden in the Land further reinforces the circular structure of the story as it mirrors an earlier scene in which the father visits the diasporic imaginary garden. If in the imaginary garden, the father humours the girls by pretending to enjoy the taste of a "bag of stones" as if it was fruit, in the last scene, the father tastes an orange from his daughter's orchard, and the story concludes with him relishing "the real nectar" of the real fruit.[101] According to Pinsker, the mirroring between the diasporic and Zionist gardens may be read as a sign of the subversive inseparability of the past and present, diaspora and Land. And yet, I would suggest, this very circularity also obscures the very different political meanings of the two gardens, and thus naturalizes the appropriation of the Land. If in the diaspora, the expansion of the children's garden into the neighbouring yard takes place against the backdrop of Christian dominance vis-à-vis

Jewish marginality, in Palestine, Gittel's plot of land is part of the project of appropriating the indigenous space.

As in much of the early Hebrew literary canon, the Palestinians are completely absent from the story. In fact, while in the diaspora, the Jews must contend with their non-Jewish neighbours and constantly worry that they would destroy the garden, Gittel and Reuven-Asher's plot of land is described as a safe haven that is detached from the contentious political space around it, so that "the couple hardly felt the war that broke. Somewhere, far, the winds storms – they said – the land raged, but their piece of land remained calm as ever."[102] Strangely, despite initially emphasizing the detachment of the couple's plot from the faraway violence of war, the text immediately continues with a description that undermines this picture: "To be safe, the two build a high fence and kept the blinds always open in their shed, so there was no more barrier between them and the yard, and with the intuition given to every devoted heart, they would always wake up whenever there was any danger there, and always came out at the right moment."[103] While the war referred to in the text is presumably World War I, the safety measures that the couple take – such as building a fence and ensuring surveillance of their territory at night – seems to address a different security concern. Indeed, the protection of territory from invading Others described in this passage more likely responds to the growing tensions between Arabs and Jews in Palestine with the rise of Palestinian nationalism and its growing resistance to the prospect of Jewish sovereignty in the Land. The timing of the story's publication in 1939, after the clashes of 1920–21, 1929, and 1936–39, suggests that Baron, in fact, had these tensions in mind. Without ever naming the enemy against whom the fence is built, the story, in this reading, narrates the establishment of a bordered and surveyed Jewish territory. The remark that the couple would wake up "at the right moment" "whenever there was any danger" is peculiar because it directly contradicts the earlier passage claiming that the couple's land always remained calm. Instead, this passage insinuates that the yard was, in fact, occasionally invaded by "Others" whose identity remains completely obscured. While the continuity between the diasporic and the Zionist spaces reflected by the analogy between two gardens may subvert the linearity of the Zionist narrative, the erasure of the difference between the diasporic Jewish space and the Zionist space, in fact, intersects with the erasure of Palestinian presence in the Land.

The central image that Pinsker explores – the rabbinic myth of *"gilgul mehilot,"* or, the notion of Jewish souls travelling to Palestine through tunnels in order to arise there at the end of times – is also useful as an allegory for the critical approach of Pinsker and others, whose illuminating interpretations of Baron conjure up meaning from the depth of classical Jewish textuality.[104] While I value these readings immensely, I offer a different perspective that situates these stories on the nationalist "surface" in which they are written – in the space of colonization, militarization and the expulsion of the indigenous Other. Ultimately, I suggest, this reading of Baron also points to the limitations of the diasporic as a critical category in the study of Modern Hebrew culture, and, in turn, to the ramifications of the expansive understanding "negation of exile" paradigm in terms of further insulating this field of inquiry.

Of her entire oeuvre, the one exception in which Baron does significantly address the Palestinians is her story "Bney Kedar" (The Kedarites) published in the 1949 collection, *Shavririm* (Fragments). A rather brief and relatively unknown story, "The Kedarites" is comprised of three analogous moments of narration. It first depicts the relationship between the Jews and the Muslim-Tatar minority in the East European town, emphasizing the cultural proximity and social intimacy between the two ethnic minorities, as "they do not touch pork, it is abomination for them. In their house of worship, there are no statues and they too fast. They are afraid of the police, because they are, like us, in exile."[105] As the story proceeds, however, this sense of affinity between Jews and Muslims is attributed to childish naivety derived from the children's reading of the biblical story of the expulsion of Hagar and Ishmael:

> We [the children] were inclined to believe that there are family-relations between us. And alongside the biblical story of Isaac … we were drawn to the story of Ishmael (that in our imagination looked like Mahmud). Sarah's harshness of the heart, which prompted the expulsion, was not clear to us. We felt something like a guilty feeling toward these people here [the Tatars] that this is how their ancestor was treated as a boy, and despite all the sweetening explanations of the exegetes, it was hard to understand how these people, who were rich with property and slaves, did not find a place for the unbeloved son except for the desolated desert.[106]

Exegesis of the biblical story of Hagar and Ishmael read as an allegory for contemporary Jewish-Arab/Muslim relations is the story's second layer of meaning. The invocation of the traditional exegeses recalls that the behaviour of Sarah toward Hagar and Ishmael was a matter of moral concern for several of the rabbinic commentators. For example, the medieval exegete Rabbi David Kimhi (Radak, 1160–1235) maintains that "Sarah did not act according to the virtue of morality or the virtue of grace ... and what Sarah did was not good in the eyes of God."[107] Similarly, Nachmanides (Ramban, 1194–1270) comments, "And Sarai dealt harshly with her – our matriarch has sinned in this torment and Abraham too in allowing her to do so."[108] Yet, most of the commentators justify Hagar's expulsion following the major medieval commentator Rashi (Shlomo Yitzchaki, 1040–1105), who maintains that Sarah had greater power of prophecy than Abraham, and, therefore, that she knew that Ishmael would end up harming her own son's legacy.[109] This is the position that Baron ultimately upholds in the third and final moment of the story wherein the narrative shifts to Palestine.

> This is how it seemed to me then, in childhood days, over there. Yet, as time passed, after encountering these "relatives" of ours here, all these scriptures and their exegeses appeared in a new light: Ishmael did not resemble Mahmud the Tatar, not in bodily force and not in the innocence of the heart. He was humble and peace seeking while he was oppressed, like us, by tough masters. Then, we thought that amidst the sea of strangers how good it would be to work our lands side by side. Yet, as the times changed, when the burden was lifted of his shoulders, his real nature was revealed: "a wild ass of a man" – as the angel told Hagar – "his hand against everyone." Abraham, who knew the nature of this son of his, still raised him in his home, and even had fatherly loving feelings for him, as we can see ("O that Ishmael might live by Your favor!"), but his wife Sarah remained upset, *because she, the mother of mothers, with her prophetical foresight, given only to the great lovers,* knew, already then, that one day this one will rise against her son and will demand a piece of the land that God himself has given to her son forever. And in her despair (the exegetes say that already then, this boy would taunt her son and throw arrows at him) she cried her decisive and unequivocal cry: the son of that slave shall not share in the inheritance with my son.[110]

Here unfolds a national coming-of-age story marked by the evolution of the narrator's reading of the biblical story. In this process, the sign the narrator's maturation is her recognition of irresolvable rift between Jews and Arabs and the renunciation of her previous "childish" notions of affinity and solidarity between the two Others of Europe. Interestingly, if the beginning of the story discloses what seems as the narrator's perceptive understanding of the socio-historical context that links that the two minorities, the supposedly mature national consciousness developed in the later part of the story obscures the political context of national conflict and colonization, reverting to a mythical understanding of the animosity between Jews and Arabs as a function of the Arabs' innate and irrational hatred and violence. Published in the wake of the 1948 War, Baron's interpretation of the biblical story acquires a concrete political meaning that rationalizes the expulsion of the Palestinians from the territory of the newly founded Jewish state.

African-American theologian Delores S. Williams notes that "Hagar – the African slave of the Hebrew woman Sarah – has appeared in the deposits of African-American culture. Sculptors, writers, poets, scholars, preachers and just plain folk have passed along the biblical figure Hagar to generation after generation of black folk."[111] The figure of an enslaved woman, who was "treated harshly" by her mistress and raped by her master only to eventually be "cast out ... without resources for survival,"[112] Williams explains, was a source of spiritual inspiration and empowerment for African-American women and "the community's analogue for [their] historic experience."[113] This cultural affinity between Hagar and African-American women points toward the intersectional politics embedded in the biblical story as a story about racialized power-relations between women.

Dubbing Sarah's position as possessing "prophetical foresight, given only to the great lovers"[114] is reminiscent of the rhetoric that Baron uses in "Gilgulim" in which she attributes to Gittel and Reuven-Asher the "intuition given to every devoted heart." In both cases, true national love or devotion is associated with intuitive foresight that is instrumental in guarding the national boundaries against the Other. If feminist cultural theory often used the feminine experience of motherhood to extrapolate alternative ethics grounded in the blurring division between self and Other enabled by the mother-child connection,[115] with Baron the mother's devotion to her own child entails the expulsion of the Other. This "maternal nationalism" speaks to the nature of "nation-ness" as a form of "political love," as theorized by Benedict Anderson in *Imagined Communities*, that is, an emotion modelled after the emotional bond of the family, and cultivated in the national imagination to sustain the commitment of the members of the national collective to each other.[116] In its most exacerbated manifestations – and I maintain that the conclusion of Baron's story is one such instance – national love appears as inextricably bound with racist hatred. Sarah's love is construed by Baron as a force that situates the political self-interest of the nation in the "zero-sum" dynamics that characterize settler-native conflict in a settler-colonial framework,[117] in which no co-existence is possible, as "the son of that slave shall not share in the inheritance with my son."[118] The "great lovers" are inevitably the "great haters."

Postscript: Femininity, Particularism, Power

In the summer of 2014, I attended a protest in Tel Aviv against the military operation "Protective Edge" that took the lives of over two thousand Palestinians, most of which civilians, among them hundreds of children. The protesters carried signs with pictures and names of the children who were killed. As usual in such occasions, the response from the Israeli street ranged from indifference to ferocious hostility. One moment in particular remains etched in my mind. At some point during the protest, a car slowed down on the road next to the boulevard where we were marching, and a woman shoved half her body through the sunroof and shouted something. Her loud voice overcame the noise of the busy street and the anti-war chants. My partner, who was walking with me, does not understand Hebrew, so she asked me to translate, which I did. The woman was shouting, "Kill all their children. Kill them all." Such expressions of hate are, unfortunately, not unusual in the Israeli public sphere. I suspect that I would not have even made any special note of the incident, were it not for the act of translation. The rage of a presumably normative woman calling for the murder of children seems related to Baron's maternal lesson in "The Kedarites." It is an extreme commitment to the self that radically trumps all ethical sensibilities, and an intense conviction that the Other needs to be annihilated, for its very existence is always at the expense of the self.

In an essay about diasporic Jewish identity, Daniel and Jonathan Boyarin examine Christian vs Jewish cultures in relation to the categories of universalism and particularism:

Our thesis is that Judaism and Christianity, as two different her-
meneutic systems for reading the Bible, generate two diametrically
opposed and mirror-image forms of racism and also two dialectical
possibilities of antiracism. The genius of Christianity is its concern
for all the peoples of the world; the genius of Judaism is its ability to
leave other people alone. And the evils of the two systems are the precise obverse of these genii. The genies all too easily become demons.[119]

The ethically defining factor, Boyarin and Boyarin stress, is not the distinction between universalism and particularism, but rather, the presence of
power, for "if particularism plus power tends toward fascism, then universalism plus power produces imperialism and cultural annihilation as well
as, all too often, actual genocide of those who refuse to conform."[120] This ob-
servation, I believe, is relevant to the discussion of gender as a constitutive
dimension of Jewish and Zionist identity, as scholars have often articulated
women's inherent Otherness within the nation in terms of the particularity
of the feminine vis-à-vis the universality of the masculine.[121] Indeed, both
Pohatchevsky's and Baron's work are read as subversive precisely because
they privilege the contingent, the concrete, the private over the universal-
ized ethos of the nation.[122] Yet, the Zionist imagination always vacillates
between particularist and universal vantage points, namely, between the
commitment to defend the Jewish self, on the one hand, and, on the other
hand, the desire to universalize Jewish identity and become "a People like
all other Peoples."[123]

What we see in the nationalist writings of Ben-Yehuda, Pohatchevsky,
and Baron is that Hebrew women authors were in fact able to occupy both
universalist (Ben-Yehuda) and particularist (Pohatchevsky and Baron) positions to construct gendered narratives that reinforced the Zionist project
of colonization. This, of course, does not undermine the value of the rich
and sophisticated readings through which feminist scholars have identified
the subversive potential of Hebrew women's writing. Indeed, I recognize
that for the contemporary feminist reader, reading is a political action performed through the interaction between the reader and the text, not an
attempt to decipher an objective truth embedded in the literary work. In
the same vein, my readings in the previous pages do not aim to expose an
unknown "truth" about Zionist women authors, but rather to offer an interpretation that considers not only the Otherness entailed by their gender but

also their ideological commitment to the Zionist self and the implications of their position within the intersectional dynamics of power in which they constituted themselves as subjects.

3

THE NATIONAL CAREGIVER
Gender and Ethnicity in Zionist Women's Writing

———

The association had cultural and national goals, but life had other
demands, calling women's attention to the material needs of the
community. New immigrants came to the colony ... and were in need
of help and advice. Who will care for them, if not women who are
more attentive to the suffering of others than men are?[1]

In an essay about the contribution of women to the building of the colony
of Rishon Le-Zion, Nehama Pohatchevsky recounts a paradigmatic
story about women's activism in the Zionist public sphere. The women's
association founded by Pohatchevsky and the other women colonists,
we are told, aspired to contribute to the nation's important "cultural and
national goals," but ultimately came to do the work of "caring" for new
immigrants arriving at the colony because such a division of labour seemed
like a natural extension of women's work in the private sphere as mothers
and wives. The fact that this early association was named "Dvora," after
Dvora Ben-Yehuda, is meaningful in the context of the present discussion,
since the story of Zionist women as "national caregivers" indeed constitutes
a point of access to the national space in which women became subjects of a
particular kind of national sacrifice that is defined in many ways in relation
to the kind of selfless mother-martyr figure that Dvora symbolized.

What I refer to in this chapter as "care work" or "caregiving" (from the
Hebrew verb *letapel*, which means to care for or to treat) denotes a range
of roles and endeavours that Zionist women undertook – as community
volunteers, nurses, social workers, educators etc. – vis-à-vis the Yishuv's
growing socio-economic, often ethnically-marked, disparities. Of course,
the case of Zionist women is by no means unique. Women's engagement

with social caregiving seems almost universally present as part of processes of modernization, nation-building, and colonization. Examples range from women's essential contributions to building the German welfare system in the late nineteenth century,[2] to the establishment of women-led communal charity organizations as part of the emergence of the Palestinian women's movement in the early twentieth century.[3] Indeed, social welfare was one of the main avenues through which women entered the public sphere in various very different settings. Yet, although it is seemingly universal characteristic of women's presence in the nation, care work is also a site in which specific dynamics of social and cultural power always manifest themselves, especially at the intersection of race, ethnicity, class, and gender. As postcolonial feminist scholarship has shown, in imperial and colonial settings white women were often cast as principal agents of the colonizer's civilizing mission. This mission often allowed them to acquire new positions of freedom and authority which were not necessarily available to them in their home countries.[4] In this sense, the site of care work may be usefully described through Mary Louise Pratt's concept of the "contact zone" – "social spaces where disparate cultures meet, clash, and grapple with each other, often in highly asymmetrical relations of domination and subordination."[5] It is in this light that I read the writings of three Zionist women authors and activists, Nehama Pohatchevsky, Shoshana Bluwstein, and Hannah Thon, who, in three different socio-political settings, have assumed caregiving roles in relation to Yemenite, Sephardi, and Mizrahi communities in the pre-state Zionist society. While this reading is inevitably critical of the way power dynamics are consolidated in what I call the "contact zone of care," it recognizes that the gendered position of women as social caregivers is often built into the ethno-gendered order as a lifeline for the communities with whom it concerns, and that women's care work is often carried out against the grain of male-dominant mainstream indifference and neglect. Thus, the following sections do not aim to implicate the women whose work is discussed here, but rather, to interrogate the ways in which specific architectures of power and ethnic hierarchy are reflected, reinforced, and sometimes subverted, through their work and writings.

Throughout this book, we have already encountered the bifurcated cultural place of motherhood in the Zionist imagination: on the one hand, as is typical of national cultures, the mother appears as a metaphor for the Land and the nation as a whole, and, relatedly, associates with cultural and biological reproduction, sustenance, and expansion of the nation;[6] on the other hand, Jewish motherhood in particular also constitutes a metonym for diasporic Otherness that represents the state of dependency and weakness that the Zionist subject strives to overcome.[7] The kind of "social motherhood" discussed in this chapter resonates with both meanings of motherhood.[8] On the one hand, in their practice and writing, the "national caregivers" work to expand the scope of the nation by bringing more subjects into the national "family". On the other hand, Zionist culture often expresses ambivalence toward what was called women's "philanthropy" as an expression of diasporic mentality – an extension of the abject Jewish mother and all that she represented. The agency of the caregiver thus opposes the same power that she also represents vis-à-vis the receivers of care. This duality, I suggest, relates to the particular misrecognition embedded into the "contact zone of care," a blind spot within the apparatus of power where one can fully identify herself as *giving*, when she is, in fact, participating in a system of dispossession.

One of the primary sites of intervention for social care work is the family of the Other, especially the Other mother. In the Zionist context, the horrifying horizon of Zionist women's care work is the disappearance and alleged abduction of Mizrahi children from the immigrant transit camps in the early days of the State, in which "care institutions" operated by Zionist women's organizations were significantly involved.[9] I conclude this chapter by addressing the affair and its implications for thinking of the history of Zionist women. However, while the 1950s mass immigration of Jews from the Middle East and North Africa is often considered the point of origin of the Ashkenazi/Mizrahi divide in Israel, the bulk of this chapter sheds light on the processes and depth structures that defined ethnically marked hierarchies in the Zionist pre-state society as of the beginning of the Zionist settlement in Palestine. Adding a literary perspective to the work of Israeli historians and social scientists who have in recent years begun to critically interrogate Zionist institutional discourses on Mizrahi families, women and children,[10] I situate women's "care work" and what I call "care writing" at the threshold between the Zionist imagination and the material social reality evolving in Palestine in the wake of Zionism. If "care work" was often framed as a mode of bringing marginalized communities into the national fold, "care writing" – writing that depicts or derives from the setting of care work – often involved reiterating and expanding the national narrative in a way that would incorporate the Other. As is often the case, the frictions between the narrative that Zionist writing produces and the realities of history and politics tell another story, one in which the inherent self-misrecognition of the caregiving subject often becomes undone as her built-in place within the ethnic divisions of space, labour, and power comes to light. Ultimately, as I show in this chapter, the contact zone of care is a juncture in which self-making, nation-making, and the making of the ethnic Other are entangled in a way that has left deep and often unacknowledged marks on the make-up of identities, narratives, and counter-narratives of Israel/Palestine. Thus, notwithstanding the marginality of some of the writings discussed here, I contend that they reflect an important moment in the genealogy of gender and the history of women in the Zionist space.

"Why Should We Always Give and Give?": Nehama Pohatchevsky and the Threshold of Giving

The figure of Nehama Pohatchevsky, the writer and colonist from Rishon Le-Zion, has already been discussed here in the context of her attitudes toward the Palestinians. I have mentioned her response to the famous essay by Yitzhak Epstein (1908) in which he suggests that the Zionists should be more mindful of the Palestinian claims to the land.[11] In response, Pohatchevsky vehemently cries – "why should we always give and give?" – arguing for the cultivation of national egoism exclusively privileging the needs and interests of the Jews in Palestine.[12] I have also noted that Pohatchevsky's specific use of the language of "giving" and her adamant objection to any form of "altruism" in relation to the Palestinians is curiously at odds with the central theme of feminine altruism in her literary writing. In the Zionist space, as narrated by Pohatchevsky, "everything, from the smallest plant to the pioneer, is in need of her care," as one of her female protagonists exclaims.[13] In this context, many of her stories invoke what I would call the "threshold of giving," the point in which "giving and giving" coincides with near self-negation, as, for example, in the story "Regret" which dramatizes the excruciating dilemma of an exhausted woman colonist called to take care of a neighbour's sick child at night. Here, the threshold of giving is materially marked by the doorstep, where the woman agonizes over whether to go do her caregiving duty or stay in and sleep. Similarly, in "Flora Sporto," a story published under the pseudonym "Bat Tzvi," who was recently identified as Pohatchevsky,[14] the protagonist bitterly elaborates the position of being worn out by giving: "Goodhearted Flora – that is how they call her from an early age – she was created only to serve others, to care for others, to give them her soul! Flora suffers in silence – so why wouldn't they exploit her? Why wouldn't they take everything that she has to give?"[15] The cry "why should we always give and give?" at the national level, echoes the same emotional rhetoric that is often employed by Pohatchevsky's feminine protagonists. The threshold of the nation, in this sense, is modelled after the threshold of the feminine self. Within Pohatchevsky's world, as discussed in chapter 2, this emerges as a porous threshold that must be strictly guarded against the national Other, who always threatens to destroy the fragile self. But vis-à-vis the internal Jewish Other, especially the non-Ashkenazi Jew, that threshold becomes a border zone in which the subject emotionally grounds her identity.

The story "In Solitude" illustrates the threshold of giving as marked at the racialized national boundary lines in Tzipora's resentful soliloquy concerning a young Palestinian boy employed on the farm with his pet foal:

> The son of Mustafa, Khalil, is also among the gang. I cannot stand that spoiled corrupted boy, and each week, on payday, I ask Amram to give him what he deserves and fire him, but my brother keeps silent and doesn't do what I ask. And Khalil does not even make an effort to deceive us and openly walks around doing no work counting on his forefathers-right to play on his behalf every time. He brings over his little foal, and let him in straight into the stable to eat from our feeding stalls. And he sneaks over a dessert – ground bran or barley that he has hidden for the foal – and Khalil learns the "art" of thievery.[16]

Tzipora's fury at Khalil's and his foal is especially glaring given the prevalent theme of kindness toward animals in Pohatchevsky's stories. As Moshe Behar observes in the story "Flora Sporto," where upon discovering that the heifer has suckled the milk of its mother cow leaving nothing for the farmer to milk, Flora compassionately comments, "it is just that the weak heifer will enjoy her mother's milk from time to time," which Behar sees as a testimony of Pohatchevsky's overall ethical sensibilities.[17] In "In Solitude" Tzipora herself expresses empathy toward a flock of "tiny sparrows" who feed off the seeds she throws for the chickens. She initially wants to drive the birds away with a stick, but then she is reminded of "faraway days" in the diaspora, where her mother used to feed the birds as customary on the Jewish day of "Shabbat Shira."[18] Tzipora continues: "I think this was the first time in my life I felt the desire to look closely at these little creatures that fly in the air, and from then on there was a covenant between us."[19] The contrast between Tzipora's overall kindness toward small animals and her utter resentment of the Palestinian boy and his foal illustrates giving as the threshold of the national space. It is within that national space that Pohatchevsky constitutes herself as a caregiver vis-à-vis the nation's ethnic Others – the Yemenite Jews. In this sense, the threshold of giving is drawn between the nation's internal and external Others, or, in other words, between those who are completely excluded from any kind of giving and those whose position in the nation's social hierarchy is cemented through the benevolence of the feminine caregiver.

Nehama Street: Pohatchevsky and the Yemenite Community

Before I proceed, a brief survey of the history of Yemenite Jews in Palestine is warranted here. The Yemenite immigration to Palestine began in the early 1880s with a large group of approximately 5000 immigrants. This community is often considered as part of the first Zionist immigration wave (*Aliyah Rishona*), albeit only a few of these immigrants ended up in the colonies while most settled in the urban centres of Jerusalem and Jaffa.[20] Pohatchevsky was reportedly involved in assisting the few families of this early group that did reach the colony of Rishon, but it seems that her engagement with the community increased with the arrival of the later smaller immigration waves, settling mostly in the colonies as of 1908. The 1911 publication of Pohatchevsky's first collection of stories, which included five "Yemenite stories," namely, stories about the Yemenite immigrants in the colony, coincided with these waves. Some of these immigrants arrived through the operation titled the *Yavneeli Aliyah*,[21] which was a deliberate effort coordinated by the Zionist leadership to bring Jewish Yemenite workers to Palestine to compete with the Palestinian workers, and thus assist the Zionist Labor Movement in its campaign for exclusive Jewish labour in the colonies ('*avoda 'Ivrit*).[22] The operation's main actor was Shmuel Yavneeli, member of the core ideological group of the second Zionist immigration wave (*Aliyah Shniya*). In 1910, Yavneeli was sent by the Zionist leadership to Northern Yemen masqueraded as a Sephardi rabbi to persuade the community to immigrate to Palestine. The Orientalist masquerade was intended to trick Yemenite Jews into perceiving the Zionist agent as a messianic emissary. Yavneeli's travel journals and letters (in contrast with his later public writings) attest to the reversal of his Orientalist prejudice during this trip, in which he found a mostly thriving community living at peace with its Muslim neighbours. "In all of these places," wrote Yavneeli, "Jews live securely, happy with their lot, and healthy, why would they go to Eretz-Yisrael?"[23] Indeed, as historian Bat-Zion Eraqi Klorman stresses, this immigration was not motivated by economic difficulty or political persecution, but rather by a desire to own and cultivate a portion of the "Land of Israel" to fulfil both economic and spiritual aspirations. [24] Ultimately, Yavneeli convinced a group of approximately 800 Yemenite Jews to make the difficult journey to Palestine. Sixteen families from this group settled in Rishon Le-Zion and joined the few families from the earlier waves who already lived there under wretched conditions.[25] As Eraqi Klorman underscores, "from the start, all the activities of the colony with regards to the Yemenites were based on voluntarism and charity, with no funds from the colony's budget,"[26] despite the fact that the heads of the colony had requested that Yemenite immigrants would be dispatched to the colony as workers. In this way, we should understand how what was framed as philanthropy was really a function of systematic neglect, indifference, and dispossession.

An archived interview with Pohatchevsky's daughter Efrat Cohen recounts Pohatchevsky's early intervention with the Yemenite community in the colony:

> Mother received them. We lived in this house, a solitary house, mother settled them in tabernacles, not tents, God forbid. They set them up on the roof of the "Talmud Torah," it was by our house. She took care of them until the day she died. To this day there are Yemenite women who remember mother...families with children came, they settled them in the tabernacles ... and then in sheds, in Nehama Street, amidst the Eucalyptus trees ... I remember mother taking care of them in those sheds. This is why they called the street after her ... She also wrote stories about the Yemenites. She took care of them like a good mother. Listen to their stories, Tabib can tell, her husband was a shoemaker in Jerusalem Street; she also worked for us, her sister also worked for us.[27]

The context of the housing arrangement of the Yemenite immigrants should be further unpacked because it illustrates the entanglement of charity and dispossession. As Eraqi Klorman recounts, "The immigrants did not arrive to the colony accidently. Before their arrival, the colony's council expressed interest in bringing over Yemenite immigrants to work in the colony."[28] The council's plan was to "receive ten families at the beginning, and give them a place to live free of charge, and if the experiment with them goes well, to bring in more families and give them a place to live as well."[29] What is framed as charitable "free of charge" housing is, in fact, a vehicle of the community's disempowerment considering that the "free" residence ended up being impoverished dwellings that exacerbated the community's suffering:

> After a few days of living outside, when winter rains have already started, the council cleared the basement of the town hall, and put the immigrants there. Dozens of people lived there in impossible conditions for five months. Many suffered from diseases and two children died. Tabib recounts that they missed their life in Yemen: "they remembered how they were owners of houses of 4-5 floors in Yemen, and the specious rooms, and the large flat roof, and the plants on the roof, spreading heavenly scent ... and now they dwell in garbage, 62 people in one room, in terrible stench."[30]

After many pleas and especially after the death of two children, as Eraqi Klorman further records, a public plot of land was assigned to the community "and they put three old shacks on it, and this is where the seven largest families were settled, each family in a room. This was a significant improvement of the housing conditions. The rest of the families found shelter in yards, cowsheds, stables, and warehouses."[31] Naming the street bordering the Yemenite "neighbourhood" "Nehama Street," encapsulates the logic of the "contact zone of care" illustrating the benefactor's domination over the site of the Other's dispossession and disempowerment.[32]

Pohatchevsky's "Yemenite stories" – the five stories in her first collection that centre on Yemenite protagonists and the later story "Aphia's Plight" (1925) – are stories written in great proximity to the contact zone of care. As Yaffah Berlovitz has noted, many of these stories are likely based on conversations that Pohatchevsky had with the immigrants during the course of her engagement with them as a benefactor, arbiter, and employer.[33] Indeed, the stories are often composed of two realms of narration: a realm of testimony, seemingly grounded in actual stories Pohatchevsky had heard, and a realm of ideology through which concrete stories are integrated into the national narrative.

The story "Ruma," the first in the collection, may illustrate this duality. The story includes a long narrative depicting the community's arduous journey from the city of Hidan in the North of Yemen to Palestine. The details of the story, with specific cities and locations in Yemen, speaks to its origins in concrete testimony. Notably, Pohatchevsky's commitment to these realistic details is quite unique against the backdrop of the early Zionist imagination, in which the Yemenites were often represented as metaphoric figures symbolizing a primordial Jewish identity grounded in the "East" as a mythical space.[34] The opening of the story, however, marks the limits of Pohatchevsky's realism:

> The moon that rose at this late hour behind the Judea Mountains shed its light on the Yemenite neighborhood, playing a magical game amongst the trees – hiding behind them, peeking out of branches, painting different pictures: a glowing web between the branches of one eucalyptus tree; diamond and sapphire shine between the leaves of another tree, and the top of a third one suddenly glow with wondrous light, for the magician has climbed and floated upward, with its glowing circle, and smiled. And the sky is full of pale stars, deep dark blue; faraway, beyond the grove, thin clouds have gathered, silvery with indigo crowns, paused there for a moment and dispersed. The croaking of the frogs and the chirping of the crickets are carried out by the air in the grove, disrupting the silence of the quiet neighborhood, which is sweetly sleeping after a day of labor.[35]

The realism of the Eucalyptus grove next to the Yemenite "neighborhood" serves as a reminder of the concrete place at the edge of the colony near the grove where the Yemenite immigrants were settled in wretched shacks "free of charge." Yet, in relation to the racialized history of the division of space in the colony, Pohatchevsky's poetics here have the effect of decontextualizing this history, especially as she proceeds to frame the distress of the main protagonist in the next sentence: "Only Ruma is not sleeping. Her cough overcomes her, and does not even let her lie down in peace."[36] If according to the historical accounts, the physical and medical conditions of the immigrants were a function of the poor housing conditions in which they were made to live in the colony, Pohatchevsky poetically detaches the body of her protagonist from this history in this opening of her first "Yemenite story."[37] In this pastoral and serene environment, Ruma's cough, which eventually brings about her death, emerges as a lone disruption in an otherwise "sweet" scene of a restful neighbourhood.

Along the same lines, the benign reference to the end of "a day of labor" in this idyllic surrounding obscures the oppressive terms in which Yemenite men and women were exploited in the farms and households of the colony's bourgeoisie.[38] When Ruma's husband Saeed is brought "dangerously ill" from the fields, her inner response – "who knew that Saeed would be brought from the field dangerously ill, and will not enjoy life anymore, ah, her misfortune!"[39] – emphasizes the randomness of his death as if unrelated to the harsh conditions in which Yemenite bodies were put to work. Zionist leadership, as we recall, expected that the Yemenites would replace the Palestinian workers in the colonies. This vision was based on the perception of the Yemenites as "natural workers" that are used to manual labour and would settle for lower pay in contrast with the Ashkenazi idealistic workers. This notion, however, did not reflect reality since most of the Yemenite immigrants were artisans and city dwellers and not at all used to agricultural work. Further, many of the immigrants became exhausted and ill after the long journey afoot from Yemen to Palestine. Those who were put to work in agriculture received about half the salary of an Ashkenazi worker and were subject to abuse and harsh treatment by both the colonists and their fellow workers.[40] This reality, however, is often sublimated or obscured in Pohatchevsky's "care-writing."

A powerful approach to Pohatchevsky's poetics is offered by literary scholar Orly Lubin. Lubin provides a rich and sophisticated interpretation of one of Pohatchevsky's later stories and shows how by privileging contingent and coincidental temporalities, Pohatchevsky subverts the teleological determinism of the national narrative.[41] Pohatchevsky's tendency to confront her protagonists with what seems like arbitrary misfortunes is read through Lubin's deconstructive perspective as dismantling the Zionist meaning-making process. In this sense, I would argue that Pohatchevsky's Yemenite stories operate differently. Here, the arbitrariness of the disasters befalling the protagonists has the effect of decontextualizing the way in which their situation is determined by history.

In "Ruma," notably, the protagonist's death is framed through a different narrative in which Ruma's husband Saeed places a curse on her so that she joins him in death on the one-year anniversary of his passing. While the curse would most likely not be a plausible rationale for Ruma's sudden death from the perspective of Pohatchevsky and her readers, it draws the attention of the readers to gender relations within the Yemenite community as the context for Ruma's suffering and death. As both Yaffah Berlovitz and Goni Kasuto Ben-Yisrael have noted, Pohatchevsky's first collection of stories, which is divided symmetrically into five "Ashkenazi stories" and five "Yemenite stories," features gender criticism only in the Yemenite stories. Arguably, early in her career Pohatchevsky could only master the confidence to be critical toward a community which was not her own, whereas her second collection from 1930 is explicitly critical of the Zionist patriarchal system.[42] Yet reading the stories, I suggest that it is not merely that Pohatchevsky experiments with the possibilities of gender critique through the Yemenite family before she can direct the critical gaze to her own society, but also that the focus on gender oppression in the Yemenite family serves in her stories as a kind of diversion from ethnic and racialized oppression.

In the story "G'alut" (Exile), the agricultural worker protagonist Musa protests the exploitative labour relations in the colony, noting: "a person is sold as a slave to his brother."[43] Musa's dubbing of the Zionist space *"Galut"* (exile) grounds the story in actual reality, as it echoes specific rhetoric that was indeed used by Yemenite immigrants at the time to describe their agony over their dire situation in the Zionist space. Historian Yehuda Nini cites an immigrant that has returned to Yemen because of the harsh conditions in Palestine: "if here in Yemen is exile, then in the Land of Israel it is exile within exile. If here it is exile among other peoples, there it is exile among the People of Israel. Very bad!"[44] Nini observes that, "it was relatively easy for the Yemenites to endure abuse by Muslims, as they saw it as part of the sanctifying suffering of exile,"[45] but the humiliating and abusive treatment by the Jewish colonists was harder to endure since it could not be rationalized in this way. By invoking this critique, Pohatchevsky sheds light on the reality of ethnic hierarchy and exploitation. Yet, here too her critique is disarmed. First, it is marginalized through another "gender diversion" as what is presented as Musa's main cause of distress in the story – he cannot earn enough money to pay the bride price for the woman he loves – pivots the Ashkenazi readership's attention away from Musa's conditions of labour to the bride price as a sign of the patriarchal Yemenite society. Furthermore, the end of the story further blurs the poignancy of the Musa's protest through ideological superimposition. In a cathartic scene, taking place during the workday in the field, Musa forgoes his resentment and reconnects to the Land:

A bird is flying, jumping from branch to branch on the tree, tweeting cheerfully. Musa raises his head, looks at the branches looking for the mischievous bird. Soft sunbeams reach his eyes, enter his heart with their warmth, and soften the bitterness in it. On the windowpanes of the master's home, he suddenly sees another golden sun, and here also, on the tin of his own shed, the sun is smiling as a silver ball. A great joy spreads all over his heavy limbs, and along with the blessing of food, he blesses God for the beautiful world he has made, and he changes his mind about going back abroad. It is better for him to work here and not move from here.[46]

As in the poetic opening of "Ruma," the landscape itself appears here as a reconciling force which negates Musa's earlier protest bringing him back into the national fold. The term "Galut" is thus disarmed of its critical edge, appearing instead as a falsity corrected in the final scene. Even more striking is the way in which nature is endowed with the capacity of blurring the hierarchical labour relations. While the employer lives in a house with windowpanes, whereas the worker lives in a tin shed in the field, Pohatchevsky's poetic description of the sun reflecting on both the employer's house and the worker's shed naturalizes the material hierarchy by subsuming both homes into the unified and continuous space of the Land, whose ideological significance gives "labour" its meaning and precludes its understanding as exploitation. Thus, in the story's conclusion, Musa forgoes his plans to leave Palestine, and instead decides to remain in the colony to work under the conditions that earlier in the story he had named "slavery." Reinforcing the Zionist understanding of labour as a vehicle of spiritual regeneration, rather than a site of exploitation and class struggle, the story ultimately erases Musa's critique.

As may be gathered by now, the Yemenite immigrants in Rishon Le-Zion were effectively made into a homeless community in the Zionist national home. This situation is referenced in the stories a few times in the context of the relationship between employers and workers. As mentioned, many of the Yemenite immigrants ended up living in makeshift dwellings on their employers' property. In "G'alut," after the redemptive scene discussed above, Musa's sudden optimistic mood at the end of the story is invigorated when he recalls, "maybe the master was not joking when he said, 'these bricks we are tending to are for you, Musa. I want you to make yourself a nice room.'"[47] This remark fleshes out the ambiguous position of the employer-as-benefactor which Pohatchevsky herself also occupied. In "Ruma," this theme is developed as Ruma seeks to imitate the Ashkenazi home, and builds furniture out of wooden boards she finds in the colonist's yard. The boards are given to her as an act of charity with the "lady" (*gveret*) "stroking her cheek and promising her with a smile that if she is hardworking, she would get even better gifts than those boards."[48] In another story, "Pe'amim" (Steps), the Yemenite domestic worker Tuvia regards her employer Mrs. Havin as "beautiful, nice and more than a mother to her."[49] However, when Tuvia does not show up to work because she has to take care of her sick husband, the lady causes Tuvia distress by "not showing her a smiling face."[50] While witnessing Tuvia crying while she works, however, Mrs. Havin once again shows her kindness and consoles her. Mrs. Havin's wavering kindness and anger expose the hybrid nature of the relationship in which the Yemenite worker is dependent on her employer not only for employment but also for "maternal" emotional support which is contingent upon satisfactory labour.

The attribution of "maternal" qualities to the employer brings us back to Pohatchevsky's own position vis-à-vis the Yemenites. Indeed, Pohatchevsky was called the "mother of the Yemenites" and her daughter Efrat testifies that "she took care of them like a good mother."[51] In the semi-autobiographic novel, *Ke-'esev ha-sade* (Like the Grass of the Field), Mordechai Tabib, an author of Yemenite descent from Rishon Le-Zion, includes a scene where the protagonist calls out a woman-colonist: "you have spoken about women's rights … what does the lady do with Rumia the child who works for you from dawn to dusk."[52] Eraqi Klorman notes that Tabib most likely refers to Nehama Pohatchevsky herself in this scene. Indeed, as was common in the colony, Pohatchevsky did employ young Yemenite girls in her household. It seems that she understood employment as a mode of "care-work" in which she takes the girls in and provides them with both employment and sustenance. Pohatchevsky's archive includes interviews with women who have worked for her as girls. One of the interviewees recounts the incident in which she came to work for Pohatchevsky. Upon seeing the girl peeling almonds in the yard, Pohatchevsky reportedly announced, "*You* will not peel almonds outside, *you* will be in my home,"[53] implying that the girl's employment in the family home, rather than outside, is an act of benevolence. To an uncited interviewer's question, another interviewee responds, "Did she love me? I was just a child, she gave me something to eat, something to drink, good breakfast, lunch and dinner."[54] This testimony proceeds with an anecdote that seems to encapsulate the complex and fraught position of the Yemenite girl worker within the Ashkenazi family home:

> She [Pohatchevsky] used to cook. She had a big oven. She would cook the food, put it in the oven and close the oven. I really liked sweet and sour cabbage … once, when she made sweet and sour cabbage and took it out of the oven, I stole a little bit. She happened to have a beautiful daughter dressed in a skirt and white shirt, nicely dressed, she was wonderful. Her name was Efrat. She walked behind me and I did not see her. I went to the pot, took a little bit of cabbage and ate it. She said to me, "Yona'le dear, if you like cabbage, get a plate and get some before dinner. If you like it, I give you permission to take some."[55]

While this story is framed as a story about the kindness bestowed on the Yemenite girl-worker in the Ashkenazi home, it also discloses the problematic liminal position of the child-employee, whose labour is tied with the benevolence of the employer. This scene is particularly poignant as it stresses the class relations between two children: the child of the owner who is dressed well and has the authority to give the other child permission to eat, and the child worker whose ambiguous position as a guest/worker/sister/daughter/charity-receiver leads her to "steal" the cabbage. In this context, Efrat's testimony that her mother took care of the Yemenites "like a good mother" ought to be juxtaposed with her testimony that "one Yemenite woman came to work for us. She worked and got a room in the basement. She was with us ten years … she raised me, not mother."[56] In the context of the entanglement of philanthropy and labour relations, a series of substitutions among women seem to define the organization of class, power, and the division of labour within and outside the home, as one woman's "social motherhood" is contingent on the employment of the other as a substitute mother. In this way, the overlapping labour and care-work relations also coincide with the disintegration of the Yemenite family whose mothers and daughters are forced into problematic liminal positions in the Ashkenazi household.

To further unpack this, it is worthwhile to look at the account by Yemenite community leader Yisrael Yeshayahu wherein he describes the immigration crisis of the Yemenite family in the context of its integration into the Yishuv's hierarchic labour market:

The work of the Jewish man in Yemen – be him a goldsmith or a shoemaker, a carpenter or a weaver – is done at home alongside his wife and children. He sets his work schedule as he pleases with no supervision and teaches his craft to his sons ... his wife manages the household and sometimes helps with his work. The daughter helps around the home as well, either to her mother or to her father, of her own free will. In Palestine, the father becomes a hired worker in other people's farm ... he works eight to ten hours under supervision of the employer. Calm and rest are taken away from his body and soul. In the evening, he runs around from person to person and from institution to institution – register here, wait in line there – in order to get a day's work. In the morning, he rushes to work. Therefore, he is deprived not only of his personal freedom but also of his joy in life. He does not have time to spend with his friends, even an hour of joy ... the wife and mother is no longer at the position of the one governing her own home. Here most of the Yemenite mothers go to work as hired domestic workers, and this is the origin of the crisis. The mother must be with the other family during all hours of the day, a family that is alien to her in its lifestyle, character, culture and language, and she needs to give this family, the lady employer and her children, her own maternal energy for meagre salary. And when she comes back home ... she has no energy left to give to her children who were abandoned during the day.[57]

While Yeshayahu analyzes the disintegration of the Yemenite family as a result of its difficult transition from a traditional home-based economy to the bourgeois capitalist framework of the colony, in Zionist discourse, the Yemenite family is rendered as innately deficient and in need of restructuring at the core. The process by which Yemenite women become liminal subjects caring for the Ashkenazi family is thus often framed as a process through which they are in fact initiated into the more advanced Ashkenazi society.[58] In this context, as Pohatchevsky's case illustrates, Zionist women's "care-work" and "care-writing" facilitate the integration of Zionism's ethnic Others into the symbolic and material structures of power that sustain Zionist culture.

Shoshana Bluwstein – Buddha of the Yemenites

The tale of Buddha. In those days, I liked the tale about the young prince who never knew any sorrow or grief. All shadows were kept away from him. He did not know that there is pain and sickness in the world; did not know the lacking order of the world. Only beauty, perfectness and purity ruled around him. … And one day, he snuck out over the fence of his garden, outside of his wonderful palace, and went out into the world. And behold, on the road, the road of life, pain after pain: sickness, ugliness, sorrow and death. His bewilderment was unmeasurable – all these monstrous phenomena – what are they? … and the rest is known: he had a turn of heart and became a saint. … Kinneret seemed to me to be a world that is entirely good. The beauty of the surrounding, the labour which seemed to me to be crowned with a glowing wreath of primordial power, the dream of revival that I have experienced through ecstatic faith – all this cast a fairy-tale-like cloak over life. … Why was I reminded of the legend of Buddha? Because I too was struck by the monstrous phenomena of life … old age, sickness and death – all that I encountered when the Yemenites came.[59]

Born in 1889 in the Russian city of Saratov, Shoshana Bluwstein is mostly known as the sister of the renowned poet Rachel Bluwstein (known as Rachel the Poet).[60] The two sisters arrived in Palestine together in 1909 as tourists, but ended up being infatuated with the idealism of the second Zionist immigration wave, and stayed on in the Kinneret commune by the Sea of Galilee. They later enrolled in the women's educational farm established in Kinneret by the famous Zionist educator Hannah Meisel.[61] Shoshana Bluwstein wrote two memoirs about her experience in Kinneret. The first *Aley Kinneret* (*Of Kinneret*) is a glorifying account of pioneer life described as a cathartic experience in which the ideology of spiritual regeneration through work of the land encompasses every aspect of life.[62] While the second memoir *Ali Teyman* (*Ascend Yemen*) was published three years after *Aley Kinneret*, it seemingly describes events that happened concurrently with the experience depicted in the first memoir. As the Buddha story above discloses, pioneer life and caring for the Yemenites constituted two dichotomous realms for Bluwstein; on the one hand, the "entirely good" world of the commune, and, on the other hand, the realm of "monstrous phenomena" introduced by the Yemenites. The point of convergence between the two realms is the caregiving self that according to the Buddha analogy is sanctified through the experience. While Bluwstein separates the two stories, the two memoirs share the same intensely ideological, cathartic tone ripe with something akin to religious excitement, wherein both life on the Land and care work are described as experiences in which the self loses itself, purified, and regenerated.

Elsewhere, she remarks: "The 'I' was not at the centre of the action, not even the 'we.' The scope was wider, and at the centre 'the very core of things.' And we – were we delegates of the great 'unknown'? With great humility, we carried out our role: we worked for the 'People,' we are simple workers in the great work of building our land."[63] Ironically, like the Buddha story, the inflated rhetoric in this statement ultimately reveals how much in fact the work of "care" is entrenched with the making of the self, and, in particular, the Zionist feminine self. Bluwstein's rhetoric contains a mix of ideas about femininity, including the revolutionary Russian image of the self-sacrificing radical "working for the people,"[64] the altruist "angel of the home,"[65] and the selfless Jewish mother. Unlike Pohatchevsky who postulates an innate feminine inclination to care for others, Bluwstein is committed to ideas of gender equality taken from the context of Russian radicalism, often underscoring the desire of the pioneer women to do the same work as men. Yet, as we have seen with Pohatchevsky's memory of the mother feeding the birds, for example, writing about her care work seems to be an outlet through which Bluwstein conjures up feminine contents connected with the diasporic mother as an emotional and ideological source of inspiration. In a moment of poetic rumination, she reminisces, "In my faraway childhood, and we are under the wings of mother, she planted in our hearts the love of God, purity, and charity to others."[66] The religiose ethics of the mother, she continues, has developed into her adult political passion to "fight human suffering and then fight the suffering of the 'People.' Wipe away tears, alleviate pain – the banner of the 'nurse.'"[67] Work with the Yemenites appears here as a climax of a gendered story that begins with a spiritual connection to the abandoned diasporic mother, continues through the image of the revolutionary martyr, and culminates with the identity of the caregiving "nurse." It is a story that, on the one hand, fulfills the Zionist trajectory of sacrifice and regeneration, but, on the other hand, connects to the Othered diasporic motherhood as an emotional undercurrent. In this sense, representing the Yemenites allows Bluwstein to reconcile the rift created by the negation of exile ethos and its emotional toll; in a sentimental scene in *Aley Kinneret* wherein the women-pioneer are missing home, she laments: "we are all 'exiles,' and there, in the Diaspora, 'abroad,' are dearly beloved hearts. Sisters, brothers and parents."[68] If here, Bluwstein immediately negates the emotion of exile in the Land – "we have to live in the new world, because who else will build it if not us, the pioneers"[69] – the context of care work in the second memoir allows reminiscence of the "feminized" old world to be incorporated into the ideological present.

In comparison to Pohatchevsky, Bluwstein's writing is generally much more implicated in the ideological mystification of the Yemenites. As typical of Zionist rhetoric, she depicts them as mythical personifications of "ancient Judaism"[70] embodying the narrative of national redemption in which "our brothers, exiled for thousands of years in their harsh desert, are now redeemed by us."[71] The rhetoric regarding the Yemenites being saved from the darkness of exile by Zionism is, of course, at odds with the historical reality. As historian Yehuda Nini explains, the group of Yemenite immigrants that arrived in Kinneret were part of the *Yavneeli Aliyah*. As such, they were not in fact saved by the Zionists; rather, they were members of a thriving community in Yemen who were recruited to come and work in Palestine to save the Zionist Labor movement's failing project of Hebrew Labor by replacing the Arab workers in the colonies. In this context, the redemption narrative served to obscure the real circumstances of the Yemenite immigration.[72]

As in Rishon Le-Zion, in Kinneret as well, no preparations were made to house the immigrants because they were not deemed as needing a proper place to stay. As Bluwstein notes, it was assumed that they can sleep outside in the summer, but "in rainy days (it was in the winter), they must be under some kind of roof, and there is none. So, they emptied a warehouse out of crops and gave it to the Yemenites, but it did not have windows and it was dark there all the time."[73] Her impressions of this inadequate dwelling are emblematic of her overall poetics in this text:

I remember the first impression I had when I entered that darkness. Is it day or night? Is there darkness in the whole world, or maybe just here, and outside, it is a bright day, a Kinneret day, beautiful and calm … my heart wrenched out the heaviness of the darkness. I looked at the life teeming. In the corners, bodies folded. Why are there no lights? … if I could open the windows of their prison and tear up the wicked darkness, and waves of sunlight and warmth would come in, and suddenly the world is bright, and life is welcoming. Oh! It was only an illusion, that darkness – the shadow of darkness? We are in the "homeland," in the sacred land of light and glow.[74]

Transposing the concrete living conditions caused by prejudice and negligence into the symbolic realm, Bluwstein incorporates the darkness of the warehouse into the national imagination by deeming it the "darkness of exile," thus also casting herself potentially as bringing the light of the "homeland" to the immigrants. This allegory seemingly allows her to reconcile the harsh reality that unfolds alongside the perfect Zionist utopia, where families with children, as well as old and sick people, were crowded into a dark warehouse. Further, she proceeds to imagine the Yemenite consciousness as a liminal site of battle between light and darkness, where "hope and faith push away the darkness of exile and its shadows, but they may be hiding in the corners, not left yet," worrying that because of the harsh conditions in which the Yemenites were forced to live in Kinneret, "the shadows" will prevail, and "the spark of liberation in the heart will burn out, God forbid."[75] Through the poetic strategy of allegorization, material suffering is reconstructed as an ideological-psychological drama in which the immigrants are imagined as not yet fully present in the Land, still battling the shadows of exile, thus allowing the "caring" Zionist self to deflect the dissonance between the story of redemption and the reality of neglect.

Another defining characteristic of Bluwstein's representation of the Yemenites (which sets her apart from Pohatchevsky) is her tendency to depict them as a collective. While according to her testimony, she had close relationships with the Kinneret families, she rarely names the individuals with whom she interacts, nor does she address any biographical background of their life before their immigration. One episode in which the setup of Bluwstein's selfhood vis-à-vis a nameless Yemenite collective is most glaring concerns the death of a Yemenite woman in the warehouse. The scene begins with an instance of self-centredness on the part of Bluwstein that seems most endemic of her near adolescent age. One evening she arrives at the Yemenite camp after having been absent for a day because of "urgent work" in the women's farm.[76] Feeling guilty for her absence, she notices the group's behaviour is strange and alienated: "why are they not answering my greeting, and their speech seem sad, is it really ... because of my absence? Are they resentful, sad or angry at me?"[77] Yet, as she soon reveals, her absence is not the cause of the immigrants' sadness:

> I go from one sickbed to another almost in complete darkness. "Tomorrow morning, I will be here ..." I decide in my heart. "With you again, my dear patients ..." I stood in one corner. There is a sick woman there. She has a fever. I have not seen her today. I felt guilty. I should have come to see her, even in the middle of work [...] I ask about her... I come closer, I want to take her hand in my hand ... but they stop me with a feeble gesture. "No need." Why? I don't understand, I say. And, suddenly, did I feel it or did I hear the word: dead.[78]

As the text was published, and presumably written, years after the events, it is striking how close Bluwstein's narration remains to her own consciousness. Here, the individual emotional drama of guilt and benevolence revolves around her one-day absence, while the Yemenites all appear as nameless, dark figures, only present in the scene through their reactions to her. Later, in sharing her sense of guilt and distress over the woman's death with another member of the cooperative, she is told, "maybe she was already ill, in her faraway step-motherland. Nobody knew anything. Maybe she was old and weak? Who knows? They all look old."[79] Such a response seems emblematic of the Ashkenazi gaze at the Yemenites as an undifferentiated collective of bodies. Notably, this approach is reinforced in Bluwstein's various depictions of her visits to the warehouse, whose darkness becomes the textual vehicle of this undifferentiating gaze. The story of the deceased Yemenite woman proceeds without naming or revealing any other specific information about her or the circumstances of her death. In response to the racist remark by her friend, Bluwstein responds, "Perhaps she did not receive food all day?" then brings the narrative back to the drama of her absence, "Please, God, forgive me! I abandoned them, I walked away, devoted myself joyfully to work in the field. Now I know: I will never have another day of such forgetfulness."[80] Yehuda Nini mentions in his study the grave of a Yemenite woman buried in 1912 in Kinneret of whom we know nothing about apart from the name carved on her gravestone, "Badra, daughter of Moshe Afgen."[81] The burial, like the name, remains outside of Bluwstein's narrative: "I was not at the actual burial. I was too busy with the patients. Also it was too hard for me, the vision of this shadow, going back to the land of shadows, leaving the hopeful shore of life, which she has

just now reached and did not get to root herself in."[82] Deeming Badra Afgen
as a shadow "going back to the land of shadows," Bluwstein concludes the
story with complete detachment of Badra's life and death from its concrete
history; "burying" her, so to speak, in the national narrative where she can
only be seen as shadow.

While Bluwstein grapples with the dissonance between the Yemenite
experience and the ideal of life in the Zionist cooperative, her story in fact
connects to a much deeper disruption of the Zionist ideal associated with
the Yemenite settlement in Kinneret. The story of the ultimate expulsion
of the Yemenites from Kinneret in 1930 by orders of the Zionist leadership
and the subsequent appropriation of their lands by the Ashkenazi kibbutz
Kvutzat Kinneret exposes a reality of racism, exclusion, and cruelty behind
the Labor Zionism's utopian façade of the new ideal and just society.[83] While
the 1930 affair is better known by now, Bluwstein describes an earlier event
of expulsion. Her narrative concerns the first group of Yemenite immigrants
that were expelled from Kinneret just a few months after their arrival in
1912.[84] While there is little historiographic material on this event, it seems
to be a precursor of the final expulsion, manifesting the politics of ethnic
segregation in the ideological centres of the Yishuv. Nini recounts that this
first group (like the second one) arrived at the Kinneret at the initiative of
the Zionist "Eretz Yisraeli Office"[85] in order to strengthen the workers' farm
that was at the time in need of working hands.[86] While they were subject
to harsh living conditions, and received half the pay of the Ashkenazi
workers, the group acclimated to the place "faster than expected ...
they mastered the work and became according to all accounts 'a productive
element,' good workers."[87] A few weeks after their arrival, however, the work
was finished, and the leadership of the farm decided that the Yemenites
would be moved to the village of Yavneel. At that point, Nini recounts,
Bluwstein, who objected to the expulsion, remained the only "bridge
between them and another world [the world of the pioneers], an alien and
strange world, which seemingly lost its social values, its systems of beliefs,
its national dreams, turning into a utilitarian and bureaucratic world."[88] As
a Zionist historian of Yemenite descent, Nini himself writes out of a sense of
sadness and disappointment, viewing the Kinneret affair as contradictory
of the Labor movement's leftist worldview, which has shaped his own
political perspective.[89] In many ways, his approach echoes Bluwstein's own
predicament in negotiating the rift between the "two worlds," which is,
in essence, a rift between myth and reality. Bluwstein reconciles this rift

through the same poetic strategy noted earlier, by construing the expulsion in terms of the a-historical cyclical story of Jewish wandering. Depicting one of the community's elders made to walk from Kinneret to Yavneel, she remarks: "I look at him, this *Israel-saba*,[90] this elder, with the travelling cane and his bible. What does this poetic sad figure remind me of in its serenity? Are you the eternal Jew?"[91] As earlier, the reality of racism and injustice is transposed into mythical terms; arguably the only way in which the contradiction between the expulsion of the Yemenites and Bluwstein's "entirely good" commune may be reconciled.

A comparison between Bluwstein and Pohatchevsky may be useful here to situate the gendered caregiving subject within the different socio-political settings of the colony vs the socialist cooperative, as two distinct geographies of ethnic marginalization. Notably, both women were referred to as "mother of the Yemenites," and Bluwstein's testimony that "their camp was called after me: Shoshana and the Yemenites"[92] is reminiscent of the naming of "Nehama Street." However, Pohatchevsky operates in the context of the bourgeois first immigration wave colony where the Yemenites are "absorbed" into the work world as manual labourers and domestic workers, while Bluwstein works in the Second *Aliyah* cooperative – the vanguard communal experiment of Labor Zionism – which enforces segregation between the Yemenites and the Zionist Ashkenazi pioneers as two separate "worlds" that cannot be integrated. In the following section, we shall see how dynamics of power revolving the figure of the national caregiver come into play in yet another setting – the Zionist urban space.

Hannah Thon and the Forgotten Neighbourhood

As a social worker, journalist, and editor of *Ha-isha*, the first Zionist women's journal, Hannah Thon was one of the most articulate advocates of Zionist women's care work. As a German Jewish woman of an upper-class family who came of age around the turn of the twentieth century, Thon's national and gendered consciousness evolved in the context of the massive involvement of German Jewish women in social welfare organizations at the time. This phenomenon, discussed extensively by Marion Kaplan, enabled Jewish women to redefine their place in Jewish society while negotiating the tension between their commitment to the Jewish community and the new intellectual and professional opportunities offered by the modern revision of gender-relations.[93] It was also part of the larger

phenomenon of "maternal feminism," referring to a strain of liberal feminism evolving in Western Europe and the United States that framed women's
intervention in the public sphere as extrapolation of their domestic roles as
caregivers and nurturers.[94] While this proto-feminist activity significantly
contributed to the evolution of the modern welfare state, it is also tied to
the development of apparatuses of power and regulation that devalued impoverished families and communities, subjecting them to assessments and
policies developed by the hegemonic group with the underlying aim of con-
forming the Other to its standards.[95] The efforts of German Jewish women
targeted the communities of East European Jewish immigrants who were
mostly traditionally ultraorthodox, and seen as threatening for the German
Jewish project of assimilating into modern non-Jewish German society. In
the German Jewish context, as in the Zionist context, the enterprise of rede-
fining women's social identity and role intersected with the emerging need
to engage with the Jewish Other.

Born in the German city of Dresden in 1886, Thon was raised in an
assimilating household with little Jewish education.[96] Her first meaningful
encounter with Jewish identity, which would eventually lead her to
Zionism, occurred when visiting with Christian relatives in London in 1907,
where she picked up the novel *Children of the Ghetto* by the English Jewish
author Israel Zangvil. The novel, a nostalgic representation of London's
impoverished East End, drove Thon to visit the Whitechapel neighbourhood
where many Jewish immigrants from Eastern Europe settled throughout
the nineteenth century. The vision of these Jews, which were so different
from the assimilated German Jews, reportedly drove her to contemplate
the Jewish return to the homeland, "where they will no longer dwell as
strangers in alien surroundings."[97]

Thon's involvement with Zionism evolved concurrently and interde-
pendently with her social welfare projects. One of the projects she was involved in was Bertha Pappenheim's "home for 'endangered and morally
sick' Jewish girls," an institution established in 1907 by Pappenheim, one
of the leaders of German Jewish women's social activism, for "reform-
ing" of East-European Jewish prostitutes.[98] While Thon's connection with
Pappenheim seems minor and inconspicuous, it brings to mind a seminal
moment in the history of Jewish gender studies, namely, Daniel Boyarin's
ground-breaking work on Jewish masculinity, Zionism, and psychoanalysis which largely blazed the trail for gendered critique of the Zionist
project.[99] Concluding Boyarin's analysis is a chapter titled "Retelling the Story

of O; Or, Bertha Pappenheim, My Hero," where he introduces Pappenheim as a model for successful integration of feminism and orthodox Judaism.[100] For Boyarin, Pappenheim forms an antithesis to the Zionist resolution of the modern crisis of gender and Jewishness. Traditional Orthodox Judaism, according to Boyarin, offers models of masculinity that are different and more fluid than Western conventions of gender that Zionism has adopted. Yet, in excluding women from the realm of the study of the Torah, the sacred centre of Jewish spiritual life, traditional Judaism does enforce a patriarchal gender hierarchy. In this context, Boyarin claims, Pappenheim was a woman "who figured out how to combine – however tensely – militant feminist protest and demand for radical change within Judaism with continued commitment to the existence of vibrant, full traditional Jewish life."[101] Boyarin contrasts Pappenheim with the figure of the "New Hebrew Man," the Zionist man who engages in "colonial drag," seeking to imitate the position of the Western colonizer as a way of normalizing Jewish manhood in line with the modern stereotype of masculinity.[102] While Boyarin's admiring evaluation of Pappenheim is compelling, the connection between Pappenheim and Thon highlights the continuity between Pappenheim as a model of Jewish feminist intervention and Zionist women's activism. The type of care work advanced by Pappenheim and Thon could be said to mirror western women's intervention in colonial spaces as primary agents of the civilizing mission. Thus, in many ways, I suggest, care work is Zionist women's "colonial drag."

Dafna Hirsch has insightfully analyzed Thon's biography and writings as illustrating the "conjunction of gender and ethnicity in the Zionist nation-building project."[103] According to Hirsch, Thon and the middle-class women's organizations in which she was involved redefined the national boundaries by operating as "agents of 'nationalization' and westernization" among the Mizrahi and Sephardi communities.[104] "In her writings," Hirsch shows, "Thon defined the role of middle-class women's organizations in the nation-building project as one of 'unifying the nation' and specifically of doing social and cultural work among Mizrahi Jews."[105] Ultimately, Hirsch continues, Thon's work should be understood through its dual political meaning: on the one hand, she operates as a civilizing agent of the nation within a colonial context in which the Orientalized ethnic Other is to be transformed and integrated into the nation; on the other hand, she, and women like her, offered a much more inclusive vision of the nation than that held by male-dominant Zionist leadership.

While I agree with Hirsch's interpretation, my close reading of Thon's short story "Yom Geshem" (Rainy Day) in the following pages seeks to further unpack the meaning of Thon's intervention as part of the genealogy of women's care writing charted in this chapter. As in the analyses of the works of Bluwstein and Pohatchevsky, I seek to situate Thon's gaze at the Other within the evolving geography of the Zionist space as marked by intersectional hierarchies and divisions. In this context, the Jerusalemite neighbourhood of Shimon Ha-tzadik, the site of Thon's first project in Palestine and the setting of this story, is particularly evocative. The neighbourhood was established in 1875 when the "Committee of the Sephardi Community" purchased lands by the sacred gravesite of Shimon Ha-tzadik (Shimon the Sage) in order to build houses for impoverished Sephardi families. During the late nineteenth and early twentieth centuries, Jewish immigrants of various Middle Eastern and North African origins – who arrived in Palestine mostly out of religious motivations – moved into the neighbourhood. Importantly, unlike in the cases of Pohatchevsky and Bluwstein, Shimon Ha-tzadik was not an Ashkenazi Zionist space into which Jews of Arab descent entered, but rather, a non-Zionist Sephardi/ Mizrahi space into which Ashkenazi women entered with the aim of improving the lives of the residents, but also acculturating them to the dominant Zionist culture. In the first issue of the women's journal *Ha-isha*, of which Thon was the chief editor, an anonymous writer published an essay titled "Shimon Ha-tzadik," in which she calls for Zionist society to "bravely" turn its gaze beyond "the beautiful and the good" of Zionism, and "see the ugliness in the cities of the Land ... the distress and the misery in the cities, whose residents dwell in narrow and crowded rooms with no light and no air."[106] As Hirsch explains, Thon's investment in Mizrahi and Sephardi communities in the 1920s took place against the backdrop of overall Zionist indifference toward these communities who were considered part of the Old Yishuv and thus not under the "jurisdiction" of the Zionist leadership.[107] The Zionist gaze that the anonymous writer seeks to direct at the neighbourhood may be considered, as Hirsch argues, in terms of the inclusive agenda of the Hebrew Women's Organization, the middle-class women's association of which Thon was one of the leaders. Yet, at the same time, this gaze is also a vehicle for expanding Zionist domination over spaces and communities that were not initially identified with Zionism. The caring gaze in this sense is always also a controlling and regulating gaze.

Thon's 1927 story "Yom Geshem" dramatizes the operation of the caring gaze, as it vividly presents a particularly miserable scene from the life of the neighbourhood. The main drive of the story seems to be in line with the goal of the anonymous essay to draw the attention of the Zionist audience to the neighbourhood. The opening passage underscores the act of seeing as the organizing principle of the narrative, first, setting up a panoramic outlook of Jerusalem in the storm: "Three days a storm is blowing over the bare Jerusalem Mountains. Three days angry rains, the mountains, the desolated lots at the centre of town, the streets, everything is wet and foggy."[108] Then, gradually narrowing the view the text summons the reader's gaze to the neighbourhood itself, which is crumbling – "the tents and sheds by the grave of Shimon the Sage are starting to rot and crumble. Through the windows with no windowpanes and through the crooked doors, the winds blow and the chill comes in. The muddy puddles on the floor are feet deep."[109] Finally, the implicit gaze settles on a community dwelling in a dark basement:

The basement of Eliyahu the Persian shoemaker bustles with many blurry figures: in the middle of the room stands a large table and under it, a pan full of burning coals. Around the table, in the darkness, the people of the neighborhood sit and warm their feet, which are either barefoot or wrapped in worn-out sandals. Oh, these stiff legs under the large table – they crossed the wilderness of Mesopotamia, wandered through the desert of Syria, through the dunes by the Red Sea, through the mountains of Persia and the valleys of Morocco. Weeks and months they wandered, hurting, wounded, blistered but full of strength aspiring to finally step on the soil of the Holy Land and put an end to their wandering.[110]

Here, the writer introduces the feet as a metonym for the body as a whole through which the figures are placed in the larger narrative of Jewish "homecoming." Through the image of the feet, she joins the various Middle Eastern and North African origins into one ideological collective. Implicit in this description is the rift between the idea of national homecoming and the reality of the physical unhomely place which is wretched, porous, and collapsing. The paragraph concludes by delivering Thon's social critique: "That here too they must keep wandering through the city streets from one workplace to another, and walk from neighborhood to neighborhood, and here their feet are under the large table of Eliyahu the shoemaker. Filthy, wounded and bare like before."[111] While Thon is much more explicit than Bluwstein in her critique of the Zionist establishment, like her, she subtly renders the socio-economic dispossession of the Mizrahi immigrants as an extension of exile. The foot imagery is a double-edged metonym that delivers Thon's social critique of the Zionist society's treatment of the immigrants but also disintegrates and allegorizes their bodies as a way of incorporating them into the national story.

The next paragraph proceeds to follow the story of the gaze, "when the eye has gotten used to the moist fog in the basement, it can start noticing the different figures around the table."[112] While the previous paragraph situates the bodies through the feet in the grand narrative of exile and return, the reader is now asked to imagine that she is physically in the room witnessing the realistic scene. All of the figures listed in the following passage are physically marked by their suffering: "Here is Rachel the young Yemenite with her baby on her shrunken breast, here is strong David with his right hand amputated, here is fat Leah with the marks of smallpox of her face, here is Hannah the madwoman ... here is Barukh the merchant startled by a feverish cough."[113] Thon's depiction of the way the space marks the bodies and souls of the characters may have drawn on the book that inspired her in her youth, Israel Zangvil's *Children of the Ghetto*. While Zangvil's novel is a nostalgic piece, it also presents the ghetto as a dark place, which deeply shapes the people in it to the point that people cannot leave the ghetto since they are "their own ghetto gates."[114]

While the main objective of the piece seems to be to expose the Zionist reader to the "dark" reality of the neighbourhood, as in Zangvil's novel, it also features a forbidden love story. Thus, against the almost grotesque backdrop of misery, we are introduced to one exceptional figure: "In the grim darkness of the room, it is as if Mazal's face is glowing, as if here in the basement of Eliyahu the shoemaker, there blooms a tropical flower full of foreign tenderness and purity."[115] Dubbing Mazal "a tropical flower," Thon detaches her from the misery and degeneration that seem to mark the other characters. We later learn of Mazal's forbidden love for David the water-drawer, whom she cannot marry since her family sees him as unable to provide for her because of his amputated arm which he lost in a labour related accident. Generally, however, although the story of Mazal and David provides the only real dramatic plotline, it is pushed back as the writer continues to highlight the various idle and at times vulgar conversations between the different characters in the basement, conversations which reveal the miserable circumstances of their life – one husband incarcerated and the other an abuser – and the neighbours are taunting each other about their troubles. Through Thon's gaze, the community seems physically and spiritually impoverished as material degeneration seems to overlap with mental degeneration. The misery reaches its peak as snow begins to fall and the room becomes even colder while the community begins to lament: "why did we come here? Is it better for us here than there? There we were poor and here we are beggars."[116] Shortly afterward, the story concludes with Mazal's sudden death. The tragedy is explicitly blamed on the situation in the Land, as Mazal's father cries, "my child, my child, why did we come to this land, where cold and hunger devour us?"[117] The question that reoccurs a few times throughout the last part of the story – "why did we come here?" – is meant to provoke and impress upon the Zionist reader the urgency of turning her gaze toward the neighbourhood and address its distress.

The more recent history of the neighbourhood, which is today part of the Palestinian neighbourhood of Sheikh Jarrah, creates an irony of history which is hard to ignore. While throughout the pre-state period, the neighbourhood remained a liminal site at the margins of the Zionist space, today it has become a focal point of the project of colonization. The Jewish residents of the neighbourhood were displaced during the 1948 War when East Jerusalem came under the control of Jordan which settled Palestinian refugees in the abandoned Jewish houses. When East Jerusalem was occupied by Israel during the 1967 War, the neighbourhood came under Israeli control. During the 1990s, a group of right-wing Jews purchased the rights to the formerly Jewish houses and began pushing for the Palestinian residents to be expelled as part of the effort to expand Jewish dominance in the city. The politics surrounding the neighbourhood should be understood against of the massive displacement of Palestinians during the 1948 War, as the attempt to reclaim the Jewish residences contrasts with Israel's uncompromising rejection of any claim in favour of repatriating Palestinian refugees.

Michael Ben-Yair, who was born in the neighbourhood of Shimon Ha-tzadik in 1942, recounts that before the 1948 War, "The relationship between Arab and Jews in the neighborhood were very good,"[118] recalling, "On the seventh day of Passover we would have a picnic by the grave, where there was open space, in nature, Jews and Arabs together."[119] From this perspective, arguably, the ultimate assimilation of the neighbourhood into the Zionist space ended up severing the possibility of Jewish-Arab cohabitation, which ultimately led to the displacement of Jews in this case. In a letter she asked to be opened only after her death (1953), Thon wrote:

> Let me bid farewell to this world believing that my children and grandchildren will have better, purer and safer life … But I am afraid it is not time yet, and I am not referring at the moment to the dangers that threaten us from outside, but to those from within … We are lacking any measure of consideration and attention to people who are not part of our nation, in the land and outside it. We are lacking any measure of goodness and humane attitude toward the Arabs that live in the territories that we have occupied. We also do not show any good will to sacrifice something in order to solve the problem of the Arab refugees that constitutes a great threat to them and to us![120]

While the language of care and "consideration" is endemic to the patronizing position Thon often occupies vis-à-vis the Others of Zionism, her words resonate eerily against the grain of the recent history of the neighbourhood. As I complete this book in the summer of 2021, tensions surrounding the Sheikh Jarrah neighbourhood have culminated in a war that took the lives of 256 Palestinians and 13 Israelis.[121] The formerly "invisible" neighbourhood is once again claimed as a Zionist territory, although this time it is not through the caring gaze but rather, through state and settler violence. In this context, we may view the neighbourhood as a "border zone," in Gloria Anzaldúa's terms, namely, as a site in which different histories of dispossession and displacement intersect,[122] recalling the structural imbrication of the national and ethnic hierarchies marking Israel/Palestine and thus the affinity between the "unhomliness" of the Mizrahim in the Zionist space and the dissolution of the Palestinian homeland.

The Missing Children: Looking Back at the Contact Zone of Care

> In 1949, he was about three years old and perfectly healthy, when she was ordered to bring him to the infant-centre in the Rosh ha-'ayin transit camp. Even though she did not understand the point of it, it did not take much for her to obey the nurses in the white uniform. My grandmother says there was a lot of pressure to do that, leaving her no choice. Like other women in the camp, she convinced herself

that the nurses know what they are doing. They are in charge. The
nurses were among the good Jews that devoted themselves to bring
her and her family to the Holy Land.[123]

In the account above, anthropologist Tova Gamliel tells the story of the
disappearance of her uncle Hayim, the youngest son of her grandmother
Sʿaada, from the Rosh ha-ʿayin transit camp in 1949. Gamliel's testimony
refers to "the kidnapping and disappearance of thousands of toddlers from
families of new immigrants, mostly from Yemen, but also from Iraq, Tunisia,
Morocco, The Balkans and other countries, mostly in the 1950's."[124] This
affair received renewed attention in recent years as a result of the work of
third-generation Mizrahi activists.[125] According to scholars and activists, a
range of women's organizations as well as medical and childcare facilities
were involved in the disappearance of Mizrahi babies in the transit camps.
The children were in most cases taken from the camp's "infant centre" (beit
tinokot) for medical treatment, although in many cases the parents testify that
their child was perfectly healthy. Subsequently, parents were told that their
child had died in the hospital but were not shown a body or a grave.[126] In fact,
according to the activists, the children were likely put in foster institutions
and then given to Ashkenazi families (often abroad) for adoption.

Gamliel's story begins, like many of these stories, at the infant centre in
the transit camp, which was often the place where parents saw their children
for the last time. In an essay tracing "the method" by which the alleged
abductions were carried out, Nathan Shifriss explains that the Yemenite
babies in particular were systemically taken from their parents as soon
as they arrived in the Land (or when babies were born) and concentrated
in mandatory infant centres.[127] Shifriss describes the infant centres as
instrumental in the initial removal of children from the custody of their
parents. These facilities were run as inpatient institutions where contact
between parents and babies was limited. Only mothers were allowed to
access the babies at specific times to breastfeed and all interaction was
monitored and regulated by nursing staff, composed of mostly Ashkenazi
women, who often manifested patronizing and condescending attitudes
towards the Yemenite mothers.[128] In many cases, a child was reportedly
transferred during the night from the infant centre to the hospital where
parents would lose track of them. Thus, the infant centre emerges in many
of the testimonies as the site of the initial trauma; the site where the child is
separated from the body of the mother.

Activist Nʿaama Katiʿee underscores the involvement of the early Zionist feminist organizations, Hadassah, Witzo, and the Working Mothers Organization, in the management of the infant centres as well as the foster institutions from which the children were arguably dispatched for adoptions. "This affair," Katiʿee rightfully argues, "explains a lot about the complicated relationship between the local feminist discourse, Mizrahi women, and Mizrahi communities more generally."[129] She alludes to the discourse of care surrounding the missing children, in which nurses and caregivers saw themselves as saving the children from the unhealthy setting of their families. As Katiʿee discerns, this discourse was cultivated within the organizational setting of early Zionist feminism, and, thus, the affair calls for critical retrospection of Israeli feminism. "Israeli feminism," Katiʿee says, "must recognize the crime that was done and take responsibility for its part in the affair. It must stand before the parents in their final years, the siblings who remained and grew up under the terrible shadow, and admit – we were collaborators in the crime."[130]

While Pohatchevsky, Bluwstein, and Thon are by no means personally implicated in the abduction affair, they each represent a moment in the cultivation of the particular ethno-gendered order which generated the organizational and ideological apparatuses enabling and facilitating the affair. In this light, the testimonies by parents and siblings of the missing children offer an "oppositional gaze," in bell hooks' terms, at the Zionist contact zone of care.[131] Sarah Tzarum's filmed testimony about the disappearance of her daughter Tzyona illustrates this:

She was put in the infant centre. "Forbidden!" They did not leave any baby [with the mother in the tent]. You know, some women hid the baby under the bed in the bedpan so that no one knew that their baby is with them. "Here [in the tent] there are many people, here people are coming and going, here there is no care, here they will not bring me her food, here they will not let me have a bed for her." They had beds. Every child had a bed. Baby-beds … it was the first separation… it was the worst disruption for me. I give birth and they take my baby… but I accepted this. "It's important, it's good, it's healthy, it's healthy, it's healthy and all that." Okay, we accepted. I tell you, she was very healthy. I would take her and play with her at the infant centre. There were nurses who used to tell me "It's very nice, how you play with her!"[132]

Later, Tzarum describes herself as mute when medical authorities informed her the child had died. Knowing very little Hebrew, she was dependent for translation on the hospital's Arabic-speaking cleaning lady while she was desperately looking for her baby. In her testimony cited above, we may note how she quotes fragments from the institutional discourse used to convince her to put her daughter in the infant centre. Tzarum's tone is ironic as she repeats the phrases ("It's important, it's good, it's healthy") as if through ironic reiteration of the language of power, she is able to speak back to the forces that rendered her mute at the time of the trauma. Emphasizing the repetition of the same phrase-structure, her testimony subtly calls the attention of the listener to the oppressive ubiquity of the institutional discourse of care. If, at the time, hegemonic discourse imposes itself on her as absolute truth – "It's important, it's good, it's healthy, it's healthy, it's healthy and all that" – she now exposes its malicious falseness. The repetition of "it's healthy" now points to the Zionist healthcare institutional discourse as the perpetrator of violence. The cited praise by the nurse, "It's very nice, how you play with her," which Tzarum pronounces with sharp sarcastic tone, becomes an outlet of her silenced anger connoting the oppressive context in which the nurses saw themselves as instructing the Yemenite mothers how to mother their babies.

The frequent mention of nurses as agents of care in relation to the children's disappearance brings to mind Shoshana Bluwstein's excitement about the title "a nurse." Bluwstein is especially attached to the white uniform of the nurse as a marker of this glorified identity: "It is so good! It wraps me like a dress with long sleeves. When I wrap myself in it, I feel that the entire external world is beyond me. I have only calm and the power to endure."[133] Gamliel's remark about her grandmother – "it did not take much for her to obey the nurses wearing the white uniform"[134] –reflects back on the construction of the "nurse" as a gendered identity through the eyes of those for whom she is a figure of authority, one of the first agents of state power that the immigrants encountered, an encounter that constitutes a disruption of what seems natural to the mother and the family, but that they accept largely because of what that white uniform symbolizes. Reading Bluwstein retrospectively in this context, we may discern an awareness of the position of power enforced by the white uniform: "When I would appear wearing my white uniform – it seems that the patients would relax, as the purity of the outfit glows with light and peace … and *they would not refuse* [treatment], daylight and the white uniform relaxes them."[135] The reference to the patients "relaxing" and "not refusing" treatment because of the white uniform implies that there were at other times conflictual situations between the caregiver and care receivers. Bluwstein indeed recounts that there were unsuccessful visits in which the Yemenite patients would express distrust toward their caregivers and refuse treatment and medication. While she attributes a calming effect to the symbolic value of the white uniform, we may also frame the situation through what Gamliel and others present as a situation of authority and power that is experienced as breaching the patients' autonomy over their own bodies.

Shlomo Jahsi, whose two brothers went missing, recounts a story that further highlights the figure of the white-dressed nurse as a symbol of altruism turned into a figure of authority and institutional power:[136]

The moment we got off the plane, we kissed the soil, the Holy Land, and later this image came to me of two angels that approached, supposedly, two nurses, well dressed, clean, white, everything, with two blankets. Each nurse took one of the twins, both twins. So I, as a child, I say, "This is the Land of Israel? This is how they welcome my baby brothers? In such a respectable manner? Blessed be his name that we have come to such a State." And then they put them in this concrete structure, yes, a nursery, and we are in the tents. I used to tell my mother, "I want to see my brothers." She said, "They don't allow taking them out." I said: "Try doing it, take them out, bring them over, and then return them." There was a nurse there. Mother said: "Do me a favor; I'll take the kids only for half an hour. They'll play with their brothers, and I'll bring them back." She said, "Okay, but try to get back quickly." She brought them, such happiness inside the tent to see them, all of us gathered around, like flowers ... Suddenly they came into the tent. They burst in, rudely, into the tent, the two nurses. They did not say hello or anything. "What have you done? Why did you take the children?" Immediately each one grabbed a child, like a rag, in a way that was not gentle. They told my mother, the two nurses, "We'll teach you a lesson," gesturing like that with their hand, "We'll teach you a lesson." I got scared. Where are those angels God sent us? Eventually, they took them back. In the morning, when she came to breastfeed, one of the twins, Shalom, is no longer in bed. "Where is my son?" They said, "He's at the hospital." A day or two later she came to breastfeed Yosef, who was still in the infant room.

Doesn't see Yosef either. "Where is Yosef?" "He's at the hospital." Like that, the two of them … From that very week they kept their word, "We will teach you a lesson." She did not see her twins ever again to this day.[137]

Jahsi's story, through the perspective of the child, illustrates the site of care as one of disillusion. The "angels in white," who initially symbolize the new society's benevolent care for the children, become agents of institutional authority that violently intrudes on the Yemenite family's space, undermining the parental autonomy over the care of their children, ultimately punishing the Yemenite mother for breaching their authority. The disintegration of the "angels" marks the disintegration of the broader vision of the "maternal State" that cares for the immigrants and for their children, and sets the ground for what Gamliel calls "civil melancholia," namely, overwhelming grief and loss over harm perpetrated by the hegemonic society which ultimately destroys of the victim's sense of belonging to the national collective.[138]

In writing about this affair, I am aware of the voices in Israeli society that reject the claims that babies were deliberately taken from their families. I recall the first time it occurred to me that this affair may be relevant to my work on Zionist women, when, as part of my dissertation research, I was going through volumes of *Dvar ha-po'eelet*, the monthly women's publication of the Zionist Labor Movement from the late 1940s and early 1950s. There, I encountered various reports about women's involvement in care work with Mizrahi families, children and girls. While at the time (2007-08), the conversation surrounding the affair was much less prominent in the Israeli public sphere than it is today – and I personally have not given it much attention until then – as I was reading the dominant attitudes among proto-feminist Zionist activists toward Mizrahi families, I found myself thinking, "it does make sense now." What had previously seemed to me as exaggerated claims that could be explained away by the chaos of newly founded state now seemed very much inline with what I was finding in women's writing. The prevalent discourse in these writings marks the Mizrahi and Yemenite family as a problematic and even harmful site that holds the children back from being cultivated into the nation. In this context, the message that Mizrahi children would be best separated from their families is often implied and sometimes explicit.[139] While I cannot engage with questions of archival documentation and proofs often demanded by the detractors, I seek to push back against the "chaos hypothesis" wherein babies disappeared in the context of the chaos that characterized the absorption of massive immigration waves by the young state. In this context, I join others to point to a deeper ethno-gendered order into which the kidnapping of children fits perfectly.[140] As part of this order, I argue, Ashkenazi women activists were poised to intervene in the Mizrahi family as employers, philanthropists, nurses, and community volunteers in ways that at times facilitated the disintegration of the family. Situated within this ethno-gendered order, I see the missing children affair as a cultural event that needs to be grappled with even by those who do not believe the numerous testimonies and evidence gathered by activists. That is to say, apart from the investigation of the crimes that were allegedly committed, the fact that thousands of families perceived themselves as having experienced a trauma perpetrated by the State that brought about such deep sense of alienation and disillusionment calls for an interrogation of the culture in which such affair was deemed plausible. In this sense, I contend, Zionist women's stories of "national caregiving" shed light on the intersectional architectures of power that form the cultural infrastructure of the missing children affair.

METAPHORS OF DIMINISHMENT
From Women's Writing to National Security

To my Land[1]

אֶל אַרְצִי

I did not sing to you, my land
I did not glorify your name
with tales of bravery,
from many battlefields;
Only a tree – my hands planted
on the peaceful shores of the Jordan River
Only a pathway – my feet paved
in the fields

לֹא שַׁרְתִּי לָךְ, אַרְצִי,
וְלֹא פֵּאַרְתִּי שְׁמֵךְ
בַּעֲלִילוֹת גְּבוּרָה,
בִּשְׁלַל קְרָבוֹת;
רַק עֵץ – יָדַי נָטְעוּ
חוֹפֵי יַרְדֵּן שׁוֹקְטִים.
רַק שְׁבִיל – כָּבְשׁוּ רַגְלַי
עַל פְּנֵי שָׂדוֹת.

Very meager, indeed
I know, my mother
Very meager is
the offering of your daughter;
Only a roar of joy
at daybreak
Only a secret cry
for your poverty.

אָכֵן דַּלָּה מְאֹד –
יָדַעְתִּי זֹאת, הָאֵם,
אָכֵן דַּלָּה מְאֹד
מִנְחַת בִּתֵּךְ;
רַק קוֹל תְּרוּעַת הַגִּיל
בְּיוֹם יִגַּהּ הָאוֹר,
רַק בְּכִי בַּמִּסְתָּרִים
עֲלֵי עָנְיֵךְ.

Like many of Rachel Bluwstein's poems, "To My Land" (*el artzi*) had a long afterlife in Israeli culture. The poem, a seemingly simple lyrical articulation of the poet's love of the Land, was put into music and is often performed at national ceremonies by choruses of *kibbutzim* and Zionist youth movements as well as by some of Israel's major singers.[2] Hebrew literature's prominent scholar Dan Miron brings the poem as an example of how traits such as modesty, poverty, and simplicity, ushered Hebrew women's poetry into the emerging literary canon.[3] In this poem, the minor interventions of the Zionist subject ("only a tree ... only a path") align with Bluwstein's aesthetic preference for poetic simplicity, which, according to Miron, formed a poetic standard for women's poetry that only a few poets would later exceed. This gendered reading of Bluwstein's poetics was criticized by later scholars for perpetuating stereotypes about women's poetry, ignoring Bluwstein's deliberate artistic choice of "understated poetics," which, according to Michael Gluzman, derived not from her gender, but from her modernist sensibilities, particularly those drawn from a specific strain of Russian modernism associated with poet Anna Akhmatova.[4] While I concur with Gluzman's critique, here, I am less interested in the gendered historiography of Modern Hebrew literature, than I am in the genealogy of gender, femininity in particular, as a Zionist subject matter. In this context, I return to the gendered understanding of Bluwstein's poetics as a point of departure for investigating the discourse I term "metaphors of diminishment," that is, flexible network of contents, images, and narratives that express the meaning and legacy of "the feminine" as a "national metonym" in terms of smallness, asceticism, and reduction of excess.[5] I suggest that the reception of Bluwstein's "understated poetics," and what it came to represent in the Zionist consciousness, is a significant moment in this genealogy, even as it does misconstrue the poet's ground-breaking poetics.

Oz Almog discusses the norms of austerity and asceticism as an important aspect of Zionist culture.[6] While this culture was shaped in part by "objective economic scarcity,"[7] Almog explains, it was also an expression of the new system of values connected with "life on the Land" as opposed to the excesses of urban European culture. Like many other studies of early Zionist culture, Almog places the masculine figure of the New Jew at the centre of the new sabra culture, but, like others, his analysis elides the way in which gender difference operates within this culture. In fact, I suggest, the set of values connected with asceticism in Zionist culture had a particularly poignant meaning for shaping femininity as a cultural category.

While the rhetoric of feminine diminishment and smallness, whose coordinates are traced in the following pages, has been a generative cultural force in Hebrew culture, there are notable examples of women authors that challenged and breached the norms set by this discourse. We may note poets from Esther Raab and Yocheved Bat-Miryam to Yona Wallach whose poetics were far from succumbing to the code of smallness and diminishment.

Furthermore, Bluwstein's poetry itself often features a productive tension between its subdued, understated tones and its moments of eruption (such as the "roar of joy at daybreak") that point back to inner richness and expansiveness.[8] Yet, I contend, the poetics of feminine diminishment is worth investigating not as a testimony of the limitations of women's poetic capabilities, but as part of a discourse of the feminine, whose scope, as I show in the following pages, spans from women's writing to women's bodies to the Zionist politics of ethnicity and the geopolitics of the Israeli-Palestinian conflict. While, as discussed earlier in this study, scholars often underscored how women writers pushed back against Zionist gender ideologies, here, I am interested in how women have positively engaged with, elaborated, and expanded the ideological scope of femininity as a Zionist field of meaning. As scholars have noted, while women's subjectivity is often relegated to the margins of the national public sphere, femininity is cast as the nation's "most internal Other, through which the nation defines its uniform and coherent identity."[9] The following pages interrogate the poetics of women writers as they engage with the production of both selfhood and Otherness through the realm of gender, probing the ways in which these poetics are imbricated into the politics of the national project.

To consider this further, I return to Bluwstein's "To My Land." The poem, I suggest, may generate two possible readings. In the first reading, the speaker's position reflects the marginality of women poets in the national space. Bluwstein's life story, which in itself acquired mythical stature, is of relevance here. As mentioned in chapter 3, Rachel Bluwstein and her sister Shoshana arrived in Palestine as tourists in 1909. They fell in love with the idea of living on the land and the landscape of the Sea of Galilee and became immersed in the ideas of the charismatic Zionist thinker A.D Gordon about the "religion of labor."[10] In 1913, however, Rachel departed from Palestine to study agriculture in France and ended up stranded in Europe for the duration of World War I. During that time, she contracted tuberculosis while working with refugee children. When her illness was revealed, after she had finally gotten back to the Land, she was asked to leave the kibbutz and her beloved Sea of Galilee for fear that she would infect the community. She thus spent the final years of her life in Tel Aviv and Jerusalem, alone and mournful. It was during this period, however, that she also wrote the bulk of her poetry. Reading "To My Land" through the voice of the abandoned poet who is exiled from the ideological locus of the nation, means reading her as speaking from the margins of the Zionist ethos of heroism and glory, and as confessing the limitation of her own contribution to this ethos ("I did not sing to you ... I did not glorify your name").[11] The national standing of the poem, however, derives from a different reading. In this reading, the poetic "I" is not a marginalized voice of a lonely, exiled woman,[12] but rather, one that encapsulates the self-image of the emerging nation. In other words, the "I" is "the image that the Zionist labor Movement adopted for itself," as Anita Shapira has argued, that of a Zionist subject who is "simple in its manners, modest in its speech, identified with the Eretz-Yisraeli landscape, lover of work – a peaceful movement."[13] This subject represents what Shapira refers to as the Zionist "Defensive ethos," a term she coined to refer to what she sees as a stage in the development of political Zionism, characterized by the denial of the prospects of violent conflict in Palestine and the cultivation of the self-image of the Zionist settler as a peaceful worker of the Land who is never an aggressor, and might only defend himself against the violent attacks by others. Palestinian nationalism is negated in this framework, and any Palestinian resistance to the Zionist colonization of Palestine is construed as deriving from an irrational hatred of the Jews rather than valid national claims.[14] Here, the diminished poetic subject of "To My Land" is not the Other of the nation; rather, she represents a crystallization of the imagined collective self. While according to Shapira, the Zionist leadership abandoned the "Defensive Ethos" in the 1930s, realizing the inevitability of military confrontation with the Palestinians, the long afterlife of "To My Land" speaks to the persistence and resonance of the emotional and ideological underpinnings of this ethos in the Israeli collective consciousness well beyond 1930s. The poetic frames of poverty, smallness, and meagreness, attributed to both the self and the Land, constitutes a depth structure of Israeli culture which forms an invaluable "flip side" of the masculinist ideology of heroism and strength. The scholarly and popular readings of "To My Land" point toward the reverberations of its poetics in Zionist culture which span from the discussion of the conditions of women's literary expression to women's bodies, and, finally, to the politics of settlement and dispossession in Israel/Palestine.

Halokh ve-Tafof, Mincing Steps: Misogynistic Trajectories

To support the argument that Bluwstein's minimalist poetics derived from a conscious modernist vision rather than her relationship with her gender, Gluzman invokes some of her meta-poetic works, including the modernist manifesto "On the Mark of Our Times" and her poem "Phrase" (*niv*) in which she articulates this poetic vision.[15] In "On the Mark of Our Times," Bluwstein writes:

> It is clear to me: the sign of contemporary times in poetry is the simplicity of expression. Simple expression means the expression of the primordial fluttering of the lyrical phrase, before it had time *to cover its nakedness in silk costumes and golden jewelry*; expression, clear of literariness, that touches the heart with its human truth, that revives the soul with its freshness.[16]

While the manifesto articulates Bluwstein's poetic vision, the poem "Phrase" articulates similar ideas, loading them with intimate emotional significance:

Phrase[17]   נִיב

I know many beautiful idioms,	יוֹדַעַת אֲנִי אִמְרֵי נוֹי לְמַכְבִּיר,
Endless poetic expressions,	מְלִיצוֹת בְּלִי סוֹף,
Walking with mincing steps,	הַהוֹלְכוֹת הָלוֹךְ וְטָפוֹף,
and arrogant gaze	מַבָּטָן יָהִיר.

But my heart belongs to the simple phrase	אַךְ לִבִּי לַנִּיב הַתָּמִים כְּתִינוֹק
Innocent as a baby and humble as earth.	וְעָנָו כֶּעָפָר.
I know countless words–	יָדַעְתִּי מִלִּים אֵין מִסְפָּר—
therefore, I keep silent	עַל כֵּן אֶשְׁתֹּק.

Will you hear even through silence	הֲתִקְלֹט אָזְנְךָ אַף מִתּוֹךְ שְׁתִיקָה
my timid phrase?	אֶת נִיבִי הַשָּׁח?
Will you cherish it as a friend, as a brother,	הֲתִנְצְרֵהוּ כְּרֵעַ, כְּאָח,
as in a mother's bosom?	כְּאֵם בְּחֵיקָהּ?

While Gluzman fleshes out Bluwstein's modernist agenda evident in these texts, I would like to draw attention to the feminine antagonist emerging from these pieces; the feminine figure whose body is covered "in silk costumes and golden jewelry" and who "walks with mincing steps." While these are metaphors undoubtedly geared at making a meta-poetic point against the use of excessive formulaic literary tropes in Hebrew literature,[18] these images also resonate with the early Zionist misogynistic discourse on women's bodies. The allusion to the women "walking with mincing steps" (*halokh ve-tafof*) is taken from *Isiah* 3, where it is used by the prophet to chastise the haughty and adorned daughters of Zion. In the biblical text, the sinning women are metonymic of the People's overall hedonistic and promiscuous behaviour. As typical of prophetic rhetoric, sexualized and gendered violence emerges as an allegory of God's wrath, "The Master shall blight the pates of Zion's daughters and expose their private parts."[19] The text proceeds to describe at length the stripping of "the splendid ankle bells and the headgear, and the crescents, and the pendants, and the bracelets and the veils, and the necklaces, and the armlets, and the sashes," etc.[20] This gesture of stripping women's physical or intellectual excess resonates in multiple terrains of Modern Hebrew and Zionist culture, and forms a misogynistic history, which I would like to briefly chart here.

The accusation of Modern Jewish women of being "*gandraniot*" – overly invested in self-adornment – was integral to the discourse on women already in the *Haskalah* period. Tova Cohen discusses the derogatory stereotype of the "false *maskilah*," the woman who studies foreign languages, which was used to ridicule the educated Jewish woman as excessive and vain. Here, the intellectual pursuits of the "false *maskilah*" were considered expressions of women's vanity. This figure was contrasted, on the one hand, to the ideal of the traditional and chaste "daughter of Israel," and, on the other hand, to the modern bourgeois figure of the "angel of the home."[21] While this form of misogyny mostly targeted women's education in foreign languages and cultures deemed as a gateway for assimilation, as mentioned in chapter 1, women who learned Hebrew were also initially mocked as pursuing it out of interest in self-aggrandizement.[22] Indeed, as a rule, it seems, the charge of excess was directed at any woman who defied the casting of women as small, delicate, diminished figures.

In the Zionist context, the public discourse on early women settlers also brands them with hedonism, vanity, and excess. Yisrael Dov Frumkin, editor of the first Hebrew newspaper in Palestine *Ha-havatzelet*, for example, describes the women of the colonies as "a bunch of novel-reading women farmers with two Arab maids each,"[23] and the journalist Avraham Moshe Luntz writes critically of the daughters of the colonists who occupy themselves with "fashionable clothing, playing the piano and crochet work."[24] The recurrent denunciation of women for occupying themselves with leisurely cultural activities was endemic of the dramatic change in social expectations from women entailed by the transition from the *maskilic* bourgeois home to the Zionist settlement in Palestine. As discussed in chapter 1, the model of the ideal woman in *maskilic* homes was the bourgeois "angel of the home," a woman proficient in leisure arts and crafts and European vernaculars who was not expected to assume any responsibility for the sustenance of the home. When fathers and husbands transferred their ideological investment from the *Haskalah* to early Zionism and settled in Palestine, the leisurely "angel of the home" was replaced by the figure of the woman settler inspired by the figures of the German and Slavic peasants, a model that was foreign and virtually unattainable for most women and girls of bourgeois households that populated the colonies.[25]

In the context of Labor Zionism and the growth of the Jewish settlement in Palestine during the 1920s and 1930s, a similar discourse was framed by the tensions between the ideological centres of the settlement project, the agricultural *kibbutzim* and *moshavim*, and urban society constituting the bulk of Zionist society in Palestine. In 1927, for example, critic and literary editor Yaakov Rabinowitz published, in the women's publication *Ha-ishah* of all places, a vehement diatribe against "The Intelligent Woman" (*ha-ishah ha-intiligentit*), namely, the educated urban women of the civil sector, which constituted most of the readership of the publication. Using harsh rhetoric, Rabinowitz denounces the figure he calls "the educated, the musical, the theatrical, the subtle, the stylistic, the liberated, the revolutionary woman."[26] As in the earlier discourse on the "false *maskilot*," educational, cultural, and political pursuits are all construed as external luxuries that women pursue out of greed, selfishness, and vanity.[27] The categories serving to define femininity then remain constant in different moments in Jewish and Zionist history. It is against this fixated figure of the "excessive," "greedy," "adorned" woman that the Zionist ideal of femininity evolves.

Pure Patient Poverty: Poetics of Diminishment and the Diminished Writer

In a eulogy to writer and friend Rivka Alper,[28] editor and critic Rachel Katzanelson discusses Alper's transition from writing early realistic and semi-autobiographic fiction to writing Zionist biographies that constituted the bulk of her oeuvre in later years. Describing Alper's poetics, Katzanleson states that if at the centre of Alper's early fiction "stands not the glory of life, … [but] the troubles, weaknesses and desires haunting an average person,"[29] in the later work, suffering and poverty are also present, but "everything is overshadowed by the glory of pioneer life, and even poverty seems as *'pure patient poverty'* [dalut savlanit u-vara]."[30]

The line "pure patient poverty" is taken from another poem by Bluwstein. Cited below, the poem "A Visit" (bikur), describes the speaker's visit to a worker's dwelling:

A Visit[31]   ביקור

In the evening, in autumn, in a worker's   בָּעֶרֶב, בַּסְּתָו, בִּצְרִיף-פּוֹעֲלִים, בַּמּוֹלֶדֶת,
shack, in the homeland,   עֲפַר הָרִצְפָּה, סִדְקֵי הַקִּירוֹת הַדַּקִּים,
The earthen floor, cracks in the thin walls,   בְּקֶרֶן-זָוִית עֲרִיסָה בִּלְבָנַת כְּסוּיֶיהָ,
In the corner, a cradle with white sheets,   בַּחַלּוֹן – מֶרְחַקִּים.
In the window – distances.

Guide me, as you did then, honest toil   הַנְחוּנִי כְּאָז, עָמָל עַקְשָׁנִי וְתוֹחֶלֶת!
and purpose!   שֶׁלָּךְ אָנֹכִי, דַּלּוּת סַבְלָנִית וּבָרָה!
I am yours, *pure patient poverty!*   נִגְשׁוּ תִינוֹקוֹת, הִסְתַּכְּלוּ, הֶחֱרִישׁוּ, עַל מַה זֶּה
The children came near, and grew silent   נֶעֶצְבָה הַדּוֹדָה הַזָּרָה?
Why is the strange auntie so sad?

The first stanza of the poem paints the physical space of the home as the ideological locus of Labor Zionism, which is simple and impoverished, yet features the hopeful purity of "a cradle … with white sheets," and connection to the vastness of the land ("In the window – distances"). In this context, the cry "I am yours, pure patient poverty" expresses both the speaker's emotional affinity with this place and her acute sense of estrangement as someone who is exiled from this home, and leads to the final lines which sharply break from the ideological realm, bringing into the scene the lowbrow perspective of the children, who are perplexed at the sight of the tearing "strange auntie." The scene is then charged with the painful self-recognition of the speaker through the eyes of the children.

Katzanelson's allusion to Bluwstein's "pure patient poverty" in her commentary on Alper transposes the phrase from the scene of the poet's complex relationship with the Zionist home to the realm of Zionist aesthetics and women's writing. The quotation of one woman writer's words by another to refer to the writing of a third woman invokes all three women's fraught relationship with women's writing and the prescription of feminine "diminishment." Katzanelson herself was ambivalent about women's writing, which she saw as implicated with erotic excess at odds with the austere principles of Zionist culture. According to Dan Miron, Katzanelson's intellectual life was shaped by willed ideological repression of parts of the psyche consciously conceived as excessive and disruptive of the Zionist ethos of a simple and ideologically committed life.[32] An aspiring writer in her youth, like Alper, Katzanelson ended up not pursuing the path of a literary author largely because she conceived of literature, and especially women's literature, as inherently excessive. In this context, Miron notes Katzanelson's ambivalence toward Bluwstein herself, whom she perceived as revealing, in her poetry and behaviour, erotic and emotional excess. According to Miron, vis-à-vis Bluwstein, Katzanelson experienced an internal conflict, which was actually a conflict with "a mirror image of her own unfulfilled self. The results of this conflict were the repression of Katzanelson's creativity, the diminishment of her selfhood, and denunciation of the spiritual energies that she could have released within herself, had she not forced herself 'to conquer the heart.'"[33] In light of this, Katzanelson's assessment of Alper's writing using Bluwstein's words appears to be a way of grappling with the creative excess of all three women.

The tensions surrounding women's writing as excess notably shaped the reception (or rather rejection) of Alper as an author, especially with regard to her first novel *Pirpurey Mahapekha* (*Quivers of Revolution*, 1930) which follows the trials of a young Jewish woman named Batya in Russia at the wake of the 1917 revolution concluding with her immigration to Palestine.[34] A salient aspect of the novel is the representation of sexual and gendered violence. The novel opens with the death of Batya's mother and proceeds with her father's attempt to sexually abuse her. Later in the novel, Batya's abuse and harassment by her boyfriend and father lead her to immigrate to Palestine. Her immigration appears in this context less as an ideological endeavour and more as a form of escape from a reality of gendered violence. The critic Yaakov Rabinowitz was one of Alper's early literary mentors and wrote one of the first reviews of the novel. The novel, he writes, "fits the measurements of the storyteller, her size and height, no more no less, simple, straightforward. The narrator, like Batya, the protagonist, has healthy senses. She is not sickly or nervous, and not sentimental, but has natural, simple, emotions."[35] Rabinowitz's evaluation of Alper's literary writing aligns with the ideas of his 1927 essay cited earlier. While presuming to be positive and encouraging, he reinforces the standards of impoverishment, simplicity, and modesty as criteria of women's writing. The woman writer is praised here for embodying the correct diminished form of feminine presence in the public sphere. Curiously, in contrast to Rabinowitz, an anonymous critic writing under the pseudonym V. Tomer challenges Alper's novel, referring specifically to the striking representations of sexual violence, as "literary pioneering [ḥalutziyut sifrutit] that we have not seen yet in such an excessive way."[36] Notwithstanding the opposite views of the two male critics, they both measure the novel on the spectrum of excess and diminishment, invoking questions that are often uniquely applied to women's writing in the Zionist sphere and beyond: how much space is she allowed to take for herself? How much may she reveal of her reality? How much of the world may she expose?

Alper's second novel, *Ha-mitnahalim ba-har* (*Settlers in the Mountain*, 1944) may be read as a self-diminishing response to these questions. The novel presents the biography of Leah Cohen, one of the first settlers in the colony of Motza near Jerusalem. Cohen's story appears as diametrically contrasted to Alper's own life-trajectory. Like Bluwstein, Alper may be deemed as "a failed pioneer." While she arrived in Palestine to join a Kibbutz and work the Land, she ultimately left agricultural work for health-related reasons, choosing instead to devote herself to writing and editing. Moreover, breaching the norms of the national-patriarchal culture she remained unmarried and did not bear children (although she ended up adopting a relative girl refugee after World War II). Conversely, Leah Cohen has overcome many challenges in order to stay on the Land, while also exemplifying the ideal of Zionist motherhood by raising four sons who themselves became farmers and soldiers. In this context, *Settlers in the Mountain* seems as a manifestation of willful self-erasure, hiding the creative self behind the idealized subject of the biography.

Settlers in the Mountain received less critical attention than the first novel, but the tone of the reviews was overall positive, praising the author for her choice of subject and her contribution to the commemoration of the life of the pioneers. Yet, as the following comments by critic Immanuel Ben-Gurion demonstrate, concerns with the category of simplicity inform the critical response to this novel as well:

A modest act of conquering, but an exemplary one, the beginning of the settlement in the mountain, is described by Rivka Alper. The book tells the reality as it is, it gives the story's contents to the reader without any "make up," a report of a hard life story that has become a model. The narrator has given up her artistic privilege to subtract from or add to the story. She did not cut in places where conciseness may have been needed in order not to lose any drop of the heavy burden of fate. She also did not add anything, but left it to the reader to reveal the lesson learned.[37]

Although framed as praise, Ben-Gurion's employment of the attributes of modesty, simplicity, and asceticism ultimately disqualifies Alper as a literary author, an artist, and instead posits her as a mere reporter of a model story. We may observe here the elasticity of the ideal of simplicity as it refers to women's writing. If the critique of Alper's first novel charged her with "excessive realism," namely, of exposing the reader to too much contents that destabilize the patriarchal structure, here her commitment to reality "without any make up" is celebrated since it aligns with the dominant ideology.

The use of the gendered metaphor of "make up" to refer to poetic excess invokes the analogy between the feminine body and the literary text. Eulogizing Alper on the first anniversary of her passing, the poet Zelda critically notes: "I sometimes saw her as a 'Rusalka' [mermaid] wandering a midst concrete walls … she tried for some reason to blur her signs. Her long hair, the hair of a mermaid, she would strictly fold, and she would eliminate the mystery and the boldness from her blue eyes, and wore a 'uniform' of a political activist, a 'uniform' of a writer."[38] For Zelda, Alper's long hair serves as a metonym of her creative qualities that are strictly confined by what she calls "a uniform of a writer." The analogy between the regulation of women's writing and the regulation of the feminine body frames Alper's largely forgotten literary career as a paradigmatic case illustrating the restrictive gendered field in which Zionist women's prose has evolved. At the same time, Zelda's "uniform of a writer" metaphor visualizes the way Alper's own self-fashioning as a nationalist writer includes the willful imposition of the Zionist norms of diminishment.

A series of scenes taking place toward the end of *Settlers in the Mountain* may be useful in further unpacking this analogy. The first scene is set in Syria, where Leah travels to meet a potential bride for one of her sons:

The girl came out. Beautiful, eastern beauty, foreign, with no Jewish flair. She was wearing jewelry and make up. She is not a mate for her son. He does not need a woman to look at ...

"It's a shame," they said, "we wanted for our daughter, who is very educated, speaks French and English, an Ashkenazi man, to whom we would be very generous."

"Never mind," she consoled them, "you'll find one."

"But why don't you want her?"

"I need Rivka,"[39] she said to them, "I want Rivka, who goes down by herself to the fountain with the pitcher, who would be a *fellaha* for my son the *fellah*."[40]

The Syrian Jewish girl is rejected because her excessive adornment conflicts with the image of the simple *fellaha*, the Arab female peasant. The invocation of the Arabic term recalls two contrasting meanings of "Eastern" femininity in the Zionist imagination: first, it is connected to the Zionist fascination with the indigenous Palestinian peasant as a model of the kind of grounded simple existence of life on the Land they sought to emulate; and secondly, it denotes the excessiveness of Eastern femininity as metonymic of the Orient itself as a site of excess.

A few chapters later, Leah severely reproaches a teacher for wearing makeup and painting her fingernails red: "I have seen how teachers like you teach . . . walking with the girls . . . they lunge at the Geranium bush, pluck the red leaflets of the flower and stick them to their nails and lips."[41] Here, the adorned woman's body becomes a destructive force. The teacher's self-adornment makes the nature walk lose its ideological and educational value, and renders it instead as the setting of a grotesque scene of feminine excess. In another scene, the hardy pioneer also chastises a woman painter for engaging in "amusement and art" when the People is in need of "hands to work in building and rescuing the nation."[42] This series of encounters culminates in the final scene of the biography where Leah scolds a woman writer who proposes to write a story about the heroic family from the mountain:

In a hundred years, we will have time to write books. Now we need workers of the land, now we first have to set the ground for the People, and the important books will be written when our lives grow from the ground. First, we have to resurrect the body of the People. God too first created the body and then put spirit into it. The People of

Israel has written enough books. The spirit of the People needs to rest. The People has been uprooted for two thousand years from the roots of life; it has lost its sense of life. We have to return it first to the origins of creation.[43]

While the protagonist of the Zionist narrative of the body is typically the Zionist man, Cohen's speech quickly shifts to a critique of the feminine body:

In Tel Aviv, women walk all painted and adorned. It is disgusting to look at their faces. When I come to Tel Aviv, I walk the streets hastily looking down in shame, because I cannot see these monsters with the plucked painted eyebrows and the horrible outlandish fingernails and lips. These eye-shadows and the blown-up hair, which they leave untied on the nape so that they can look like little girls. And men too. The image of God is effaced from the faces of these human beings. They were supposed to build a home for the People, and they are making themselves into dolls.[44]

If the inadequacies of the Jewish masculine body are often depicted in terms of lack, with the diasporic masculine body described as underdeveloped, weak, neglected, deficient, and sometimes castrated,[45] the bad feminine body, in contrast, is overly made-up, overdressed, blown-up, and monstrous in its excessiveness. At stake are often the limits of the body – the fingernails, the hair – emerging as hectic and expansive frontiers of the body that require regulation. Men's transgressions appear as secondary in this context (Leah briefly comments: "and men too"); indeed, here, it is women's excess, and not men's lack, that serves as a metonym for the failure of the People to transition from text to land. The Zionist project of body-making is articulated, not in terms of building and growing muscles and phalluses, but rather through the gesture of undressing the feminine body of adornments and ornaments which emerges as metonymic of the project of stripping the People of its spiritual excess. Presumably, the writer who visits Leah Cohen in this scene is, in fact, Alper herself. Thus, the biography concludes with a denunciation of its own writing, bringing into relief the process of self-diminishment that marks Alper's writing career, a career which is illustrative of the fraught position of the woman writer in Zionist culture at large, and one in which she is often cast as an agent of an ideology that prescribes her own diminishment and renunciation.

Stripping the Bejewelled Body: Diminishment
and the Intersection of Gender and Ethnicity

I will now tell you of an incident that happened to me when I was visiting home. A friend came to visit me. Her arms were covered with gold bracelets. This was strange to me, because I have not seen this kind of jewellery for a long time. I mocked her and asked her if the piece of land that many people can make a living of is less important than the ringing sound of the bracelets on her arms? My friend laughed in response to what I have said. I was sad and a thought came to my mind: how far away is our youth from the Zionist aspirations and how great are the efforts that need to be invested in this youth.[46]

In Ada Mimon's survey of *Fifty Years of the Women Workers' Movement*, she includes the above account by a female student of Syrian descent in the agricultural school Ayanot. Expressing the values of her Zionist education, the girl's testimony phrases the opposition between simplicity and adornment in terms of the conflict she sees between the national project and the bejewelled body of the Eastern woman. Illustrating this further, Mimon presents a "before" and "after" images of a girl in the same institution (figure 4.1), which visualizes the ideological reconstruction of the Mizrahi female body.

The removal of Eastern ornamentation in this image markedly coincides with a change of colour. Not only is the girl dressed in black in the "before" picture and in white in the "after", but the light on her face also lightens her complexion. This image illustrates the way the Zionist tropes of feminine diminishment intersect with a discourse on the ethnic body, in which whiteness emerges as the ultimate diminishment.

We may recall from chapter 1 Dvora Ben-Yehuda's essay about her work with Sephardi girls at the Evelina de Rothschild School, in which the removal of the girls' jewellery aligns with their overall desired cultural reform. In her study of women in the Old Yishuv, Margalit Shilo explains that Sephardi women's jewellery was a site of cultural tension in Jerusalem even before Zionism, as "a woman's jewelry, worn for display, was the antithesis to the general tendency to camouflage her as far as possible behind veils and extra layers."[47] While "Sephardi families took special care to beautify their daughters from childhood with jewelry,"[48] both the Sephardi and Ashkenazi

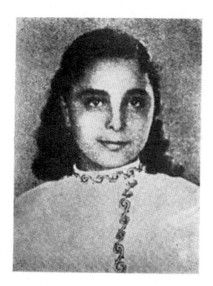 

אותה נערה לאחר אחד-עשר
חודשים בעיינות

נערה תימניה, עולה חדשה, ביום
בואה לבית-הספר החקלאי עיינות

4.1 A Yemenite girl depicted on her first day at the Zionist agricultural school Ayanot (*right*), and the same girl after eleven months at the school (*left*).

rabbis of Jerusalem intervened on the matter on several occasions during the eighteenth and nineteenth centuries and issued regulations limiting the wearing of jewelry in public for it violated the codes of feminine modesty which were especially important in Jerusalem, where women's bodies were conceived as embodying the sanctity of the city. The entry of modernizers like Dvora Ben-Yehuda into this space changed its terms. The bejewelled Sephardi body was now measured not against the traditional modesty required of the "daughter of Israel," but against the Victorian respectability of the "angel of the home." The consistency between the orthodox religious setting, the Western bourgeois project of the Evelina de Rothschild school and the Labor Zionist agricultural school speaks to the continuity of the norms surrounding femininity across the traditional, modern, and national contexts. While the masculine narrative of the Zionist body often postulates a radical break between the weak effeminate diasporic body and the virile and strong Zionist body, the process of reshaping the feminine body seems to be one in which values of religious modesty, modern respectability, and Zionist asceticism overlap.

In her discussion of Ashkenazi women's attitudes towards the bejewelled body of the Yemenite woman, Yael Guilat shows that the renunciation of traditional jewellery was a constitutive gesture of the Zionist reconstruction of Yemenite women's bodies.[49] According to Guilat, Ashkenazi women's rejection of Yemenite jewellery was related to its role in "the system of bride price and dowry,"[50] which made the jewellery "a symbol of women's oppression by husbands and fathers and as part of an ignorant, superstitious world, full of amulets and primitive spells."[51] My analysis of Dvora Baron's novel *The Exiles* in the following sections aims to expand the scope within which the removal of jewellery from the Mizrahi woman's body is probed by situating it within the broader project of shaping a Zionist femininity.

The Shape of the "Daughter of Israel": Gender, Ethnicity, and the Feminine Body in Dvora Baron's *The Exiles*

As we may recall from chapter 2, Dvora Baron was a unique figure in the Hebrew literary landscape as the only woman prose writer who was valued by her male peers as a member of Labor Zionism's literary elite. Like Rachel Bluwstein, Baron's biography may be conceived as embodying the metaphors of smallness and diminishment as it included thirty-three years of seclusion in her Tel-Aviv apartment where she wrote the bulk of her literary oeuvre. As with Bluwstein, the scholarship on Baron often engages with questions of measurements and dimensions. While Dan Miron's seminal 1959 essay about Baron argues that her stories transcend the concrete context of the *shtetl* forging a cyclical ahistorical metaphysics,[52] feminist scholars challenge this reading of Baron for its disavowal of the specific historical and political contexts from which she wrote. This argument is often phrased through emphasis on Baron's engagement with the minute and marginal elements of feminine existence. Indeed, scholars such as Naomi Seidman, Orly Lubin, Wendy Zierler, Sheila Jelen, and Shachar Pinsker highlighted Baron's poetics of the concrete, the contingent, the marginal, and the small-scale as undermining the grand narratives of Zionism.[53] My understanding of Baron's novel *The Exiles* traces a different meaning of the tropes of smallness and diminishment. Placing them in the context of the construction of feminine bodies in the novel, I show how the theme of diminishment coincides with the nationalization of these bodies.

While Baron was distinguished from other Zionist writers of her generation in placing most of her plots in the diasporic space of the *shtetl*,

The Exiles is one of Baron's few pieces that takes place entirely in the Middle East. The novel narrates the story of a community of Jewish settlers deported by the Ottomans from Palestine to Egypt during World War I.[54] Of the multiple families and individuals whose stories are entangled in *The Exiles*, I focus here on the interrelations between three young women: Ita Blokh, a new Jewish arrival to Palestine at the beginning of the novel who joins the community's exile in Egypt; Brakha Rothstein, the daughter of a bourgeois Zionist Jewish family settled in Jaffa; and Lulu, a Jewish Egyptian embroiderer, whom the deportees encounter in Alexandria, and who later travels back to Palestine with them. Ita arrives in Palestine from Lithuania at the beginning of the novel as a "tourist to the Orient"[55] accompanied by her relative Menahem Gutt, who is hopelessly in love with her. In Jaffa, the couple stays at the inn of Nehama Rothstein, whose daughter Brakha develops a fascination with the beautiful Ita. When Jaffa's Jewish community is deported by the Ottoman authorities to Alexandria,[56] Ita and Menahem accompany them aiming to continue their tours of the "East" in Egypt. In Alexandria, Ita, who lodges with the Rothsteins, falls in love with a Jewish Egyptian cotton merchant whom she follows to Cairo, where she dies in labour while giving birth to their daughter. In the wake of Ita's death, in the hopes of learning more of her tragic fate, Brakha Rothstein pays a visit to Lulu the embroiderer who is a relative of Ita's Egyptian lover. This meeting, where Ita's figure is reconstructed as a feminine ideal, is the point of departure of my reading.

From the start, the visit with the Egyptian embroiderer is introduced to the reader as a transgressive venture; here, Brakha secretly enters "a forbidden courtyard", ensuring that "she wouldn't see anyone she knew"[57] to meet Lulu,[58] whom she "would usually avoid ... because of Lulu's adornment and outlandish dress."[59] The architecture of the "Oriental" space coincides with the description of Lulu's physical appearance; in Brakha's view, it is excessive and disorienting with its "dizzying sight of countless spinning roofs, laundry blowing in the breeze, domes and towers suspended over the void."[60] While she herself is described as a subject of "Oriental" excess, Lulu describes Ita Blokh as a feminine model of European respectability and simplicity, "and what a beauty ... everyone thought she walked around in satins and silks, when all she wore was simple cotton, unadorned cotton and flannel. She had no need for anything fancier."[61] Further, the unadorned body is assigned moral significance here as a metonym of Ita's virtuous nature: "she was so good, so good ... she saw into everyone's heart and pitied them."[62]

Significantly, this postmortem idealization of Ita contradicts earlier
accounts of her as a frivolous young woman, or, "a tourist to the Orient"
that hunts after pleasures and adventures, while paying no attention to
the suffering of her travel companion Menahem Gutt. Through Brakha's
envious eyes, Ita, as presented in the early chapters of the novel, models
European luxury, for she possesses "marvelous objects, among them a tiny,
delicate manicure kit, and a hand-embroidered handkerchief bordered
by an azure thread,"[63] which Brakha encounters while cleaning her room.
Brakha's fascination with Ita develops in the community's early days
in Egypt alongside the young woman's discovery of new possibilities of
femininity in the cosmopolitan space of Alexandria:

During her days here, in the city, she had become more sophisticated.
Just as in their house in Jaffa, Brakha washed floors and dishes, peeled
eggplants and zucchini for frying, and listened to her father's – or
the Lithuanian boy's – history lessons on the Sabbath. But all this –
she now knew – wasn't in the least bit interesting. It was interesting,
rather, to stand and gaze through the window of "Modern," a giant
store, or to look at the boys skating on the sidewalks, or to watch the
group of attractive English girls rolling tennis balls along grassy fields.
In the morning, on her way to the vegetable market, she sometimes
stopped outside the beauty shop called "Paris" and was surprised to
observe for the first time that all the young women emerging from
there looked the same: they had the same loose, almost sloppy curls
in their hair, the same white powdery countenances, and the same red
tinge on the cheekbones, which made them look strangely cunning.
But after some time, she understood on her own that they did all this
on purpose, because this is what the seamstress from the basement
apartment called "fashion."[64]

It is in the context of Brakha's new interest in cosmetics that she also
notices Ita's most alluring feature – her natural white clear skin tone – of
which she is envious since her own complexion bears the marks of the
Middle-Eastern sun and is all covered with "pimples, freckles, and light
spots."[65] Brakha's admiration of Ita's whiteness prompts one the most
grotesque scenes in the novel, in which she tries to cosmetically whiten her
own skin complexion:

Brakha, after conversation with the Italian seamstress about Ita's glowing face, asked if she wasn't using some kind of make-up that she had bought at "Paris." But the young woman strenuously asserted that with Ita it was natural ... It is possible, however, to create the same effect – she said – artificially.

In a beauty salon? "Brakha asked."

"No, with drugs that can be purchased at the drug store," she said ... "You just buy a bottle of cream: 'Belladrama' or 'Metamorphosis' or 'Disappearing Cream.' You apply them to your face according to the directions on the bottle. If you have any pimples, freckles, or light spots, they all disappear, and your skin becomes as soft as a baby's."

By the light of the street lamp, she squeezed out some of the cream and rubbed it, precisely according to the directions, on her face. Then she waited for it to sink into her skin ... But suddenly, the door creaked open ... Her mother, in her nightdress, entered with the kitchen lantern in her hand. When she saw the bleached face of girl ... she asked, in a thundering voice:

"Have you gone mad? Are you out of your mind?" ...

After she had put the lantern down of the table, she clapped her hands and cried out:

"Woe is me. A daughter of Israel, this is a daughter of Israel?!"[66]

In his seminal work on whiteness, Richard Dyer recounts how "much of the history of Western makeup is a history of whitening the face."[67] According to Dyer in the colonial context, "to be a lady is to be as white as it gets."[68] Brakha's unfortunate attempt to clear her complexion is embedded in this racialized history which stems from the cultural construction of white femininity as the beautiful and virtuous epitome of Western civilization and the embodiment of racial superiority.[69] As Jews were never completely included in the Western notion of whiteness, the painfully ridiculous result of Brakha's experiment seems parodic of the Jewish girl's desire to occupy the "white" position in the colonial politics of colour. The comical scene, however, arguably clarifies something essential about the cultural meaning of whiteness. In the terms suggested by Dyer, Brakha's "error" is mistaking whiteness for a "hue" that she may artificially acquire, rather than understanding its symbolic place as the "norm" which is essentially transparent.[70] Culturally, as Dyer theorizes, the superiority assigned to whiteness in white cultures derives not only from the marking of whiteness as "good" as opposed to blackness as "bad," but also from the cultural perception of white as transparent, or as no colour at all, namely, as a universal essence in relation to which all colours are to be understood.[71] This point is further illustrated in a scene where Lulu and Brakha meet again in Jaffa after the exiles' return to the Land; as Brakah observes, "I see that you do not use lotions anymore ... I too have pushed all those creams and powders away, because ... here there is no need for all this."[72] The ideological terrain of the Land here emerges as a force that naturalizes women's complexion, and therefore makes cosmetics redundant. The project of whitening the skin becomes obsolete as the cultural essence of whiteness as naturalized universal transparency is gained.

Returning to the initial scene in Lulu's room, the reconstruction of Ita as a model of feminine simplicity begins a process by which the bodies of both Lulu and Brakha are reshaped. As she speaks of Ita, Lulu is "unmade-up" through Brakha's eyes, clearing the ornamentation which at first marked her as Other: "the rouge on her face and the blue eye shadow becoming no longer visible to Brakha, only her sad good eyes."[73] Moreover, when Brakha leaves Lulu's home, she notices that the space itself is simplified as she goes down the stairs "without feeling at all dizzy."[74] Later in the day, she contemplates her disillusionment from the excessive possibilities of femininity found in exile:

> This was the first time since they had been here that she did not put her hair in curlers before going to bed. She saw no need to. In order to keep her hair out of the way she braided it, as she used to, in Jaffa, and she felt as she did this that she had returned to the way she had been in those days: A simple girl, helping her poor mother with the housework so they could provide food and shelter to the family.[75]

The process by which the young women are reinvested in the aesthetic and ideological values of simplicity set the stage for the return of the community to Palestine. Shortly after the return, we learn that Lulu, having joined the returning deportees and immigrated to Palestine, has indeed "taken off the last of her jewelry: the earrings, the bracelets, the corals, and has combed her hair in a simple manner," thus achieving, according to Nehama Rothstein, "the shape of a daughter of Israel."[76] We may note the repetition of the title "daughter of Israel," which is usually associated with

4.2 Still from Otto Preminger, *Exodus*, 1960.

the traditional Jewish values of feminine modesty, and which Nehama, as we recall, uses to reproach Brakha for her failed cosmetic experiment. The reiteration of the phrase in relation to Lulu's integration into the Zionist Ashkenazi community in Palestine marks not only the continuity between the religious and Zionist conceptions of femininity in terms of asceticism, purity and modesty but also the Europeanization of the Zionist feminine body as conformed to the cultural norms of white femininity.

Sacrifice, Victimhood, and White Femininity

Otto Preminger's 1960 film *Exodus*[77] depicts one of the most iconic representations of Zionism on screen where Zionist aesthetics are schematically formulated as a system of gendered colour coding.[78] Notably, the visual appearance of each of the main characters dovetails with their ideological role, particularly in terms of their complexion. Thus, Ari Ben-Canaan, the male protagonist played by Paul Newman, who models the figure of the sabra, has blonde hair and blue eyes that ostensibly contrast the image of the old diasporic Jew, but also tan skin that signifies his "nativeness" to the Middle Eastern space. The other male protagonist of the film, Dov Landau, an angry and tormented survivor who turns to the extreme right-wing para-military group, the Irgun,[79] has a darker skin tone, a feature which matches his "darker" psychological character. Conversely, the two female leading characters, Kitty and Karen, mirror each other physically as blondes with fair complexions. The colour differences between men and women here visualize gender differences that cast men as heroes and fighters, and women as pure, vulnerable, and victimized figures. The character that embodies this feminine ideal most clearly is Karen Hansen, who is played by Jill Haworth. Depicted in the original novel by Leon Uris as tall with brown hair and green eyes, Karen appears in the film as an "Aryan looking Holocaust survivor"[80] with a blindingly white complexion and very light blonde hair. Her whiteness coincides with her purity and innocence as well as with her role as a martyr who is killed by Arabs toward the end of the film. In the frame depicting her dead body (figure 4.2), she is powerfully constructed her as a visual embodiment of the white martyr. Her body, blended with the white rocks, is placed in a soft and vulnerable posture but is still completely intact despite the violence it supposedly endured, thus maintaining the wholesomeness of her body, white and untarnished, as a visual sign of the nation.

Interrogating the mutually constitutive construction of whiteness and femininity in the colonial space, scholars have noted the narrative in which the white woman is victimized by "brown" men.[81] The vulnerability of the feminine body substantiates the colonizer's fear of being contaminated by the threatening "native," and thus obscures the colonial relations of power while rationalizing and naturalizing colonial violence. While the relationship between the East-European community of exiles and the Egyptian Jewish community in Baron's novel is not a colonized-colonizer relationship, it is interesting to observe how the context of the colonial spaces of Egypt and Palestine reverberates in the story of Ita's ruin by the Egyptian cotton merchant Morris Levy, in a plotline that echoes the racialized premise of the white woman's victimization narrative. From his very first appearance in the novel, Morris is marked as a "dark man," by way of "his expressionless brown face – the face of an Egyptian"[82] which "startles" Nehama Rothstein in a scene that in many ways foreshadows Ita's ultimate fate. In another scene, Ita's forsaken lover, Menahem Gutt, sits alone in a Cairo hotel room while Ita and Morris explore the city. At that point he has a hallucination in which Ita is "carelessly too close to the edge of the open balcony" with "no one to warn her to be careful not to fall into the abyss that lay beneath her."[83] Often entangled with the plot of white women's victimization in the Orient, the image of the "fallen woman" that emerges from this scene is also bound with the construction of the sexuality of the modern white woman in the colonial space.[84] Ita's character arch shifts her from the position of a transgressor, whose illicit affair the community finds "shameful,"[85] to the position of the innocent martyr-like victim of whom Nehama Rothstein remarks as "That good girl. Beautiful and good. Why did this happen to her?"[86] Dyer comments that the whiteness of death, encapsulated by the death of the white woman, culminates the symbolic significance of whiteness as absolute vulnerability.[87] It is within this logic of whiteness that we may locate Ita's death, given that in this economy, the ultimate role of the "white" Zionist woman is to diminish herself to the point of disappearance. Intriguingly, Lulu plays a significant role in bringing resolution to this story. Upon returning to the Land with the exiles, she marries Menahem Gutt, Ita's rejected suitor, and adopts Ita's daughter. The pattern of the substitution of women, which we observed on several occasions in this book, appears here as a way of resolving the ethnic tensions surrounding the feminine body. The Eastern woman as a substitute for the dead white woman further coincides with the cultural structure of sacrifice; as Ita is largely construed as a martyr, whose death eventually allows the community to come together.

The intersection of white femininity with victimhood and sacrifice brings us back to the figure of Rachel Bluwstein, who is often marked as the quintessential embodiment of feminine martyrdom in Zionist culture. As Miron notes, the colour white was ostensibly associated with the poet[88] through "her gentleness; her pureness; her physical weakness (paleness) ... ; her simple style (simplicity – whiteness); her connection with tuberculosis 'the white disease'; perhaps even her tendency – common to gentle young women of the time to wear white."[89] According to Miron, Bluwstein's choice of white and simple design for the covers of her poetry collections is endemic of the code of simplicity that she has bequeathed to Hebrew women's poetry. The colour white also appears prominently in her commemoration, as in Bialik's condescending eulogy likening her poetry to "white flowers, eternally whitening,"[90] and in Yokheved Bat-Miryam's poem dedicated to her memory, which invokes the image of the "white solitary stone" of her grave.[91] While Miron does not read Bluwstein's whiteness in a racialized/ethnic context, I would note that in many ways her affinity with the colour white derives from the same cultural norms that constitute Victorian feminine whiteness as a central trope of Western femininity. We may revisit Bluwstein's whiteness through its resonance with the figure of Ita Blokh, both of whom are "tourists to the Orient" that are eventually marked as white martyrs: Bluwstein through the "white disease" of tuberculosis (notably also connected to the image of the "fallen woman"), and Ita through her sexual contamination by the "dark man." Like the image of the dead white woman-martyr in *Exodus*, both, I would argue, constitute moments in the genealogy of Zionist femininity as white femininity through which the Zionist ethos of sacrifice is imbricated into the intersectional politics of gender and ethnicity.

"Our Tiny Land": From Poetics to Politics

To conclude, we shall return one last time to Rachel Bluwstein's "To My Land." In the poem, the impoverished self is analogous to the impoverished Land itself. Indeed, along with many other Zionist cultural representations, "To My Land" participates in the production of the ubiquitous image of Palestine as an "empty land," that is, as a land that is vacant and available for the Jews to settle in (as encapsulated in the popular slogan, "a land without for a People for a People without a land"). Reinforced through countless Zionist cultural representations in literature, cinema, art, and music, this image had dramatic geo-political ramifications in rationalizing the colonization of Palestine. In the context of the "empty land," diminishment signifies both weakness through the metonym of the impoverished poetic subject and power manifested by the capacity of the same subject to erase indigenous history and presence in the Land.

Bluwstein's "To My Land" resonates with various other poetic depictions of the Land as impoverished, desolated, barren, and empty. While poems such as Alexander Penn's "Oh Land, My Homeland" (*ho artzi moladti*), Shlonsky's "Behold" (*Hineh*), Esther Rabb, "Upon Your Nakedness a White Day Celebrates" (*Al maarumayikh hogeg yom lavan*), Yocheved Bat-Miryam's "The Land of Israel" (*Eretz Yisrael*), and Lea Goldberg's "My Homeland"[92] (*Mekhora sheli*) each contain their own complexity that would exceed the scope of this chapter, we may note shared characterization of the Land in these poems through a variety of Hebrew synonyms used to describe impoverishment, such as *Dala* (meagre), *Evyona* (impoverished, wretched), *Aniya* (poor), *Shdufa* (dry), and *Hareva* (barren). Like Bluwstein's poem, these poems also mark the Land as a feminine figure – a bride, a sexual partner, a mother. While maternal and feminine figures are often represented in culture as nurturing and giving, it is significant that in Zionist culture the land-as-woman metaphor almost always goes hand in hand with the characterization of the Land as impoverished and barren.

To close this discussion, I would like to follow the discursive dissemination of an adjacent term to that of the "empty land" whose poetic-political trajectory also tells a story about the cultural meaning of the diminished features of the Land as a gendered trope. The phrase "Our Tiny Land" (*Artzenu ha-ktantonet*) first appeared in Zionist culture as the title of a 1940s popular song. The feminine diminutive form *ktantonet*, deriving from the Hebrew word for feminine-small *ktana*, gives the phrase an endearing and comical meaning. Although its poetics are far less sophisticated, the lyrics of "Out Tiny Land" associate it with the group of poems mentioned above. The poem starts with a classic Zionist depiction of the Land, "Blue sky, red rock / clod of earth, desolated soil / our valley, Negev, sea / the blessing of the plowed fields," highlighting the contrast between the desolate bare land and the fields cultivated by Zionist settlement. Proceeding in the same poetic tradition, the song then professes love to the Land as a mother and a bride:

> Our tiny land, our tiny land,
> My land
> My soul yearns for you
> Our tiny land, our tiny land
> My mother, my little mother
> You love your son so much
> After 2000 years of exile
> I have returned to you
> You are my only one,
> Our tiny land, our tiny land
> I wedded you forever,
> Live, live forever, our land.[93]

The image of the tiny desolate land is at odds with the expansive function of the Land as an all-encompassing feminine figure who is both a lover and a mother. In this sense, the song encapsulates the paradox of femininity as a cultural category; although it is constituted as marginal and diminished, it also holds, as we have seen throughout this chapter, a remarkable capacity to stretch and encompass a wide range of meanings. This elasticity of the feminine mirrors of the expandability of the Land itself. As noted by Oren Yiftahel and Batya Roded in their study of the imagery of the Land in Israeli popular music, "this geographic flexibility expands the borders of the land according to the location of the last settlers or last soldiers and separates between the real and concrete disputed landscape, and the imagined exclusively Jewish geography."[94]

While the song joins the poetic discourse on Zionist rootedness and nativeness, it has a hybrid cultural trajectory, as illustrated by its Tango melody, which connects the song to very different landscapes than that of the "tiny" desolate land. The song originated in a casual meeting between two immigrant musicians-performers Shmuel Fisher (lyrics) and Henrik (Tzvi) Gold-Zehavi (music), "in an out-of-the-way shack, after a few glasses of cognac."[95] Both musicians notably ended up leaving Palestine/Israel in the hopes of cultivating an international music career (Fisher returned in 1966; Gold-Zehavi never returned). The tension between the song's international aura and its pathos-full ideological lyrics was arguably noticed by poet and dramatist Nathan Alterman who collaborated with Fisher and Gold-Zehavi in adapting the song into a satirical sketch in 1947. The sketch, performed as part of a satirical review titled "Our Tiny Land," featured a recording studio where different grotesque characters attempt to record the song.[96] Thus, the original performance of the song in fact consisted of a parodic representation of the Zionist ideological poetics of claiming the Land.

A crude "street" version of the song appeared around the same time, undermining the original version's lofty lyrics and exacerbating its gender politics. Mocking the Zionist establishment's cooperation with the British authorities, this version reads, "Our tiny land / take off your shirt / and if you have a sweat / take off your bra as well / the British are prepared / take off your underwear / and they will screw you to the bone."[97] The contrast between the gentle image of the impoverished, barren, yet beloved, virgin Land and the vulgar representation of the Land as a degraded rape victim fleshes out the tension embedded in the gendered relegation of power and weakness in Zionist rhetoric. On the one hand, as we have seen, feminine vulnerability as a trope is often used to bolster the moral gravity of the national project, framing it, as in Bluwstein's poem, as a modest endeavor of a peaceful subject. On the other hand, the gendered weakness implicit in the imagery, appearing in the "street" version of "Our Tiny Land" as an allegory of the Zionist leadership's political weakness, runs the risk of inflicting on the Zionist subject the shame of sexual vulnerability, which has long been associated with the diasporic situation.[98]

In 1956, a columnist, writing under the penname Hagai, offered a related critique on the proliferation of the phrase "our tiny land" in popular discourse:

There is nothing wrong with self-deprecating humor but this jargon of "our little itty-bitty tiny land" etc. etc. sometimes gives me a bad sour taste of contempt, self-pity, disrespect and some masochism … this jargon, when it appears in an essay or an article, or as a feeling in the heart of a citizen, there's something unhealthy about it, I believe. This "our tiny land" feeling has something diasporic about it, contrasted to the very essence of the Land, her appearance, her destiny, her power, her past. This land even as it is torn apart, even with its temporary borders – always brings to mind something bold, full of hope, something that palpitates with pain and vision – very far from this cute pastoral resignation of "our tiny land." [99]

Hagai's comments align with the tensions vulgarized in the "street" version of the song. If the smallness of the Land may seem endearing, Hagai claims, it is simultaneously degrading. What remains clear is that the attribute "tiny" is not read here as referring to the real measurements of the Land, but rather reflects a cultural characterization, which Hagai discerns as being at odds with the prescription of Zionist culture as "it has something diasporic about it." In other words, "Our tiny land" is a perplexing signifier that illustrates Zionist intimacy with the Land, while also evoking "unhealthy" diasporic associations that carry "a bad sour taste of contempt, self-pity, disrespect and some masochism." [100]

A digital search of the phrase "our tiny land" in the *Historic Jewish Press* database of Israel's National Library shows that despite this criticism, the use of the phrase continued to expand over the years in dozens of ads, news articles, letters to the editor, and opinion editorials. While it continued to be used as an expression of the intimacy and familiarity of the Israeli space, after the 1967 war, in which Israel tripled its size, the phrase also began to figure prominently in geo-political debates over borders and territory. Indeed, according to the metadata, the months just after the war saw a distinct increase in the use of the phrase. For example, an editorial piece in the Labor Movement's newspaper *Davar* that appeared a month after the war in July 1967, complains, "Every day we see new advocates of international justice demanding that we give up this or that, and even that or this, to give up, for world peace, and for our own benefit. Only by giving up [the occupied territories], can the People of Israel dwell peacefully in *our tiny land*." [101] Around the same time, an editorial from the right-wing paper *Hatzofe* published in August 1967 celebrates the territorial expansion: "The

Israeli state has expanded and is filled with inhabitants ... Geo-politically, we now control a territory of respectable size and no longer a narrow strip ... we are no longer a miniature state, or as the song goes – *our little tiny land.*[102]

Typical of the general use of the phrase in Israeli popular discourse, the contradiction between these two iterations – one denoting the smallness of the Land and the other its expansion – again demonstrates the function of "our tiny land" not as a realistic assertion about the dimensions of the Land, but as an expression of alternating cultural attitudes toward vulnerability and power. Here, we may note how the Labor Movement's publication, still invested in what Shapira has named the "defensive ethos,"[103] emphasizes the smallness and thus vulnerability of the Land, whereas the right-wing publication allows for the celebration of the newly expanded territories and the strength it represents. Yet, both share the same argument against the idea of forgoing the occupied territories.

This duality is also evident in two popular Israeli songs of the mid-1980s, a time in which debates over the status of the occupied territories intensified in light of the 1979 peace agreement with Egypt in which Israeli gave back the Sinai Desert, as well as the Lebanon War, and the growing tensions in the West Bank and Gaza that culminated with the break of the first Intifada (Palestinian uprising) in 1987. "Our Tiny Land" (1986) and "Your Wonders are not Yet Gone" (1987) both invoke the phrase "our tiny land," and allude to the original song. While curiously sharing the same lyricist, popular Israeli songwriter Yoram Teharlev, the two songs are very different from each other in tone, and yet, as with the two editorials cited above, they partake in the same discourse about the meaning of the Land's dimensions. The first song, performed by Yigaal Bashan, has a satirical tone.[104] From its opening lines – "Our tiny land, our tiny land / with American head / and Japanese stereo-system" – the song criticizes the Americanization of Israeli society and its associated hedonism and consumerism. It continues: "this is the land we inherited from our ancestors / this is the land bequeathed to us by Moses / where the mountains are dripping juice and orange soda / and my people are settled in Hilton and Ramada." Parodying biblical narratives and imagery, the song mocks the excesses of capitalist Israeli reality, contrasting it with the Zionist ascetic ideals, perceived as connecting the Land and the people to their ancestral origins.

"Your Wonders Are Not Yet Gone," first performed by a military entertainment band and later by its composer Rami Kleinstein, offers a much more solemn and lyrical tone.[105] As evident in the recurring opening line "our tiny land" of each stanza, there is a clear allusion to the original song by Fisher and Gold-Zehavi, although this song is devoid of the irony created by the tango melody of the original. Instead, Kleinstein's melody is a slow ballad that corresponds with its sentimental lyrics. The song further invokes the Land as an impoverished female figure: "our tiny land, our beautiful land, shirtless homeland, barefoot homeland, accept me into your songs, beautiful bride." As in the early poetic representations of the Land, the poverty of the Land mirrors the speaking subject, reading, "here, together we will root, graceless homeland and an orphan gypsy," and, the figure of the Land is imagined in multiple feminine roles. Indeed, while the first stanza reads "A beautiful bride," the refrain reads "to me you are a mother and daughter / you are the little that is left for me." Once again, we see the femininity of the Land as doubly representing its smallness and vulnerability, on the one hand, and the expansive comfort it offers to the male subject, on the other. As Yifthael and Roded note, "Your Wonders" is a paradigmatic example of "the rift, that has become common in Hebrew song-lyrics, between the Jewish Land as tiny and threatened, and a spatial reality of Jewish expansion and Arab-Palestinian diminishment."[106] The rhetoric of feminine diminishment is thus instrumental in ensuring and justifying the real diminishment of the Palestinians who are rendered completely invisible in these poetics.

With the cultural trajectory of "our tiny land" in mind, let us return to Bluwstein's "To My Land":

Only a tree – my hands have planted
on the peaceful shores of the Jordan River
Only a pathway – my feet paved
in the fields.

The repetition of "only a tree" and "only a pathway" articulates the small feminine position in terms of its modest modes of intervention in the space of the Land. In contrast with the heroic "tales of bravery, from many battlefields," the ideal Zionist intervention in space depicted in the poem is quiet, modest, impoverished, and non-violent. Reading the poem in light of its geopolitical aftermath reveals its relation to network of cultural signifiers reinforcing feminine diminishment, which, rather than signifying feminine Otherness, furnishes the feminine as a poetic double-edged sword professing peacefulness and vulnerability while quietly erasing the presence of the indigenous Other.

In this context, with some deliberate anachronism, we may consider how the cry "only a tree" becomes imbued in the politics of tree planting in Israel/Palestine, where the project of forestation served to reinforce the idea of Jewish roots in the Land as well as to cover the ruins of Palestinian villages after the 1948 War.[107] Along the same lines, this perspective would intersect Bluwstein's line "only a path" with the politics of movement in Israel/Palestine from the 1948 destruction of Palestinian communities to ensure continuity of Jewish settlement[108] to the building of separate roads open to Jews only in the West Bank.[109] Through this lens, poetic diminishment and geopolitical expansion emerge as complementary phenomena. This discussion thus tells a story about the illusiveness of femininity as a category of the Zionist imagination. In the context of the regulation of women's writing and women's bodies, it marks the marginalization of women, namely, the limitation of the cultural space they are permitted to occupy. In the geopolitical realm, on the other hand, it points toward the expansive resonance of femininity in Israeli politics and culture, spanning from women's writing and women's bodies, to the politics of ethnicity, and the geopolitics of colonization and national security, ultimately showing how politics of gender in fact permeates all politics.

EPILOGUE

The Father, the Daughter,
and the Question of the *Korban*

———

I approached this study with a desire to grapple with the present, no less than to recover the past, and so I return here to the present moment, which is one of global crisis. One may learn a lot about a specific culture and society at a time of crisis, not only by the direct response to it, but also from how the culture continues to negotiate its structures and dilemmas alongside the crisis. The Israeli literary market experienced its own crisis due to the COVID-19 pandemic, as bookstores were closed during the long lockdowns, and most Israelis have not yet bought into the digital book revolution. Literary editors and publishing house staff were furloughed, literary awards were cancelled, and new book projects were revoked or postponed. By the third lockdown in February 2021, where in the USA our sense of crisis was exacerbated by the January insurrection at the Capitol, the Israeli public sphere was intensely engaged with a literary scandal: the publication of Galia Oz's short memoir-essay, "Davar she-mithapes le-ahava" (A Thing Masquerading as Love) about her relationship with her father, Amos Oz, one of Israel's most renowned authors. In the book, Oz alleges that her father abused her; she writes that he: "beat me, cursed me, and humiliated me; his violence was creative ... it was not an occasional loss of temper, not a slap here and there but a routine of sadistic abuse. My crime was being me and therefore punishment had no end."[1] The book caused a storm that spanned beyond the vast readership of the late Amos Oz, whose passing in 2018 was followed by national mourning. Dozens of op-eds, reviews, and social media responses were published in the daily press and on the web, including pieces by other members of the Oz family who denied Galia's allegations against her father, albeit admitting to a couple of isolated cases of violence. The heated debates about the book generally revolved around one of two themes: The first is the discussion of the validity and believability of the allegations, which I will not address here as my interest lies strictly with the book itself as a cultural event; and, second, the implications of the daughter's accusations for Amos Oz's legacy, not only as a prominent author but also as a public intellectual and a moral leader of the Zionist left; in other words, the question of whether this most canonic author should now be "cancelled."

One notable response to the memoir was that of literary scholar and editor Yigaal Schwartz, who, in a podcast interview, offered an interpretation of the symbolic significance of Galia's move.[2] Schwartz reads the publication of the book as activating dynamics of Oedipal rivalry in the Oz family, arguing that through this book, the daughter has sophisticatedly appropriated her father's cultural inheritance:

> I think what we have here is rivalry between the three children over the name of the father … what she does here, and this is what so brilliant about this … She took from Amos Oz his greatest asset, the fact that he is the ultimate victim (*korban*) … for example on page 45 she writes, "in our family, there was only one victim, as my mother insisted on explaining to me, and he [Oz the father] is the one with the copyrights over the suffering in the family." It's amazing. She takes the copyrights away from him … and in this way she surpasses the two other siblings.[3]

According to Schwartz, Galia has claimed her father's cultural position as "the author in the family" by constituting herself as his victim in the same way that Amos constituted his own authorial position by narrating his victimhood following the suicide of his mother in his iconic autobiography *Tale of Love and Darkness*.[4] The ramifications of this claim cannot be understood without probing the Hebrew word used by Schwartz to denote victimhood, namely the word *korban*, which, as Yael Feldman has noted, has a double meaning in Hebrew: victim and sacrifice.[5] While as used by Schwartz, the word seemingly denotes only victimhood, in the context of his argument, the word is loaded with the symbolic baggage of the Zionist ethos of sacrifice primarily associated with the sacrifice of the soldier in battle.

Taking Schwartz's hypothesis as a point of departure, there are some distinctions to be made between the father and the daughter in terms of their relationship with the dual meaning of the *korban*. The position of Oz the father as the "ultimate *korban*" cannot be separated from his position in the politics of Israel/Palestine, whose origins may be traced to his role as one of the editors of *Siah Lohamim* (translated: *The Seventh Day*). Created against the grain of the Israeli euphoria after the triumph in the 1967 War, *Siah Lohamim* was a collection of soldier testimonies that undermined the figure of the fearless and fierce hero by featuring soldiers expressing feelings of fear, grief, and guilt, over their experiences in the war.[6] The culture surrounding the book is often associated with the Israeli trope of "shooting and weeping" (*yorim u-bokhim*), which refers to the image of the "sensitive" Israeli soldier who grapples with the moral consequences of his violence. As Alon Gan mentions, the collection was even used by the Ministry of Foreign Affairs for propaganda purposes as a way of countering the growing critique of the Israeli occupation.[7] In this way, *Siah Lohamim* constitutes a revision of the *korban* ethos. In the dialectic between sacrifice and victimhood embedded in this ethos, the narrative of sacrifice gives meaning to the injury of victimhood by incorporating it into the national narrative. If in earlier representations, such as the quintessential work of the 1948 generation, the novel *He Walked through the Fields* by Moshe Shamir, violence, loss, and death are marked sacrifice for the Land, *Siah Lohamim* includes the soldier's mental pain, trauma, and guilt over the violence he has done to others in the *korban* ethos. These contents are construed as an internal wound which ultimately affirms the beautiful and ethical image of the Israeli soldier; the figure of the "shooting and weeping" soldier therefore forms a new version of the beautiful *korban* – one that innately blurs the lines between victims and perpetrators of violence.

Thus, Amos Oz connects to the figure of the *korban* not merely because of his early orphanhood, but also by his embodiment of a new model of Israeli masculinity. This masculinity is not the hyper-masculine hero whose antithesis is diasporic femininity, but a sensitive solider who has internalized the diasporic wounded mother. In this sense, the 2002 autobiographical novel *Tale of Love and Darkness* is continuous of *Siah Lohamim*. In the novel, Oz indeed comes to terms with the mother figure, a sensitive and creative woman who carried with her the memories of her youth in the Ukrainian city of Rovno, a city whose Jewish population of 23,000 was murdered by the Nazis within a span of a few days. Like the mother, who shares invented stories with her son as a way of coping with the wound of her internal exile in the Zionist space, Amos Oz grows up to be an author that often grapples with the wound of internal Otherness at the heart of the hegemonic Ashkenazi identity. As "the ultimate *korban*," he draws both on the tragedy of the mother and on the tragedy of the beautiful soldier, and therefore broadly represents two paradigmatic sites of the Israeli *korban*: war and the Holocaust.

In this context, the argument about Galia Oz's Oedipal appropriation of her father's position falls short because of its lack of differentiation between the stories of the father and the daughter in terms of their relation to the collective narrative. The daughter's story, in contrast to the father's, is a story of victimhood that does not acquire its meaning from the national story. In fact, Galia makes a great effort to detach her story from the larger Israeli story, and stresses that her father's violence was exceptional and separated from the context of the communal raising of children in the kibbutz or the traumatic wars of 1967 and 1973 that took place during the period of her early childhood.[8] At one point, she counters her mother's assertion that "your father had a difficult childhood. You had a normal kibbutz childhood" – that, "I am pretty sure he would have behaved in the same way if we were living somewhere else."[9] Indeed, decontextualization of the father's violence seems to be one of the core premises of the book.

Tamar Merin has coined the term "intersexual dialogue," which refers to a form of intertextuality in which women authors negotiate gendered and sexualized constructs through dialogue, appropriation, and revision vis-à-vis their literary fathers.[10] Arguably, in the present context, the daughter and the father are conducting such a dialogue over the meaning of the *korban*. The father's *korban* is integrated into the collective history of his hegemonic identity, which, while carrying the memories and trauma of East-European Jewry, is cultivated in the context of the Zionist intellectual and ideological elites (in the circles of the Jerusalemite *intelligentsia* and then in the kibbutz). The daughter's sense of victimhood, conversely, is framed as a de-territorialized gendered wound. From this perspective, the father-daughter dialogue ultimately constitutes a negotiation of the construction of the hegemonic Israeli position around the internal wound of the *korban*.

Regardless of the limitations of Schwartz's interpretation of the father-daughter rivalry, it aptly draws our attention to the position of the *korban* as a privileged Israeli position. Adi Ophir's interrogation of the position of the victim in the context of Israel/Palestine helps to contemplate the ramifications of this position beyond the Oz family drama. According to Ophir, the construction of Jewish identity around "a repetitive story of victimization," whose apogee is the Holocaust, creates an identification between the loss of land (exile) and the Holocaust that, in turn, frames the work of colonization as the never-ending work of compensation for an irretrievable loss.[11] After 1967, Ophir explains, "the object of loss was displaced from the destruction of European Jewry to the destruction of the Temple and the dispossession of the Land."[12] Every loss since then is understood as an extension of this catastrophic loss. "The point," according to Ophir, "is not to ask how Israeli Jews have become victims and heirs of victims ... the point is to understand how the victim position functions in Israeli culture; in the state's ideology; the apparatuses in which it is embodied; and in the construction of the constituting narrative of the Jewish state."[13] I believe that when Ophir speaks of the victim, he, Like Schwartz, has in mind the word *korban* with its double meaning of victim and sacrifice. And, like Schwartz's argument, the kind of questions that he calls for here is very much related to my interrogation of femininity as a cultural category of the Zionist imagination. In this sense, the Oz family's scandal connects to the genealogy of femininity offered throughout this study, which, to a large extent, I argue, revolves around access to the position of the *korban*. This is evident in the way Dvora Ben-Yehuda transforms into the quintessential feminine mother-martyr, in the way authors such as Nehama Pohatchevsky construct the feminine nationalist position vis-à-vis the Palestinians, in the way the feminine "national caregiver" constitutes herself through the trope of selfless sacrifice, and, finally, in the dissemination of tropes of feminine diminishment as metonyms of the nation.

Ophir's analysis underscores that the linear narrative–from weakness to strength, from dependency to independence, and from victimhood to heroism–cannot be sustained without the circular story of repeated and unending victimhood as a moral undercurrent. In this sense, the Oz father-daughter affair brings into relief the dialectic between the masculine and feminine aspects of the narrative. Ultimately, as Schwartz implies, the father-daughter dialogue identifies the Israeli hegemonic authorial position with the position of the *korban*, a position which is bequeathed from mother to son and from father to daughter. The problem with this negotiation is that while it could potentially open the Israeli discursive field toward recognition of the victimhood of others, it mostly ends up bolstering hermetic egocentrism where the wound at the heart of the hegemony is construed as the definitive site of victimhood, overshadowing all other positions of victimhood.

The ways in which the position of the *korban* was already written into the Oz family annals through the figure of the father, I argue, load the discussions of the daughter's book with the broader significance of this position in the politics of Israel/Palestine (regardless of her intentions). Yet, as often happens in Israeli discourse, these contents remain "present-absentees" haunting the rhetoric of the book itself and the discourse surrounding it without ever being recognized.[14] Thus, following the Oz affair, which was framed by the #MeToo movement, I found myself wondering whether this new attention to victimhood in the Israeli public sphere – manifesting in calls to listen to the silenced experience of the victim, to acknowledge the long-term effects of trauma and to recognize the way power-relations produce the trauma of the Other – would somehow impress upon the Israeli collective consciousness to rethink its attitudes toward of the victimization of the other Others of Zionism.[15]

In this context, we may note that one of the main aspects of Galia Oz's abuse, as she recounts, was her expulsion from the family home as a child who was brought up in the communal children-home in the kibbutz. An important moment in the book depicts her father violently throwing her out of the home at age of 8 while calling her "filth."[16] Although Galia insists that her childhood was not "a normal kibbutz childhood," the continuity she charts between her abandonment in the children-home prescribed by the *kibbutz* system and this instance of expulsion forms an opening through which her narrative can be situated in broader historical and social contexts. As someone who spent her early infanthood in the *kibbutz* baby-home, the emotional trauma of abandonment resonates with me. I would suggest, however, that a contemporary feminist reading of this phenomenon should situate it in relation to the intersectional history of home and homelessness in Israel/Palestine.[17] In this context, Galia's expulsion from the family home invokes the various expulsions and exclusions embedded in Zionist history. We may recall that the infant-centres in the transit camps, a site of trauma for many Mizrahi families, were modelled after the kibbutz baby homes. (In fact, the same term *beit tinokot* is used in Hebrew for both institutions). While I do not wish to equate the traumas associated with the communal raising of children in the *kibbutzim* and the traumas of the families whose children went missing, both traumas are grounded in the nationalist perception of children as a collective resource of the nation.[18] An intersectional reading of Oz's memoir may highlight the way its politics are imbricated into the larger racialized and nationalized dynamics of power in Israel/Palestine. Yet, what became most evident to me following the Oz affair, is that inherent to the collective Israeli processing of gendered trauma is the preclusion of such reading. In this way, I understand Galia's insistence on decontextualizing her experience, and of separating it from any social or political context. This, I suggest, is not a contingent or idiosyncratic feature of her book, but instead a function of the national ethno-gendered order in which the privileged position of the *korban* is reserved for the colourless Ashkenazi subject.

I recall in this context another incident from my trip to Israel with my American partner during the 2014 War on Gaza, which I mentioned in chapter 2. As we were having lunch in a famous Tel Aviv bar, my partner, always a very friendly and empathetic person, entered into a conversation with a woman sitting at the table next to us. This woman told us that she is a doctor on maternity leave with her first baby and that her husband was drafted into Gaza as a military doctor. She went on to share the experience of the rocket attack from the night before and described the feelings of worry and fear while running to a secure room with her newborn baby. Afterward, my partner, with both empathy and bewilderment, asked me, "but how is it that she, a doctor and a mother, does not stop to imagine how the mothers in Gaza feel?" I was reminded of my own experience of a missile attacks during my early childhood in the *kibbutz* near the northern border. While I remember very little about it, I experienced nightmares about missile attacks well into my adulthood. From this perspective, it is unimaginable what kind of mental scars the intensive and frequent bombing leave on children in Gaza, and what kinds of consequences their trauma will continue to have for everyone who lives in the space of Israel/Palestine. My final point in this discussion in relation to Zionism and feminism is that, in the end, if all we can learn by looking at the world through a feminist lens is to identify our own Otherness and gendered vulnerability, ultimately, our feminist position remains limited. Looking at the Oz affair in this context helps me articulate that the experience of victimhood may either open oneself to grasping the victimhood of Others, or it can as serve as a paradigmatic shield that allows oneself to see only her own wound. In these terms, my aim in this book is to try to open the gendered wounds of Zionism in a way that sheds light on, rather than obscures, the wounds we inflict on Others while postulating our own *korban*.

NOTES

Introduction

1 Founded in 1941, the *Palmah* was a Zionist paramilitary group that later formed the basis for the IDF.

2 In Zionist historiography, the word "pioneers" – *halutzim* in Hebrew – typically refers to the young idealist groups that arrived in Palestine in the early twentieth century as part of the Zionist Labor Movement and established agricultural cooperatives, named *kvutzot* and later *kibbutzim*, which, for several decades, were considered the movement's ideological centre.

3 According to the records, the villagers fled in May 1948 as a result of the "whisper campaign" conducted by the IDF, whose aim was to scare the residents away before taking over the Upper Galilee in "Operation Jephthah." See "Zochrot," https://zochrot.org/. Moreover, like other kibbutzim, my grandparents' kibbutz is also part of a system of land division in Israel that allots the Jewish Ashkenazi kibbutzim – whose population now constitutes a small minority in Israel – rights to vast areas of agricultural lands. This division thus maintains the enduring economic inequality between the Ashkenazim (Jews of European descent) and the Mizrahim (Jews of Middle Eastern and North African descent). See Yossi Dahan, "Le-mi shayekhet aa-adama ha-zot: 'al zkhuyot u-tfisot tsedek halukati," *Mishpat u-memshal* 8 (2004): 223–55.

4 Hagar Kotef, *The Colonizing Self: Or, Home and Homelessness in Israel/Palestine* (London: Duke University Press, 2020), 1.

5 See, for example: Margalit Shilo, *Etgar ha-migdar: nashim ba-'aliyot ha-rishonot* (Tel Aviv: Hakibbutz Hameuchad, 2007); Deborah Bernstein, *Isha be-Eretz Yisrael: ha-sheifa le-shivyon bi-tkufat ha-yishuv* (Tel Aviv: Hakibbutz Hameuchad, 1987); Tamar Hess, *Hek ha-em shel zikhronot: nashim, otobiyografyah ve-ha-Aliyah ha-sheniyah* (Or Yehuda: Dvir, 2014). Yaffa Berlovitz, "Literature by Women of the First *Aliyah*: The Aspiration for Women's Renaissance in Eretz-Israel," in *Pioneers and Homemakers: Jewish Women in Pre-State Israel* (Albany: State University of New York Press, 1992), 49–73.

6 Hess, *Hek Ha-em shel zikhronot*, 30.

7 Daniel Boyarin, *Unheroic Conduct: The Rise of Heterosexuality and the Invention of the Jewish Man* (Berkeley: University of California Press, 1997); Michael Gluzman, *Ha-guf ha-tsiyoni: leumiyut, migdar u-miniyut ba-sifrut ha-'Ivrit ha-hadashah* (Tel Aviv: Hakibbutz Hameuchad, 2007); Tamar Mayer, "From Zero to Hero: Masculinity in Jewish Nationalism," in *Gender Ironies of Nationalism: Sexing the Nation* (London: Routledge, 1999), 283–307; Mikhal

Dekel, *The Universal Jew: Masculinity, Modernity, and the Zionist Moment* (Evanston: Northwestern University Press, 2011); Philip Hollander, *From Schlemiel to Sabra Zionist Masculinity and Palestinian Hebrew Literature* (Bloomington: Indiana University Press, 2019).

8 Jay Y Gonen, *A Psychohistory of Zionism* (New York: New American Library, 1975).

9 Lesley Hazleton, *Israeli Women: The Reality Behind the Myths* (New York: Simon & Schuster, 1977).

10 Ibid., 93.

11 Boyarin, *Unheroic Conduct*, 271–313.

12 Naomi Seidman, *A Marriage Made in Heaven: The Sexual Politics of Hebrew and Yiddish* (Berkeley: University of California Press, 1997), 114–15.

13 David Biale, *Eros & the Jews from Biblical Israel to Contemporary America* (New York: Basic Books, 1992), 1–10.

14 Each of these categories, of course, includes its own diversity and complexity that will be only partially addressed within the chapters of this book. Thus, I refer here to the indigenous Arab population of Palestine as Palestinians, although it includes the Bedouin communities, for example, who are often regarded as a separate ethnicity. The *Mizrahim* is a term adopted in Israel to refer to diverse Jewish communities that immigrated to Palestine from the Middle East, North Africa, and parts of the Balkans. Another term used in the scholarship is the term Arab Jews that carries the critical implication of pushing against the binary division between Arab and Jews prescribed by Zionism. While I value this concept, I use the term *Mizrahim* here, since it is the term most widely used by Israelis belonging to this ethnic group.

15 An early version of the discussion in this section appears in my article: "Gvulot ha-heder ve-heik ha-em: 'al bikoret sifrut ha-nashim ha-'Ivrit ve-ha-Yisraelit," *Mikan: ktav 'et le-heker ha-sifrut ve-ha-tarbut ha-Yehudit ve-ha-Yisraelit* 20 (February 2020): 287–311.

16 Tamar Hess, *Hek ha-em*, 24.

17 Ibid., 9.

18 Ibid., 30.

19 Dan Miron, *Imahot meyasdot, ahayot horgot: 'al reshit shirat ha-nashim ha-'Ivrit* (Tel Aviv: Hakibbutz Hameuchad, 1991).

20 Pnina Shirav, *Ktiva lo tama:'emdat siah ve-yitzugey nashiyut bi-ytzirotehen shel Yhudith Hendel,'Amalya Kahana-Karmon ve-Ruth Almog* (Tel Aviv: Hakibbutz Hameuchad, 1998), 37.

21 Lily Rattok, *Ha-kol ha-aher: siporet nashim 'Ivrit* (Tel Aviv: Hakibbutz Hameuchad, 1994), 261–350.

22 Tamar Merin, *Spoiling the Stories: The Rise of Israeli Women's Fiction* (Evanston: Northwestern University Press, 2016).

23 See Yaffa Berlovitz's anthology of Hebrew women's prose writing from the pre-state period, where she sheds light on the wealth of women's literary writing that was previously ignored. In the extensive afterward of the collection, Berlovitz compellingly challenges the claim that Hebrew women were "silent" during the pre-state period. See Yaffah Berlovitz, "Aharit davar: siporet mi-yabeshet avuda'," *Sh-ani adama ve-adam: sipurey nashim 'ad kom ha-medina* (Tel Aviv: Hakibbutz Hameuchad, 2003), 319–60.

24 Rattok, *Ha-kol ha-aher*, 282–4.

25 Tamar Merin, *Spoiling the Stories*, 20–1.

26 Rattok, *Ha-kol ha-aher*, 303–16.

27 Hess, *Hek ha-em*, 209–48.

28 Shirav, *Ktiva lo tama*, 267.

29 In this context, Israeli feminist scholarship was heavily influenced, on the one hand, by post-structural French feminist theory, in which motherhood emerges as a unique mode of subjectivity identified with feminine multiplicity, duality, and heterogeneity; see, for example, Luce Irigaray, *This Sex Which Is Not One*, trans. Catherine Porter and Carolyne Burke (Ithaca: Cornell University Press, 1985); Hélène Cixous, "The Laugh of the Medusa," *Signs* 1, no. 4 (1976): 875–93; Julia Kristeva, "Stabat Mater," trans. Arthur Goldhammer, *Poetics Today* 6, no. 1/2 (1985): 133–52. Israeli feminist scholarship was further influenced, on the other hand, by American radical feminist projects aimed at reconstructing matrilineal literary traditions; see, for example, Sandra Gilbert and Susan Gubar, *The Madwoman in the Attic: The Woman Writer and the Nineteenth-Century Literary Imagination* (New Haven: Yale University Press, 1979) and Elaine Showalter, *Literature of Their Own* (Princeton: Princeton University Press, 1977).

30 Seidman, *A Marriage Made in Heaven*, 114–15.

31 Hess, *Hek ha-em*, 209–48.

32 Or, what Raz Yosef has termed "the Zionist body master narrative"; see Raz Yosef, *Beyond Flesh: Queer Masculinities and Nationalism in Israeli Cinema* (New Brunswick: Rutgers University Press, 2004), 16–47.

33 On the cultural and political significance of this ethos, see Amnon Raz-Krakotzkin, "Galut be-tokh ribonut: bikoret shlilat ha-galut ba-tarbut ha-Yisraelit (Part 1)," *Theory and Criticism* 4 (1993): 23–55. "Galut be-tokh ribonut: bikoret shlilat ha-galut ba-tarbut ha-Yisraelit (Part 2)," *Theory and Criticism* 5 (1993): 113–32.

34 Kimberlé Crenshaw, "Mapping the Margins: Intersectionality, Identity Politics, and Violence against Women of Color," *Stanford Law Review* 43, no. 6 (July 1991): 1241–99. Patricia Hill Collins, *Black Feminist Thought: Knowledge, Consciousness and the Politics of Empowerment* (New York: Routledge, 1990).

35 See also, for example, Audre Lorde, *Sister Outsider* (Berkeley: Crossing Press, 2007); Anne Mcclintock, *Imperial Leather Race, Gender, and Sexuality in the*

Colonial Contest (New York: Routledge, 1995); Gloria E. Anzaldúa, *Borderlands/La Frontera: The New Mestiza* (San Francisco: Aunt Lute Books, 1987).

36 See, for example, the controversy around the inclusion of an Israeli LGBTQ rights group called "A Wider Bridge" at a San Francisco LGBTQ conference in January 2016, and the exclusion of a Star of David sign from the Chicago Dyke March in June 2017. See Debra Nussbaum Cohen, "Israel-Focused Jewish Group Booted From Major LGBTQ Event in the U.S," *Haaretz* (New York, NY), 18 January 2016, https://www.haaretz.com/jewish/.premium-jewish-group-booted-from-u-s-lgbtq-event-1.5392451. "Chicago Gay Pride Parade Expels Star of David Flags," BBC, 26 June 2017, https://www.bbc.com/news/world-us-canada-40407057.

37 "Women's Strike US," http://www.womenstrikeus.org (site no longer active).

38 Emily Shire, "Does Feminism Have Room for Zionists?" *New York Times*, 7 March 2017, https://www.nytimes.com/2017/03/07/opinion/does-feminism-have-room-for-zionists.html?_r=0.

39 Collier Meyerson, "Can You Be a Zionist Feminist? Linda Sarsour Says No," *The Nation*, 13 March 2017, https://www.thenation.com/article/archive/can-you-be-a-zionist-feminist-linda-sarsour-says-no/.

40 Excluding Dvora Baron, who is known for completely withdrawing from the public sphere as of the early 1920s, almost all of the writers I discuss in the following chapters were involved in Zionist women's organizations such as the "Women's Workers Movement," "The Hebrew Women's Union for Equal Rights," "Hadassah," the "Working Mothers Organization," and others. On Zionist women's organizations see, for example, Bat Sheva Margalit-Stern, *Geula bi-khvalim: tnuat ha-po'alot Ha-Eretz Yisraelit 1920–1939* (Jerusalem: Yad Yitzhak Ben-Tzvi, 2006); Margalit Shilo, *Girls of Liberty: The Struggle for Suffrage in Mandatory Palestine*, trans. Haim Watzman (Waltham: Brandeis University Press, 2016); Dafna Hirsch, "Gender and Ethnicity in the Zionist Nation-Building Project: The Case of Hannah Helena Thon," *Ethnic and Racial Studies* 34, no. 2 (2011): 275–92, https://doi.org/10.1080/01419870.2010.506923.

41 See, for example: Chandra Talpade Mohanty, "Under Western Eyes: Feminist Scholarship and Colonial Discourses," *Boundary* 2 12/13, no. 3 (1984): 333–58; Mcclintock, *Imperial Leather*; Crenshaw, "Mapping the Margins"; Vron Ware, *Beyond the Pale: White Women, Racism, and History* (London: Verso, 1991); Ann Laura Stoler, *Carnal Knowledge and Imperial Power: Race and the Intimate in Colonial Rule* (Berkeley: University of California Press, 2002).

42 Gayatri Chakravorti Spivak, "Three Women's Texts and the a Critique of Imperialism," *Critical Inquiry* 12, no. 1 (1985): 243–61.

43 Albeit, in the case of East European Jewish women, marginality also offered a "window of opportunities" for modernization and advancement, as argued convincingly by Iris Parush and referenced in chapter 1. See Iris Parush,

Reading Jewish Women: Marginality and Modernization in Nineteenth-Century Eastern European (Waltham: Brandeis University Press, 2004).

44 Aziza Khazzoom, "The Great Chain of Orientalism: Jewish Identity, Stigma Management, and Ethnic Exclusion in Israel," *American Sociological Review* 68, no. 4 (2003): 481–510. See also: Gil Eyal, *The Disenchantment of the Orient: Expertise in Arab Affairs and the Israeli State* (Stanford: Stanford University Press, 2006); Amnon Raz-Krakotzkin, "The Zionist Return to the West and the Mizrahi Jewish Perspective," *Orientalism and the Jews*, ed. Ivan Davidson Kalmar and Derek J Penslar (Hanover and London: University Press of New England, 2005), 162–81; Ella Shohat, *Israeli Cinema: East/West and the Politics of Representation* (London: I.B. Tauris, 2010).

45 Yael Avrahami, "Yael Avrahami mesaperet lanu 'al sugiyat ha-mikhnasayim ha-ktzarim" *Politically Koreet* (blog), 4 July 2020, https://m.facebook.com/politicallycorret/posts/3347694698624889?locale2=ar_AR.

46 *Jaffa, The Orange's Clockwork*, directed by Eyal Sivan (Israel: Momento Films, 2009), DVD. 17:41.

47 See, for example, Richard Dyer's discussion of the inherent connection between whiteness and femininity in colonial contexts. Richard Dyer, *White: Essays on Race and Culture* (New York: Routledge, 2017), 58–60.

48 Hamutal Tsamir, *Be-shem ha-nof: leumiyut, migdar ve-sobjectiviyut ba-shira ha-Yisraelit bi-shnot ha-hamishim ve-ha-shishim* (Jerusalem: Ketter Books, 2006), 276.

49 Ibid., 278.

50 Carol Gilligan, *In A Different Voice* (Cambridge: Harvard University Press, 1982); Nancy Chodorow, *The Reproduction of Mothering: Psychoanalysis and the Sociology of Gender* (Berkeley: University of California Press, 1978).

51 Irigaray, *This Sex Which Is Not One*; Julia Kristeva, *La Révolution Du Langage Poétique* (Paris: Édition du Seuil, 1974); Cixous, "The Laugh of the Medusa."

52 See, for example, Gayatri Chakravorti Spivak, "French Feminism in an International Frame," *Yale French Studies*, no. 62 (1981): 154–84; Elizabeth Spelman, *Inessential Women: Problems of Exclusion in Feminist Thought* (Boston: Beacon Press, 1988).

53 Dyer, *White*, 58–60.

54 Stoler, *Carnal Knowledge*, 41–78.

55 Ware, *Beyond the Pale*, 5.

56 Seidman, *A Marriage Made in Heaven*, 102–15.

57 Mary Louise Pratt, *Imperial Eyes: Travel Writing and Transculturation* (New York: Routledge, 1992), 7.

58 bell hooks, "The Oppositional Gaze: Black Female Spectators," in *Black Looks: Race and Representation* (Boston: South End Press, 1992), 115–31.

Chapter One

1 Yisrael Dov Frumkin, "Et ledaber," *Havatzelet* (6 April 1894), 210.

2 Yisrael Dov Frumkin (1850–1914) was the editor of *Havatzelet*, one of the first Hebrew journals that was published in Palestine. Although the publication represented the *Hassidic* community, it was also a publication venue for some *makilic* writers, such as Eliezer Ben-Yehuda. Ben-Yehuda's was first employed in Palestine as a reporter for *Havatzelet*, but he and Frumkin both parted ways following a quarrel. Thereafter, Ben-Yehuda established his own publication *Ha-tzvi*.

3 I will return to the circumstances of the arrest toward the end of this chapter.

4 Yisrael Dov Frumkin, "Et ledaber," 210. My emphasis.

5 Nissim Bekhar (1848–1931) was a Sephardi intellectual, educator, and headmaster of the Alliance Israélite Universelle's school for boys in Jerusalem.

6 Itamar Ben-Avi, *Ha-hatzuf ha-Yisraeli: prakim me-hayav shel ha-yeled ha-'Ivri ha-rishon* (Tel Aviv: Yediot Sfarim, 2016), 116.

7 Benedict Anderson, *Imagined Communities* (New York: Verso, 2006), 141–54.

8 Nira Yuval-Davis, *Gender and Nation* (London: Sage Publications, 1997), 26–38.

9 Naomi Seidman, *A Marriage Made in Heaven: The Sexual Politics of Hebrew and Yiddish* (Berkeley: University of California Press, 1997), 102–4.

10 Importantly, scholars have critiqued the notion of Ben-Yehuda as the main actor in the revival of Hebrew, pointing toward other agents, such as the Hebrew literary authors operating in Europe at the time, and the "pioneers" of the second Zionist immigration wave who popularized the use of spoken Hebrew in their communes. See Benjamin Harshav, *Language in the Time of Revolution* (Berkeley: University of California Press, 1993).

11 Seidman, *A Marriage Made in Heaven*, 102–15.

12 Ibid.

13 Yosef Lang, *Daber 'Ivrit: hayey Eliezer Ben-Yehuda* (Tel Aviv: Yad Yitzhak Ben-Tzvi, 2008), 267–72.

14 On Hemda's contribution to the dictionary, see Reut Green, "Hemda Ben-Yehuda u-"milhamta 'im ha-satan": mif'aala ha-lo yadu'a – hafakat ha-milon," *Ha-'Ivrit* 58, nos 1–2 (2009): 57–74.

15 See, for example Nurith Govrin, "Limtzo et bney rekhav – Hemda Ben-Yehuda," in *Dvash mi-sel'a: mehkarim be-sifrut Eretz Yisrael* (Tel Aviv: Misrad ha-bitahon, 1989), 42–55; Yaffa Berlovitz, "Literature by Women of the First Aliyah: The Aspiration for Women's Renaissance in Eretz-Israel," in *Pioneers and Homemakers: Jewish Women in Pre-State Israel*, ed. Deborah Bernstein (Albany: State University of New York Press, 1992), 49–73.

16 See Eve Kosovsky Sedgwick, *Between Men: English Literature and Male Homosocial Desire* (New York: Columbia University Press, 1992); Danny Kaplan, *The Men We Loved: Male Friendship and Nationalism in Israeli Culture* (New York: Berghahn Press, 2006).

17 See, for example: María Lugones and Pat Alake Rosezelle, "Sisterhood and Friendship as Feminist Models," in *Feminism and Community*, ed. Penny A. Weiss and Marilyn Friedman (Philadelphia: Temple University Press, 1995), 138–41.

18 Gayle Rubin, "The Traffic in Women: Notes on the 'Political Economy' of Sex," *The Second Wave: A Reader in Feminist Theory*, ed. Linda Nicholson (New York: Routledge, 1997), 27–62.

19 The manuscript of *Kokho shel goral* (*The Power of Fate*) is kept in the Ben-Yehuda family files in the Central Zionist Archive in the Jerusalem. Although the text is not dated, it was likely composed during the 1930s and 1940s like Hemda's other biographical writings. Hemda Ben-Yehuda, *Kokho shel goral*, 3–4. Central Zionist Archive, A43/76.

20 Parush, *Reading Jewish Women: Marginality and Modernization in Nineteenth-Century Eastern European*, (Waltham: Brandeis University Press, 2004); Paula Hyman, *Gender and Assimilation in Modern Jewish History: The Roles and Representation of Women* (Seattle: University of Washington Press, 1995); Naomi Seidman, *The Marriage Plot or How Jews Fell in Love with Love and with Literature* (Stanford: Stanford University Press, 2016); Tova Cohen, "Portrait of the Maskilah as a Young Woman," *Nashim: A Journal of Jewish Women's Studies and Gender Issues* 15 (Spring 2008): 9–29.

21 Nurit Orchan, "Mavo: ruah hadasha," in *'Omdot banisayon: reshit siporte ha-nashim ha-modernit be-Yiddish*, ed. Nurit Orchan (Jerusalem: Magnes Press, 2021), 15–19.

22 Ben-Yehuda, *Kokho shel goral*, 3–4.

23 Ibid., 5.

24 Paula Hyman, *Gender and Assimilation*, 48–9.

25 *Maskil* (m) or *maskilah* (f) is a term that was used to refer to a person involved with the *Haskalah* movement.

26 Tova Cohen, "Portrait of the Maskilah."

27 Ibid., 13–16.

28 Ben-Yehuda, *Kokho Shel Goral*, 7.

29 Ibid.

30 Ibid., 22.

31 Seidman, *A Marriage Made in Heaven*, 101–31.

32 Parush, *Reading Jewish Women*, 38–56.

33 The "New Jewish Woman" is a term used to refer to Jewish women of the turn of the twentieth century who participated in the phenomenon associated with the "New Woman" in Western Europe and in the US, namely, the investment in education for women, women's participation in the public sphere, and women's entry to the labour world. Iris Parush and Paula Hyman, among others, have offered illuminating discussions of East European Jewish women participation in modernity. See Parush, *Reading Jewish Women*; Hyman,

Gender and Assimilation. On representations of the New Jewish Woman in Hebrew literature, see Shachar Pinsker, *Literary Passports: The Making of Hebrew Modernism in Europe* (Stanford: Stanford University Press, 2010), 237–74.

34 Shira Stav, *Aba ani koveshet: avot u-vanot ba-shira ha-'Ivrit ha-hadasha* (Or Yehuda: Kineret Zmora-Bitan Dvir, 2014), 18–84.

35 Ibid., 44.

36 Shmuel Versas, *Sifrut ha-Haskalah be-'idan ha-modernizatzya* (Jerusalem: Magnes, 2000), 75–81.

37 Student of the Torah.

38 Yosef Lang, *Daber 'Ivrit*, 11.

39 Ben-Yehuda, *Kokho shel goral*, 11.

40 Ibid., 19.

41 Ibid., 22.

42 Eve Kosovsky Sedgwick, *Between Men*, 27.

43 Hemda Ben-Yehuda, *Eliezer Ben-Yehuda*, מב. Note: this appears in the appendix to the biography recounting Eliezer's life prior to immigrating to Palestine. Page numbers in this section appear in Hebrew gimatry, while pages in the body of the book, from which I quote at other points, appear in Arabic numerals.

44 Ben-Yehuda, *Kokho shel goral*, 21.

45 Eliezer Ben-Yehuda was born by the name Eliezer Isaac Perlman, but his mother changed his name in the official records to Eliezer Elianoff, the name of a childless neighbour, in an effort to avoid him being drafted to the Russian army (since by law an only child was not required to enlist). Later he changed his last name to the Hebrew name Ben-Yehuda.

46 Ibid.

47 Ibid.

48 Emily Bilsky and Emily D. Braun, *Jewish Women and Their Salons: The Power of Conversation* (New Haven: Yale University Press, 2005).

49 Eliezer Ben-Yehuda, *Ha-halom ve-shivro* (Tel Aviv: Mosad Bialik, 1978).

50 Ben-Yehuda, "Zikhronot," *Ha-'am* (12 July 1931), 3.

51 We should note here the transition from the setting of private tutorship offered to Dvora to the setting of the college for women that allowed Hemda to acquire academic education less than a couple of decades later. See also, Christine Johnson, *Women's Struggle for Higher Education in Russia, 1855-1900* (Kingston: McGill-Queen's University Press, 1987).

52 Ben-Yehuda, "Zikhronot," 3.

53 Ibid.

54 Ben-Yehuda, *Kokho shel goral*, 27.

55 Ben-Yehuda, *Eliezer Ben-Yehuda*, 83.

56 Edward Said, *Orientalism* (London: Penguin Books, 2003), 115.

57 Amnon Raz-Krakotzkin, "The Zionist Return to the West and the Mizrahi Jewish Perspective," in *Orientalism and the Jews*, ed. Ivan Davidson Kalmar and Derek J. Penslar (Hanover: University Press of New England, 2005), 168.

58 Hemda Ben-Yehuda, Central Zionist Archive, A43-73.

59 Reina Lewis, *Gendering Orientalism: Race, Femininity and Representation* (London: Routledge, 1995).

60 Jay Y. Gonen, *A Psychohistory of Zionism. A Psychohistory of Zionism* (New York: New American Library, 1975).

61 Ellen Fleischmann, *The Nation and Its "New" Women: The Palestinian Women's Movement, 1920–1948* (Berkeley: University of California Press, 2003), 28.

62 Ibid.

63 Seidman, *Marriage Made in Heaven*, 109.

64 Ben-Avi, *Ha-hatzuf ha-Yisraeli*, 21.

65 Indeed, it was often the case with the *yeshiva bokhers* turned *maskilim* that European vernaculars were mediated to them by women acquaintances despite the *maskilic* anxiety about women's foreign language knowledge as a gateway to assimilation. See Parush, *Reading Jewish Women*, 174.

66 Parush, Reading Jewish Women, 38–56. See also earlier in this chapter.

67 Ben-Avi, *Ha-hatzuf ha-Yisraeli*, 73.

68 Ben-Yehuda, *Ha-halom ve-shivro* (Tel Aviv: Mosad Bialik, 1978).

69 Ben-Yehuda, *Kokho Shel Goral*, 27.

70 Seidman, *A Marriage Made in Heaven*, 106.

71 Ben-Yehuda, *Eliezer Ben-Yehuda*, 104–5.

72 Ben-Avi, *Ha-hatzuf ha-Yisraeli*, 32–3.

73 See also Maya Barzilai and Shai Ginsburg, "Ha-dibur ha-'Ivri: kriaa mehudeshet," *Mikan: ktav 'et le-heker ha-sifrut ve-ha-tarbut ha-yehudit ve-ha-Yisraelit* 20 (February 2020): 198–227.

74 Parush, *Reading Jewish Women*, 225. Mendele Mocher Sforim was the penname of the Yiddish and Hebrew author S. J. Abramowitch (1836–1917), who was considered one of the prominent figures of early Jewish and Hebrew modernism.

75 Ibid., 230.

76 Ibid., 228.

77 David Biale, *Eros and the Jews: From Biblical Israel to Contemporary America* (Berkeley: University of California Press, 1997), 161.

78 Ibid., 149–75; Seidman, *The Marriage Plot*, 188–208.

79 Tova Cohen, *Ha-ahat ahuva ve-ha-hat nuaa: bein bidyon le-metziut be-teurey ha-isha be-sifrut ha-Haskalah* (Tel Aviv: Magnes, 2002), 90–4, 336–7.

80 Parush, *Reading Jewish Women*, 227–40.

81 Ibid., 236–7.

82 Ibid., 229.

83 Ibid., 239.

84 Cohen, *Ha-ahat ahuva*, 35–6, 83.

85 Seidman, *A Marriage Made in Heaven*, 111.

86 Ben-Yehuda, "Inyaney Ha-shʿaa," *Ha-Tzvi* (7 July 1893).

87 Ben-Yehuda, "Ishut," *Milon ha-ʿIvrit ha-yeshana ve-ha-adashah*, https://benyehuda.org/dict/24412.

88 *Sephardim* was a term used to refer to Jews of Middle Eastern or North African descent (especially in the pre-state period). The term derives from the Hebrew name for Spain – *Spharad*, as Jews from the MENA area were assumed to be descendants of the Jews expelled from Spain in 1492. This assumption was challenged later on and the term was largely replaced by the term *Mizrahim*.

89 Margalit Shilo, *Princess Or Prisoner?: Jewish Women in Jerusalem, 1840–1914* (Waltham: Brandeis University Press, 2005), 158–64.

90 Gil Eyal, *The Disenchantment of the Orient: Expertise in Arab Affairs and the Israeli State*. (Stanford: Stanford University Press, 2006), 13–21. According to Eyal, the Arabs and the Sephardim were perceived by early Zionists together as part of the "East," and only in the 1950s did the discourses of the Arabs and the Sephardim/Mizrahim differentiate from one another; the former discourse became security-oriented, and the latter developed as a "civilizing" and "acculturating" discourse about the new waves of immigration of Jews from the Middle East and North Africa.

91 Itamar Even-Zohar, "The Emergence of a Native Hebrew Culture in Palestine: 1882–1948," *Studies in Zionism* 2 (1981): 172; Jack Fellman, *The Revival of a Classical Tongue* (Berlin: Walter de Gruyter, 2011), 23. On the gendered and sexualized remifications of the debate on Hebrew pronounciation, see also Seidman, *A Marriage Made in Heaven*, 113.

92 Fellman, *The Revival of a Classical Tongue*, 30–1.

93 The term the "old yishuv" refers to the pre-Zionist Jewish communities in Palestine which were comprised of religious Ashkenazi and Sephardi communities, and concentrated in the old cities of Jerusalem, Safed, Tiberias, and others.

94 Fellman, *The Revival of a Classical Tongue*, 30–1.

95 On the "Jerusalem group," a circle of Sephardi intellectuals of the Old Yishuv, see also Yaffa Berwlovitz, *Le-hamtzi eretz, le-hamtzi ʿam: tashtiyot sifrut ve-tarbut ba-yetzira shel ha-ʿaliyah ha-rishona* (Tel Aviv: Ha-Kibbutz Ha-Meuhad, 1996), 121–8.

96 Ben-Yehuda, *Eliezer Ben Yehuda*, 5.

97 Significantly, for Jewish men in Palestine wearing the *tarbush* was also a mode of asserting their belonging to the Ottoman space.

98 Ibid., 27.

99 Ibid.

100 Ibid.

101 Seidman cites a testimony about the difficulty in Hebrew communication between the husband and the wife: "When Eliezer, for example, wanted Dvora
to pour him a cup of coffee with sugar, 'he was at a loss to communicate words
such as 'cup,' 'saucer,' 'pour,' and so on. He would say to his wife, in effect: 'take
such and such, and do like so, and bring me this and this, and I will drink'
(*K'khi kakh, ve'asi kakh, ve-havi'i li kakh, ve'eshteh*)." Seidman, *A Marriage
Made in Heaven*, 108.
102 Ben-Yehuda, *Kokho shel goral*, 74.
103 We should note, however, that unlike the path taken by the Zionist Ashkenazi-
dominant women's movement in the years to come, Dvora's intervention in
the Sephardi community was a result of collaboration with Sephardi agents of
modernity, Nissim and Fortuna Bekhar.
104 Dvora Ben-Yehuda, "Takanat benot yerushalayim," *Ha-tzvi* (21 December 1888).
105 This will be elaborated in chapter 4. In the Sephardic community in Jerusalem,
as Margalit Shilo explains, women and girls' jewellery were part of an elaborate system of cultural signification through clothing which was already a site
of ethnic tension surrounding women's bodies. See Shilo, *Princess or Prisoner*,
73–4.
106 Shilo, *Princess Or Prisoner*, 162.
107 Ibid., 165.
108 On the position of Western women in the context of Orientalism and colonialism, see, for example: Reina Lewis, *Gendering Orientalism: Race, Femininity
and Representation*, (London and New York, 1995); Lisa Lowe, *Critical Terrains:
French and British Orientalisms* (Ithaca: Cornell University Press, 1991); Rana
Kabbani, *Imperial Fictions: Europe's Myths of Orient* (London: Pandora,
1994); Billie Melman, *Women's Orients: English Women and the Middle East,
1718-1918: Sexuality, Religion, and Work* (London: Macmillan, 1992); Meyda
Yeğenoğlu, *Colonial Fantasies: Toward a Feminist Reading of Orientalism*
(Cambridge: Cambridge University Press, 1998).
109 Lang, *Daber 'Ivrit*, 200.
110 Ibid., 211.
111 Eliezer's letter to Jonas, 1891, CZA A433.
112 Ibid., my emphasis.
113 Dvora's letter to Jonas, 1891, CZA A433. My emphasis.
114 Eliezer's letter to Jonas, 1891, CZA A433.
115 Parush, *Reading Jewish Women*.
116 Eliezer's letter to Jonas, 1891, CZA A433.
117 Elaine Showalter, *Sexual Anarchy: Gender and Culture at the Fin De Siècle*
(London: Vicking, 1991), 40.
118 Ben-Yehuda, *Kokho shel goral*, 101.
119 Ben-Yehuda, *Eliezer Ben-Yehuda*, 99.

120 Hamutal Tsamir, "Ha-korban ha-halutzi, ha-Eretz ha-kdosha ve-hof'aata shel shirat nashim bi-shnot ha-'esrim," in *Reg'a shel huledet: mehkarim be-sifrut 'Ivrit u-ve-sifrut Yiddish likhvod Dan Miron*, ed. Hanan Hever (Jerusalem: Mosad Bialik, 2008), 645–73

121 Rene Girard, *The Scapegoat*, trans. Yvonne Freccero (Baltimore: Johns Hopkins University Press, 1989).

122 Lang, *Daber 'Ivrit*, 159–94. The original article has been lost.

123 Hillel Cohen, "Soneim sipur ahava: 'al mizrahim ve-'Aravim (ve-'Ashkenazim gam) mi-reshit ha-tziyonut ve-'ad meora'ot tashpa," (Tel Aviv: 'Ivrit hotsaa la-or, 2022), digital.

124 Lang, *Daber 'Ivrit*, 194.

125 In Eliezer's biography, the chapter recounting Dvora's illness and death is entitled "The Ban and Dvora's death," and in *Kokho shel goral*, the chapter entitled "On her deathbed" begins with the line "the ban and the controversy distressed Dvora very much." Ben-Yehuda, *Eliezer*, 35–43; Ben-Yehuda, *Kokho shel goral*, 57.

126 Adi Ophir, "Identity of the Victims and the Victims of Identity: A Critique of Zionist Ideology for a Post-Zionist Age," in *Mapping Jewish Identities*, ed. Laurence Jay Silberstein (New York: New York University Press, 2000), 174–200.

Chapter Two

1 Tova Yaffe, "Ba-Drakhim," *Dvar ha-po'eelet* 1 (1934): 3.

2 The Women Workers' Movement (aka the women workers' council) was established in 1911 as part of the Zionist Labor Movement. The movement sought to amplify women's voices in the Labor Movement and dealt with issues such as women's employment, education, and political representation. *Dvar ha-po'eelet*, the movement's monthly publication that was attached to the daily newspaper *Davar* published from 1934 to 1977, served as an outlet for diverse and multi- genre women's writing. See also Bat Sheva Margalit-Stern, *Geula bi-khvalim: tnu'at ha-po'aalot ha-Eretz Yisraelit 1920-1939* (Jerusalem: Yad Yitzhak Ben-Zvi, 2006), 156–71.

3 Virginia Woolf, *A Room of One's Own and Three Guineas* (Oxford: Oxford University Press, 2002), 158.

4 See, for example: Hagar Kotef, *The Colonizing Self or, Home and Homelessness in Israel/Palestine* (Durham: Duke University Press, 2020); Vron Ware, *Beyond the Pale: White Women, Racism, and History*, (London: Verso, 1991); Ann Laura Stoler, *Carnal Knowledge and Imperial Power: Race and the Intimate in Colonial Rule* (Berkeley: University of California Press, 2002); Annee Mcclintock, *Imperial Leather Race, Gender, and Sexuality in the Colonial Contest* (New York: Routledge, 1995).

5 Homi Bhabha, "Of Mimicry and Man: The Ambivalence of Colonial Discourse," *Discipleship: A Special Issue on Psychoanalysis* 28 (1984): 125–33.

6 Shirly Bahar and Ilana Szobel, "Viduy hariga: vidyey hayalim ve-hayalot bi-sratim tiudiyim autobiographim tsyoniyim," *Mikan: ktav 'et le-heker ha-sifrut ve-ha-tarbut ha-yehudit ve-ha-Yisraelit* 17 (2017): 265.

7 Mary Louise Pratt, *Imperial Eyes: Travel Writing and Transculturation* (New York: Routledge, 1992), 9.

8 Yaffe, "Ba-Drakhim," 3.

9 Noga Collins-Kreiner and Nurit Kliot, "Why Do People Hike? Hiking the Israel National Trail," *Journal of Economic and Human Geography* 108, no. 5 (2017): 669.

10 Yaffe, "Ba-drakhim," 2.

11 Chandra Talpade Mohanty, "Under Western Eyes: Feminist Scholarship and Colonial Discourses," *Boundary 2* 12/13, no. 3 (1984): 333–58.

12 Yaffe, "Ba-drakhim," 3.

13 Ibid.

14 Dvora Dayan (1890–1956) was a member of the second Zionist immigration wave (the Second *Aliyah*). She was a social activist, writer, and the mother of Moshe Dayan, the renowned general of the Six Day War.

15 Dvora Dayan, "Ba-drakhim," *Dvar ha-po'eelet* (1949): 372.

16 It is beyond the scope of this study to offer a thorough analysis of the relationship between Zionism and settler-colonialism. Yet, I postulate that the objective ramifications of the Zionist project for the Palestinians were comparable with the ramifications of other settler-colonial projects for indigenous communities, namely, displacement, elimination, and replacement by the settlers. I also postulate that there are significant aspects of the Zionist gendered imagination that dovetail with the colonial imagination especially in relation to gender and sexuality. For further discussion, see Sam Fleischacker, "Interrogating the Limits of the Settler-Colonialist Paradigm," in *Social Justice and Israel/Palestine: Foundational and Contemporary Debates*, ed. Aaron J. Hahn Tapper and Mira Sucharov, 43–50 (Toronto: University of Toronto Press, 2019); As'ad Ghanem and Tariq Khateeb, "Israel in One Century – from a Colonial Project to a Complex Reality," in *Social Justice and Israel/Palestine: Foundational and Contemporary Debates*, ed. Aaron J. Hahn Tapper and Mira Sucharov (Toronto: University of Toronto Press, 2019), 51–60.

17 Dayan, "Ba-drakhim," 360.

18 On the role of the grieving mother in Israeli culture, see Dana Olmert, *Kehoma 'amodna: Imahot le-lohamim ba-sifrut ha-Ivrit* (Tel Aviv: Hakibbutz hameuchad, 2018).

19 See, for example: Orly Lubin, *Isha koret isha* (Haifa: University of Haifa Press, 2006); Tamar Hess, *Hek-ha-em shel zikhronot: nashim, otobiyografyah ve-ha-Aliyah Ha-Sheniyah* (Beer Sheva: Heksherim, 2014); Berlovitz, "Literature by Women of the First Aliyah: The Aspiration for Women's Renaissance in Eretz-Israel," 1992; Yaffa Berlovitz, "Kol ha-melakholya ke-khol ha-mehaa: 'iyun bi-yet-

zirata shel Nehama Pohatchevsky me-ha-mesaprot ha-rishonot be-Eretz Yisrael,"
in *Eshnav le-hayehen shel nashim be-havarot Yehudiyot*, ed. Yael Atzmon
(Jerusalem: Zalman Shazar Center, 1995), 325–36; Tamar Merin, *Spoiling the
Stories The Rise of Israeli Women's Fiction* (Evanston: Northwestern University
Press, 2016); Wendy Zierler, *And Rachel Stole the Idols: The Emergence of Modern
Hebrew Women's Writing* (Detroit: Wayne State University Press, 2004).

20   For example, Tamar Hess, *Hek ha-em shel zikhronot : nashim, otobiyografyah
ve-ha-'Aliyah ha-sheniyah* (Or Yehuda: Dvir, 2014). Wandy Zierler, *And Rachel
Stole the Idols: The Emergence of Modern Hebrew Women's Writing*, (Detroit:
Wayne State University Press, 2004). Orly Lubin, "Tidbits from Hehama's
Kitchen: Alternative Nationalism in Dvora Baron's The Exiles," in *Hebrew,
Gender, and Modernity: Critical Responses to Devora Baron's Fiction*, ed. Sheila
Jelen and Shachar Pinsker (University of Maryland Press, 2007), 65–78.

21   Hemda Ben-Yehuda, *Eliezer Ben-Yehuda: hayav u-mif'alo* (Jerusalem: Mosad
Bialik, 1990), גמ.

22   Margalit Shilo, *Etgar ha-migdar: nashim ba-'aliyot ha-rishonot* (Tel Aviv:
Hakibbutz Hameuchad, 2007), 191.

23   Patrick Wolfe, *Settler Colonialism and the Transformation of Anthropology:
The Politics and Poetics of an Ethnographic Event* (London: Cassel, 1999), 25–34.

24   Ibid., 34.

25   On the significance of the binding story in Zionist and Israeli culture, see Yael
Feldman, *Glory and Agony: Isaac's Sacrifice and National Narrative* (Stanford:
Stanford University Press, 2010).

26   *Ha-shomer* was the first Zionist para-military organization in Palestine that
operated in the years 1909–20.

27   Hemda Ben-Yehuda, "Htaat Ephrayim," in *Stories by Women of the First
Aliyah*, ed. Yaffa Berlovitz (Tel Aviv: Misrad Ha-Bitahon, 1985), 21–34; Hemda
Ben-Yehuda, "Havat Bney Rekhav," in *Stories by Women of the First Aliyah*, ed.
Yaffa Berlovitz (Tel Aviv: Misrad Ha-Bitahon, 1985), 43–77.

28   Ben-Yehuda, *Ha-halom ve-shivro* (Tel Aviv: Mosad Bialik, 1978).

29   Ben-Yehuda, "Hataat Ephrayim," 22.

30   Eliezer Ben-Yehuda, "Apotruposut," *Hashkafa* 4 (1902): 26.

31   In 1899, the Baron de Rothschild, who up until that point supported the colonies, decided to transfer the financial responsibility to the JCA organization
(Jewish Colonization Association). The perception of JCA management of the
colonies as stricter and profit-orientated led many of the settlers to abandon
the settlement and emigrate back to Europe or to other destinations.

32   Ben-Yehuda, "Havat bney rekhav," 43.

33   On the significance of the desert in Zionist culture, see Zali Gurevitch, "The
Double Site of Israel," in *Grasping Land: Space and Place in Contemporary
Israeli Discourse and Experience*, ed. Eyal Ben Ari and Yoram Bilu (Albany:
State University of New York Press, 1997), 212–13.

34 On the place of the Hebrew-Bedouin in early Zionist culture, see Yael Zerubavel, "Memory, the Rebirth of the Native, and the 'Hebrew Bedouin Identity,'" *Social Research* 75, no. 1, (2008): 315–52. For another literary work on the same theme, see Yaakov Rabinowitch, *Mase'ot 'Amshay ha-shomer* (Jerusalem: Mitzpe, 1929). Hemda Ben-Yehuda was probably exposed to these ideas through the members of the "Jerusalem Group" – a group of young intellectuals of Sephardi descent that sought to promote the cultural relations between Arab and Jews in Palestine – and based their arguments upon the Semitic connection between the two peoples and the history of fruitful cultural dialogue between them in Arab and Muslim countries. Another possible source of influence was the figure of Israel Belkind, who, like the "Jerusalem Group," was also a frequent visitor at the Ben-Yehudas. Belkind developed a theory of "Oriental Hebrewness," arguing that the Arabs of Palestine are in fact descendants of the ancient Jews who did not go into exile after the destruction of the Second Temple but stayed on the Land and converted to Islam at the time of Arab rule over Palestine. Notably, however, the Bedouins occupied a particular role in the Zionist imagination, distinct from the Palestinian peasants (the *fellahin*), which most of these theories reference. Yaffa Berlovitz, *Le-hamtzi eretz, le-hamtzi 'am: tashtiyot sifrut ve-tarbut ba-yetzira shel ha-'aliyah ha-rishona* (Tel Aviv: Hakibbutz Hameuchad, 1996), 121–8.

35 This perception is of course contradicted by the actual history of the Bedouins, in which they "like other indigenous peoples, developed a distinct land regime that regulates their settlement system and self-rule over property, including ownership, division, sale, and conflict resolution." Alexandre Kedar, Ahmad Amara, and Oren Yiftachel, *Emptied Lands: A Legal Geography of Bedouin Rights in the Negev* (Stanford: Stanford University Press, 2018), 8. See also Mansour Nassara, *The Naqab Bedouins: A Century of Politics and Resistance* (Columbia University Press, 2017). Notably, it is precisely the same perceptions of the Bedouins as placeless people that ultimately would serve as rationalization of Israel's appropriation of Bedouin lands and its refusal to recognize dozens of Bedouin villages.

36 Amnon Raz-Krakotzkin, "The Zionist Return to the West and the Mizrahi Jewish Perspective," in *Orientalism and the Jews*, ed. Ivan Davidson Kalmar and Derek J. Penslar (Hanover and London: University Press of New England, 2005), 169.

37 Hemda Ben-Yehuda, "Havat bney rekhav," 61–2. My emphasis. The translation is partially based on the quotation in Yaffa Berlovitz, "Literature by women of the First Aliyah: The Aspiration for Women's Renaissance in Eretz-Israel," in *Pioneers and Homemakers: Jewish Women in Pre-State Israel*, ed. Deborah Bernstein (Albany: State University of New York Press, 1992), 59.

38 Gayatri Chakravorti Spivak, "Can the Subaltern Speak?" in *Colonial Discourse and Post-Colonial Theory: A Reader*, ed. Patrick Williams and Laura Chrisman (Hertfordshire: Harvester Wheatsheaf, 1994), 66–111.

39 Ben-Yehuda, "Havat bney rekhav," 76.

40 Yaffa Berlovitz, "Literature by Women of the First Aliyah: The Aspiration for Women's Renaissance in Eretz-Israel,"*Pioneers and Homemakers: Jewish Women in Pre-State Israel*, ed. Deborah Bernstein (Albany: State University of New York Press, 1992), 49–73.

41 Lewis, *Gendering Orientalism: Race, Femininity and Representation*; Lisa Lowe, *Critical Terrains: French and British Orientalisms* (Ithaca: Cornell University Press, 1991); Rana Kabbani, *Imperial Fictions: Europe's Myths of Orient* (London: Pandora, 1994); Billie Melman, *Women's Orients: English Women and the Middle East, 1718-1918: Sexuality, Religion, and Work* (London: Macmillan, 1992); Meyda Yeğenoğlu, *Colonial Fantasies: Toward a Feminist Reading of Orientalism* (Cambridge: Cambridge University Press, 1998).

42 Lewis, *Gendering Orientalism*; Lowe, *Critical Terrains*; Melman, *Women's Orients*.

43 Yeğenoğlu, *Colonial Fantasies*, 78–83.

44 Ibid., 63.

45 bell hooks, "The Oppositional Gaze: Black Female Spectators," in *Black Looks: Race and Representation* (Boston: South End Press, 1992), 115–31.

46 Adania Shibli, *Minor Detail*, trans. Elizabeth Jaquette (London: Fitzcarraldo Editions, 2020). For an illuminating analysis of Shibli's novel, see also, Shir Alon, "The Ongoing Nakba and the Grammar of History," *Los Angeles Review of Books*, June 2021, https://lareviewofbooks.org/article/the-ongoing-nakba-and-the-grammar-of-history/.

47 Shibli, *Minor Detail*, 43.

48 Ben-Yehuda, "Havat bney rekhav," 63–4.

49 Founded in 1882, Rishon Le-Zion was one of the first Zionist colonies (*moshavot*) in Palestine. Its founders were members of the first Zionist immigration wave (The First *Aliyah*, 1881–1903). While this wave of 25,000 to 35,000 immigrants was first to settle in the Land, its influence on Zionist culture and politics is considered less central than that of the subsequent waves associated with Labor Zionism – which became the dominant political force in Zionist society.

50 Nehama Pohatchevsky, *Bi-Yehuda ha-hadasha* (Israel: Atkin Print, 1911).

51 Pohatchevsky, *Ba-kfar u-ba-'avoda* (Tel Aviv: Hedim, 1930).

52 For an extensive biographical discussion, see Nurith Govrin, "Nefesh mi-Rishon Le-Zion Homiyah: Nehama Pohatchevsky," in *Dvash mi-sel'a: mehkarim be-sifrut Eretz-Yisrael* (Tel Aviv: Ministry of Defense Press, 1989), 114–71. I will also address Pohatchevsky's philantropic work extensively in chapter 3.

53 Yaffa Berlovitz, "Kol ha-melakholya ke-khol ha-mehaa: iyun bi-yetzirata shel Nehama Pohatchevsky me-ha-mesaprot ha-rishonot be-Eretz Yisrael,"

in *Eshnav le-hayehen shel nashim be-havarot Yehudiyot*, ed. Yael Atzmon (Jerusalem: Zalman Shazar Center, 1995), 325–36.

54 Ibid., 333.

55 Lubin, *Isha koret isha*, 101–16.

56 Moshe Behar, "Meah le-Flora Sporto: sipur lo yadu'a shel Nehama Pohatchevsky ve-efsharuta shel brit feministit-mizrahit," *Pe'amim* 139–140 (2013): 10.

57 Pohatchevsky, *Ba-kfar u-ba-'avoda*, 169.

58 The campaign for exclusive Jewish labour in the colonies, called "Hebrew Labor," was one of the most intense ventures of the second and third Zionist immigration waves. It is typically understood as an ideological clash between two generations of Zionism: the agricultural bourgeois colonists of the first Zionist immigration wave (1881–1904), who employed cheap Arab labour in their farms, and the passionate youth of the second immigration wave (1905–1914), who strove to regenerate the Jewish people through the work of the Land. See Anita Shapira, *Ha-maavak ha-nikhzav: 'avoda 'Ivrit, 1929–1939* (Tel Aviv: Hakibbutz Hameuchad, 1977). Post-Zionist and Marxist scholars contested the idealist account of this campaign, describing Hebrew Labor as a colonial enterprise aimed at ensuring Jewish dominance in the Land. See, Gershon Shafir, *Land, Labor and the Origins of the Israeli-Palestinian Conflict: 1982–1914* (Berkeley: University of California Press, 1989).

59 Pohatchevsky, *Ba-kfar u-ba-'avoda*, 170. My emphasis.

60 Wolfe, *Settler Colonialism*, 1–2; Shafir, *Land, Labor and the Origins*.

61 The double meaning of the Hebrew word *'avoda*, which can denote both "worship" and "labour," make the term lend itself to Zionist usages in the context of the struggle for Hebrew Labor. In terms of Jewish religion, *'avoda zara* stands for "foreign worship" or idolatry; in the discourse of Hebrew Labor, the term emerges as "foreign labour," or, the employment of Arab workers in Jewish settlements. There are numerous examples of the employment of the term *'avoda zarah* in the discourse of Hebrew Labor. See, for example, David Ben-Gurion's remark: "The first settlers … sold the aspirations of their youth for pennies, and with them … the revival of the homeland was performed through *'avoda zarah.*" (Quoted in Shapira, *Ha-maavak ha-nikhzav*, 21).

62 Arnold Eisen, *Galut: Modern Jewish Reflection on Homelessness and Homecoming* (Bloomington: University of Indiana Press, 1986), 35–6.

63 Pohatchevsky, *Ba-kfar u-ba-'avoda*, 86.

64 Rachel Katzanelson-Shazar (1885–1975) was one of the leaders of the Zionist Women Workers' Movement and the chief editor of the movement's publication *Dvar ha-po'eelet*.

65 Rachel Katzanelson, "'Al Nenama Pohatchevsky" ["On Nehama Pohatchevsky]," *Dvar Ha-Po'eelet* 4 (1934): 96.

66 See Richard Dyer, *White: Essays on Race and Culture* (New York: Routledge, 2017), 58–60.

67 Katzanelson, "'Al Nehama Pohatchevsky," 96.
68 Pohatchevsky, *Ba-kfar u-ba-'avoda*, 175.
69 Wolfe, *Settler Colonialism*, 25–34.
70 Nehama Pohatchevsky, "Zikhronot Ahat Ha-Ikarot Be-Eretz Yisrael," *Ha-Melitz* (September 1893): 2.
71 Ibid.
72 Ibid.
73 Ibid.
74 Ibid.
75 Ibid.
76 Republished as "Mi-Rishon Le-Zion le-Marj 'ayun," in *A'avra na ba-aretz: mas'ot be-Eretz Yisrael shel anshey ha-'Aliyah ha-rishona*, ed. Yaffa Berlovitz and Rehavam Zeevi (Tel-Aviv: Misrad ha-bitahon, 1992), 299–342.
77 Ibid., 307.
78 Artur Ruppin, "Buying the Emek," *zionism-israel.com*.
79 David Gilmour, *Dispossessed: the Ordeal of the Palestinians*, (London: Sphere Books, 1983) 44–5.
80 Pohatchevsky, *Ba-kfar u-ba-'avoda*, 5.
81 Ibid., 95–6.
82 Yitzhak Epstein, "Sheela N'aalama," *Ha-Shiloah* 17 (1907): 193–206.
83 See Aharon David Gordon, "Pitaron iratzyonali," *Ha-po'el ha-tza'ir* (July 1909): 17; Moshe Smilansky, "'Al 'inyaney ha-yishuv," *Ha-po'el ha-tza'ir* (January 1908): 5–10.
84 Nehama Pohatchevsky, "Sheelot Gluyot," *Ha-Shiloah* 18, (1908): 67–9.
85 Adi Ophir, "Identity of the Victims and the Victims of Identity: A Critique of Zionist Ideology for a Post-Zionist Age," in *Mapping Jewish Identities*, ed. Laurence Jay Silberstein (New York: New York University Press, 2000), 174–200.
86 For comprehensive discussion of Baron's place in Modern Hebrew Literature, see Sheila Jelen and Shachar Pinsker, eds., *Hebrew, Gender, and Modernity: Critical Responses to Devora Baron's Fiction* (Bethesda: University Press of Maryland, 2007).
87 Ibid., 5–6.
88 Shachar Pinsker, "Unraveling the Yarn: Intertextuality, Gender, and Cultural Critique in Dvora Baron's Fiction," *Nashim: A Journal of Jewish Women's Studies & Gender Issues* 11 (2006): 244–79; Orly Lubin, "Tidbits from Hehama's Kitchen: Alternative Nationalism in Dvora Baron's The Exiles," in *Hebrew, Gender, and Modernity: Critical Responses to Devora Baron's Fiction*, 91–104 (Bethesda: University Press of Maryland, 2007); Naomi Seidman, *A Marriage Made in Heaven: The Sexual Politics of Hebrew and Yiddish* (Berkeley: University of California Press, 1997), 67–101; Zierler, *And Rachel Stole the Idols*, 228–45.
89 Amnon Raz-Krakotzkin, "Galut be-tokh ribonut: bikoret shlilat ha-galut ba-tarbut ha-Yisraelit (Part 1)," *Teorya u-bikoret* 4 (1993): 23.

90 Ibid.

91 Ibid.

92 Daniel Boyarin, *Unheroic Conduct: The Rise of Heterosexuality and the Invention of the Jewish Man* (Berkeley: University of California Press, 1997); Michael Gluzman, *Ha-guf ha-tsiyoni: leumiyut, migdar u-miniyut ba-sifrut ha-'Ivrit ha-hadashah* (Tel Aviv: Hakibbutz Hameuchad, 2007); Seidman, *A Marriage Made in Heaven.*

93 Raz-Krakotzkin, "Galut be-tokh ribonut," 51.

94 Jelen and Pinsker, *Hebrew, Gender, Modernity,* 9.

95 Zierler, *And Rachel Stole the Idols,* 130.

96 Ibid., 230.

97 Ibid.

98 Pinsker, "Unraveling the Yarn," 249.

99 Ibid.

100 Dvora Baron, *Parshiyot* (Jerusalem: Mosad Bialik, 1951), 401.

101 Pinsker's reading beautifully demonstrates the ambiguity of the figure of the father-grandfather as a sign of the overall temporal ambiguity of the story. See Pinsker, "Unraveling the Yarn," 268–71.

102 Baron, *Parshiyot,* 402.

103 Ibid.

104 Pinsker, "Unraveling the Yarn," 262–73.

105 Baron, *Parshiyot,* 423.

106 Ibid., 424.

107 See *The Hebrew Bible with exegesis by Radak, Maagar ha-keter, Genesis* 16:6, https://www.mgketer.org/mikra/1/1/1/mg/40.

108 See *The Hebrew Bible with exegesis by Nachmanides, Maagar ha-keter, Genesis* 16:6, https://www.mgketer.org/mikra/1/1/1/mg/40.

109 *The Hebrew Bible with exegesis by Rashi, Maagar ha-keter, Genesis* 21:12, https://www.mgketer.org/mikra/1/1/1/mg/40.

110 Baron, *Parshiyot,* 424–25. My emphasis.

111 Delores Williams, *Sisters in the Wilderness: The Challenge of Womanist God-Talk* (New York: Orbis Books, 1993), 2.

112 Ibid., 2.

113 Ibid., 3–4.

114 Baron, *Parshiyot,* 425.

115 Carol Gilligan, *In A Different Voice* (Cambridge: Harvard University Press, 1982); Nancy Chodorow, *The Reproduction of Mothering: Psychoanalysis and the Sociology of Gender* (Berkeley: University of California Press, 1978).

116 Benedict Anderson, *Imagined Communities* (New York: Verso, 2006), 141–54.

117 Wolfe, *Settler Colonialism,* 3.

118 Baron, *Parshiyot,* 425.

119 Daniel Boyarin and Jonathan Boyarin, "Diaspora: Generation and the Ground of Jewish Identity," *Critical Inquiry* 19, no. 4 (1993): 707.

120 Ibid., 707.

121 Mikhal Dekel, *The Universal Jew: Masculinity, Modernity, and the Zionist Moment* (Evanston: Northwestern University Press, 2011). Hamutal Tsamir, *Be-shem ha-nof: leumiyut, migdar ve-sobjectiviyut ba-shira ha-Yisraelit bi-shnot ha-hamishim ve-ha-shishim* (Jerusalem: Ketter Books, 2006).

122 Lubin, "Tidbits"; Lubin, *Isha Koret Isha*, 101-16.

123 Arthur Hertzberg, *The Zionist Idea: Historical Analysis and Reader* (Philadelphia: Jewish Publication Society, 1997), 16-104.

Chapter Three

1 Nehama Pohatchevsky, "Ha-isha be-vinyan Rishon Le-Zion," *Rishon Le-Zion Archive 5/20א*, 1932. My emphasis.

2 Marion Kaplan, *The Making of the Jewish Middle Class: Women, Family, and Identity in Imperial Germany* (New York: Oxford University Press, 1991).

3 Ellen Fleischmann, *The Nation and Its "New" Women : The Palestinian Women's Movement, 1920-1948* (Berkeley: University of California Press, 2003), 95-114.

4 Vron Ware, *Beyond the Pale: White Women, Racism, and History* (London: Verso, 1991), 126-34; Barbara N. Ramusack, "Cultural Missionaries, Maternal Imperialists, Feminist Allies," in *Western Women and Imperialism: Complicity and Resistance*, ed. Nupur Chaudhuri and Margaret Strobel (Bloomington: Indiana University Press, 1992), 119-36; Antoinette M. Burton, "The White Woman's Burdan: British Feminists and 'The Indian Woman,' 1865-1915," in *Western Women and Imperialism: Complicity and Resistance*, ed. Nupur Chaudhuri and Margaret Strobel (Bloomington: Indiana University Press, 1992), 137-57; Dea Birkett, "The 'White Woman's Burden' in the 'White Man's Grave': The Introduction of British Nurses in Colonial West Africa," in *Western Women and Imperialism: Complicity and Resistance*, ed. Nupur Chaudhuri and Margaret Strobel (Bloomington: Indiana University Press, 1992), 177-90.

5 Mary Louise Pratt, *Imperial Eyes: Travel Writing and Transculturation* (New York: Routledge, 1992), 7.

6 Nira Yuval-Davis, *Gender and Nation* (London: Sage Publications, 1997), 26-38.

7 Naomi Seidman, *A Marriage Made in Heaven: The Sexual Politics of Hebrew and Yiddish* (Berkeley: University of California Press, 1997), 114-15; Tamar Hess, *Hek ha-em shel zikhronot: nashim, otobiyografyah ve-ha-'Aliyah ha-sheniyah* (Or Yehuda: Dvir, 2014), 208-47.

8 On social motherhood, see Seth Koven and Sonya Michel, eds, *Mothers of the New World* (London: Routledge, 1993).

9   Naama Kati'ee, "Parashat yaldey teyman, mizrah, u-balkan: ha-shed ba-megera shel ha-feminism ha-Yisraeli," *Politically Koreet*, 2016, http://politicallycorret. co.il/ובלקן-השד-במגירה-ש פרשת-ילדי-תימן-מזרח-/#_ftn3; Dafna Hirsch and Smadar Sharon, "'Imahot Maznihot': Havnayat Ha-Imahut Shel Nashim Mizrahiyot Bi-Tkufat Ha-Mandat u-Bereshit Shnot Ha-Medina," in *Yeladim shel ha-lev: hebetim hadashim be-heker parashat yaldey Teyman*, ed. Tova Gamliel and Nathan Shifriss (Tel Aviv: Restling, 2019), 253–98.

10 See Deborah Bernstein, *Nashim ba-shulayim: migdar ve-leumiyut be-Tel Aviv ha-mandatorit* (Tel Aviv: Yad Yitzhak Ben-Tzvi, 2008); Dafna Hirsch, *Banu hena lehavi et ha-m'aarav: hanhalat higyena u-vnyat tarbut ba-hevra ha-yehudit bi-tkufat ha-mandat* (Sde Boker: Mekhon Ben-Gurion le-heker Yisrael ve-ha-tziyonut, 2014); Dafna Hirsch, "Gender and Ethnicity in the Zionist Nation-Building Project: The Case of Hannah Helena Thon," *Ethnic and Racial Studies* 34, no. 2 (2011): 275–92; Hirsch and Sharon, "'Imahot Maznihot'"; Tammy Razi, *Yaldey ha-hefker: ha-hatser ha-ahorit shel Tel-Aviv ha-mandatorit* (Tel Aviv: Am Oved, 2009).

11 Itzhak Epstein, "Sheela N'aalama," *Ha-Shiloah* 17 (1907): 193–206.

12 Nehama Pohatchevsky, "Sheelot Gluyot," *Ha-Shiloah* 18 (1908): 67–9.

13 Nehama Pohatchevsky, *Ba-kfar u-ba-'avoda* (Tel Aviv: Hedim, 1930).

14 Moshe Behar, "Meah le-Flora Sporto: sipur lo yadu'a shel Nehama Pohatchevsky ve-efsharuta shel brit feministit-mizrahit," *Pe'amim* 139–140 (2013), 9–54.

15 Behar, "Meah le-Flora Sporto," 17.

16 Pohatchevsky, *Ba-kfar u-ba-'avoda*, 190.

17 Behar, "Meah le-Flora Sporto," 21.

18 Shabbat Shira refers to the Shabbat in which Jews read the portion of the Torah which includes the biblical "Song of the Sea." The tradition of feeding birds on this day commemorates the story in which Datan and Aviram who objected to Moses' leadership scattered manna on the ground on a day which Moses announced as a day of fast. The birds ate the manna and thus affirmed Moses' law.

19 Pohatchevsky, *Ba-kfar u-ba-'avoda*, 175.

20 Nitza Druyan, "Skhunot hadashot le-'oley teyman bi-Yerushalayim," *Kathedra* 13 (1980): 95–129.

21 Bat-Zion Eraqi Kloreman, "Hityashvut po'aalim teymanim ve-ashkenazim: me-Rishon Le-Tsion le-Nahlat Yehuda u-be-hazarah," *Kathedra* 84 (Summer 1997): 85–106.

22 I discussed this enterprise in chapter 2. See also: Gershon Shafir, "The Meeting of Eastern Europe and Yemen: 'Idealistic Workers' and 'Natural Workers' in Early Zionist Settlement in Palestine," *Ethnic and Racial Studies* 13 (1990): 172–97; Eraqi Klorman, "Hityashvut po'aalim": 85–106; Yosef Gorni, "Kokho ve-hulshato shel ha-paternalizm ha-'erki: tadmit yehudey Teyman be-'eney manhigut ha-'aliyah ha-shniya," *Kathedra* 108 (2003): 131–62.

23 Gorni, "Kokho ve-hulshato," 139.

24 Eraqi Klorman, "Hityashvut po'aalim," 87.

25 Ibid., 89.

26 Ibid.

27 Rishon Le-Tzion Archive, Efrat's testimony, p. 5. I thank the workers of the Rishon Le-Tzion archive for their help in locating these materials.

28 Eraqi Klorman, "Hityashvut po'aalim," 87.

29 Ibid., 87-8.

30 Ibid., 88-9.

31 Ibid., 89.

32 Granted, the parallel street is named after Rabbi Saadya Sibahi who settled in Rishon from Yemen in 1930 and was a well-known public figure and social activist for the Yemenite community. This indeed attests to some effort by the city to commemorate the Yemenite community.

33 On Pohatchevsky's role as an arbiter, see: Yaffah Berlovitz, "Beit mishpat shel isha ahat: sipura shel Nehama Pohatchevsky ke-historya mekomit shel nashim (Rishon Le-Zion 1889–1934)," in *Huka ahat u-mishpat ehad la-ish ve-la-isha: nashim, zkhuyot u-mishpat bi-tkufat ha-mandat*, ed. Eyal Katvan, Margalit Shilo, and Ruth Halperin-Kadri (Ramat Gan: Bar Ilan University Press, 2010), 325-74.

34 We will encounter examples of this later in this chapter.

35 Nehama Pohatchevsky, "Ruma," *Project Ben-Yehuda*, https://benyehuda.org/read/7942.

36 Ibid.

37 Eraqi Klorman, "Hityashvut po'aalim"; Shafir, "The Meeting of Eastern Europe and Yemen"; Yehuda Nini, *He-hayit or halamti halom: teymaney kinneret – parashat hityashvutam ve-'akiratam, 1912–1930* (Tel Aviv: Am Oved, 1996).

38 Eraqi Klorman, "Yahas manhigut ha-yishuv le-yotzey teyman ke-reka le-ha-vanat tof'aat he'almut ha-yeladim le-ahar kom ha-medina," in *Yeladim shel ha-Lev: hebetim hadashim be-heker parashat yaldey Teyman*, ed. Tova Gamliel and Nathan Shifriss (Tel Aviv: Restling, 2019), 55-74; Nini, *He-hayit or halamti halom*; Gorni, "Kokho ve-hulshato."

39 Pohatchevsky, "Ruma."

40 Shafir, "The Meeting of Eastern Europe and Yemen"; Nini, *He-hayit or halamti halom*," 34-6; Eraqi Klorman, "Hityashvut po'aalim."

41 Lubin, *Isha koret isha* (Haifa: University of Haifa Press, 2006), 101-16.

42 Goni Ben-Yisrael Kasuto, "'Ve-akh evar meduldal ani': ha-guf ha-nashi be-sipureha shel Nehama Pohatchevsky," *Dvarim* (2015): 26; Yaffa Berlovitz, *Le-hamtzi eretz, le-hamtzi 'am: tashtiyot sifrut ve-tarbut ba-yetzira shel ha-'aliyah ha-rishona*, (Tel Aviv: Hakibbutz Hameuchad, 1996), 74.

43 Nehama Pohatchevsky, "G'alut," in Bi-Yehuda ha-hadasha," *Project Ben Yehuda*, https://benyehuda.org/read/7939.

44 Nini, *He-hhayit or halamti alom*, 35.

45 Ibid.

46 Nehama Pohatchevsky, "G'alut."

47 Ibid.

48 Pohatchevsky, "Ruma."

49 Pohatchevsky, "Pe'amim," *Project Ben-Yehuda*, https://benyehuda.org/read/814.

50 Ibid.

51 Rishon Le-Zion Archive, 20A – 5, Efrat's testimony, 5.

52 Eraqi Klorman, "Hityashvut po'aalim"; Mordekhai Tabib, *Ke-'esev ha-sade* (Tel Aviv: Ha-Kibbutz Ha-Meuhad, 2000), 211.

53 Rishon Le-Zion Archive. Interviews. 1980. My emphasis.

54 Ibid.

55 Ibid.

56 Yaffah Berlovitz, "'Al tsomtey mifgashim bein nashim be-reshit ha-yishuv (1878–1918): 'iyun be-kitvehen shel rishonot," *Migdar be-Yisrael* 1 (2014): 389.

57 Israel Yeshayahu, "Ha-mishpaha ve-'avodat ha-isha ba-'eda ha-Teymanit," *Dvar ha-po'eelet* 7, no. 1 (1940): 18–19.

58 Berlovitz, "'Al tsomtey," 388–9.

59 Shoshana Bluwstein, *'Ali Teyman* (Tel Aviv: Yavneh, 1943), 27–8.

60 I will discuss Bluwstein the poet in chapter 4.

61 Hannah Meisel (1883–1972) was a Zionist educator who established the first educational women's farm. See Margalit Shilo, *Etgar ha-migdar: nashim ba-'aliyot ha-rishonot* (Tel Aviv: Hakibbutz Hameuchad, 2007), 137–81.

62 Shoshana Bluwstein, *'Aley Kinneret* (Tel Aviv: Haverim, 1940).

63 Bluwstein, *'Ali Teyman*, 61.

64 On this figure as a model for Jewish women, see: Iris Parush, *Reading Jewish Women: Marginality and Modernization in Nineteenth-Century Eastern European* (Waltham: Brandeis University Press, 2004), 179–85.

65 Hess, *Hek ha-em*, 141–2.

66 Bluwstein, *'Ali Teyman*, 55.

67 Ibid.

68 Bluwstein, *'Aley Kinneret*, 30; For an analysis of this scene, see, Hess, *Hek ha-em*, 98.

69 Bluwstein, *'Aley Kinneret*, 30.

70 Bluwstein, *'Ali Teyman*, 53.

71 Ibid., 7.

72 Nini, *He-hayit or halamti halom*, 39.

73 Bluwstein, *'Ali Teyman*, 10.

74 Ibid.

75 Ibid., 11.

76 Ibid., 14.

77 Ibid., 14–15.
78 Ibid., 15.
79 Ibid., 16.
80 Ibid., 17.
81 Nini, *He-hayit or halamti halom*, 85.
82 Bluwstein, *'Ali Teyman*, 17.
83 See Nini, *He-hayit o halamti halom*; Ayelet Heller, *Dekel Shfal Tzameret*, 1992 (film).
84 Nini, *He-hayit o halamti halom*, 67–76.
85 The office that was in charge of the Labor Movement's settlement project,
86 Nini, *He-hayit o halamti halom*, 70.
87 Ibid., 74.
88 Ibid., 81–2.
89 Ibid., 13.
90 A traditional Jewish term used to speak of Jewish People intergenerational collective.
91 Bluwstein, *'Ali Teyman*, 44.
92 Ibid., 32.
93 Kaplan, *The Making of the Jewish Middle Class*, 192–227.
94 Koven and Michel, *Mothers of the New World*.
95 Sylvia Fogel-Bijawi and Anat Herbst-Debby, "Bonot merhavey tipul, hemla ve-hitmʿarvut: maternalism ve-kinun profesiat ha-ʿavoda ha-sotsyalit ba-Yishuv ha-Yehudi be-Eretz Yisrael, 1912-1948," in *Lo tsdaka ela tsedek: prakim be-hitpathut ha-ʿavoda ha-sotsyalit be-Yisrael*, ed. Jonny Gal and Ronnie Holler (Beer Sheva: Ben-Gurion University of the Negev Press, 2019), 130.
96 This biographical account is based on: Yaffah Berlovitz, "Hannah Thon," *Jewish Women's Archive*, 2006, https://jwa.org/encyclopedia/article/thon-hannah-helena; Hirsch, "Gender and Ethnicity."
97 Hirsch, "Gender and Ethnicity," 281.
98 Naomi Shepherd, *A Price Below Rubies Jewish Women as Rebels and Radicals* (Cambridge: Harvard University Press, 1993), 234.
99 Boyarin, *Unheroic Conduct: The Rise of Heterosexuality and the Invention of the Jewish Man*.
100 Ibid., 313–60.
101 Ibid., 353.
102 Ibid., 270–323.
103 Hirsch, "Gender and Ethnicity," 275.
104 Ibid.
105 Ibid., 281.
106 "Shimon Ha-Tzadik," *Ha-Isha* 1 (1925): 19.
107 Hirsch, "Gender and Ethnicity," 278.
108 Hannah Thon, "Yom Geshem," *Ha-Isha* 1 (1927): 15.

109 Ibid.

110 Ibid.

111 Ibid.

112 Ibid.

113 Ibid., 15–16.

114 Israel Zangvill, *Children of the Ghetto: A Study of a Peculiar People* (New York: The Macmillan Company, 1899), x.

115 Thon, "Yom Geshem," 17.

116 Ibid., 18.

117 Ibid., 18.

118 Ben-Yair Michael, *Sheikh Jarrah* (Tel Aviv: Hargol, 2013), 8.

119 Ibid., 32.

120 Central Zionist Archive, A148/74.

121 In May 2021, violent confrontations surrounding the impending evacuation of Palestinian families from houses in Sheikh Jarrah escalated and eventually led to a war between Israel and the Gaza Strip, in which Israel extensively bombed the besieged Strip, and caused hundreds of Palestinian casualties.

122 See Gloria E. Anzaldúa, *Borderlands / La Frontera: The New Mestiza* (San Francisco: Aunt Lute Books, 1987), 2–3. For a discussion of Anzaldúa's concept in the context of Israel/Palestine, see Smadar Lavie, "Staying Put: Crossing the Israel–Palestine Border with Gloria Anzaldúa," *Anthropology and Humanism* 36, no. 1 (2011): 101–21.

123 Tova Gamliel, "Hakhum lehum: 'al ovdan ve-melancholya ezrahit," in *Yeladim shel ha-Lev*, 369. My emphasis.

124 *The Yemenite, Mizrahi and Balkan Children Affair*, https://www.edut-amram. org/en/.

125 In particular, the Amram Association, founded by Mizrahi activists, is an organization devoted to commemorating the lost children, investigating the affair, collecting and publishing testimonies, and advocating for official recognition by the State. See *The Yemenite, Mizrahi and Balkan Children Affair*, https://www.edut-amram.org/en/.

126 This particular pattern recurs especially in the case of the Yemenite babies, as the Yemenites were put in separate camps and were obligated to put their children in infant centres. See, Nathan Shifriss, *Yaldi halakh lean: parashat yaldey teyman: ha-hatifa ve-ha-hkhasha* (Tel Aviv: Sifrey alyat ha-gag, 2019). There were, however, other testimonies that described babies taken from the delivery room or snatched from their mother's arms, and older kids kidnapped from the streets. For a comprehensive collection of testimonies, see the "Testimonies," *The Yemenite, Mizrahi and Balkan Children Affair*, https://www.edut-amram.org/en/categories/all/.

127 Nathan Shifriss, "Be-netiv he'almutam shel yaldey Yisrael ha-n'eedarim o keitsad p'aala ha-shita," in *Yeladim shel ha-lev*, 304–8.

128 Shifriss, *Yaldi halakh lean*, 77–300.

129 Kati'ee, "Parashat yaldey teyman."

130 Ibid.

131 bell hooks, "The Oppositional Gaze: Black Female Spectators," in *Black Looks: Race and Representation* (Boston: South End Press, 1992), 115–31.

132 Einat Kafah, "Interview with Sarah Tzarum," *The Yemenite, Mizrahi and Balkan Children Affair*, https://www.edut-amram.org/testimonies/sara-tzur/.

133 Bluwstein, *'Ali Teyman*, 55.

134 Gamliel, "Hakhum lehum," 369.

135 Bluwstein, *'Ali Teyman*, 55. My emphasis.

136 See also Dafna Hirsch's discussion of the nurse in Hirsch, *Banu hena le-havi et ha-m'aarav*.

137 Elad Ben Elul and Yossef Brauman, "Neviim: mivtz'a 'Amram (Episode 12)," YouTube video, 2016, https://www.youtube.com/watch?v=5KeAx9j8zkk&list.

138 Gamliel, "Hakhum Lehum"; Meira Weiss, "The Children of Yemen: Bodies, Medicalization and Nation Building," *Medical Anthropology Quarterly* 15, no. 2 (2001): 206–21.

139 See also Orian Zakai, "Girls at the Intersection: Discourse on Girl Labor in the Zionist Women Workers' Movement," *Jewish and Arab Childhood in Israel: Contemporary Perspectives*, ed. Einat Baram Eshel, Wurud Jayusi, Ilana Paul-Binyamin, and Eman Younis (Lanham: Lexington Books, 2021), 49–62.

140 See also, Razi, *Yaldey ha-hefker*, Hirsch and Sharon, "Imahot Maznikhot."

Chapter Four

1 Rachel Bluwstein, *Rahel: Ha-Hayim, Ha-Shirim*, ed. Mouki Tzur (Tel Aviv: Hakibbutz Hameuchad, 2011), 25. All translations of poems are mine unless specified otherwise.

2 Anita Shapira, *Herev ha-yona: ha-tsiyonut ve-ha-koah* (Tel Aviv: 'Am-oved, 1992), 198.

3 Dan Miron, *Imahot meyasdot, ahayot horgot: 'al reshit shirat ha-nashim ha-'Ivrit* (Tel Aviv: Hakibbutz Hameuchad, 1991), 98–9; 153–60.

4 Michael Gluzman, "The Exclusion of Women from Hebrew Literary History," *Prooftexts* 11, no. 3 (1991): 259–78.

5 The term "national metonym" derives from Dan Miron's claim that while that life stories of Zionist men of the period were assigned the status of a national metonym since they were perceived as representative of the collective story of the nation, while women's experiences were marked in the national conscious-ness as "personal private experience." Miron, *Imahot meyasdot*, 67.

6 Almog studies the figure of the *sabra* which refers to an ideal identity of those born in the Land itself as opposed to diasporic Jewish identity. It alludes to the cacti plant, which is said to be prickly on the outside and sweet on the inside,

and served as a metaphor for the personality associated with the *sabra* identity as rough and tough on the outside but tender inside. See, Oz Almog, *The Sabra: The Creation of the New Jew* (Berkeley: University of California Press, 2000) 209–25.

7 Ibid., 210.

8 On contrasts between smallness and grandness in Bluwstein's poetry, see, for example, Ziva Shamir, *Rakefet: anava ve-gaava be-shirat Rahel* (Tel Aviv: Hakibbutz Hameuchad, 2012).

9 Hamutal Tsamir, *Be-shem ha-nof: leumiyut, migdar ve-sobjectiviyut ba-shira ha-Yisraelit bi-shnot ha-hamishim ve-ha-shishim* (Jerusalem: Ketter Books, 2006), 276.

10 Aharon David Gordon (1856–1922) was a prominent spiritual figure of the Zionist Labor Movement. Influenced by Jewish Hasidism as well as the ideas of Lev Tolstoy and Friedrich Nietzsche, he preached for the regeneration of Jewish identity through labour, especially agricultural work.

11 See Hamutal Tsamir, "Ha-korban ha-halutzi, ha-Eretz ha-kdosha ve-hof'aata shel shirat nashim bi-shnot ha-'esrim," *Reg'a shel huledet: mehkarim be-sifrut 'Ivrit u-ve-sifrut Yiddish likhvod Dan Miron*, ed. Hanan Hever (Jerusalem: Mosad Bialik, 2008), 645–73.

12 Indeed, it is important to recall that while Bluwstein's final years were characterized by sadness and loneliness, she also became widely recognized during this period as a poet whose work expresses national sentiment. Bluwstein's weekly poem in the Labor Zionist newspaper *Davar* situated her at the centre of the national cultural arena.

13 Shapira, *Herev ha-yona*, 199.

14 Ibid., 17–178.

15 Gluzman, "The Exclusion of Women," 267–71. For another sophisticated reading of the poem "Niv" see also Shira Stav, "Heye li em ve-ah: Rahel ve-Bialik," *Mehkarey Yerushalayim be-sifrut 'Ivrit*, 29 (2017): 213–34.

16 Rachel Bluwstein, "'Al ot ha-zman," *Project Ben-Yehuda*, https://benyehuda. org/read/274. My emphasis.

17 Bluwstein, *Rahel: Ha-Hayim, Ha-Shirim*, 116. My emphasis.

18 The object of Bluwstein's critique here is the use of the *melitza*, namely formulaic expressions taken from the classical Jewish texts, in Modern Hebrew literary works.

19 Robert Alter, *The Hebrew Bible: A Translation with Commentary* (New York: W.W. Norton & Company, 2018), Isaiah 3:17.

20 Alter, Isiah 3: 18–23.

21 Tova Cohen, *Ha-ahat ahuva ve-ha-hat nuaa: bein bidyon le-metziut be-teurey ha-isha be-sifrut ha-haskalah*, (Tel Aviv: Magnes, 2002), 31–8.

22 Iris Parush, *Reading Jewish Women: Marginality and Modernization in Nineteenth-Century Eastern European* (Waltham: Brandeis University Press, 2004), 229.

23 Margalit Shilo, *Etgar ha-migdar: nashim ba-'aliyot ha-rishonot* (Tel Aviv: Hakibbutz Hameuchad, 2007), 38.

24 Ibid., 40–1.

25 Ibid., 39.

26 Yaakov Rabinowitch, "'Al ha-sarot ve-ha-sganot," *Ha-Isha* 1 (1927): 8.

27 Ibid., 9.

28 For a more extensive discussion of Alper's work, see Orian Zakai, "A Uniform of a Writer: Literature, Ideology and Sexual Violence in the Writing of Rivka Alper," *Prooftexts* 34 (2014): 232–70. The analysis in the following passages is partially based on this article.

29 Rachel Katzanelson, "Darka Ke-Soferet," *Dvar Ha-Poeelet* 24, no. 7 (1958): 201. My emphasis.

30 Ibid.

31 Bluwstein, *Rahel: Ha-Hayim, Ha-Shirim*, 142. My emphasis.

32 Miron, *Imahot meyasdo*, 266–7.

33 Ibid., 268.

34 Rivka Alper, *Pirpurey Mahapekha* (Tel Aviv: Mitzpe, 1930).

35 Yaakov Rabinowitz, "Ha-sefer ha-hadash: bikoret," *Moznayim* 2.5 (May 1930): 15.

36 V. Tomer, "Pirpurey mahapekha: bikoret," *Moznayim* 2 (August 1930): 13.

37 Immanuel Ben-Gurion, "'Al ha-mitnahalim ba-har," *Kneset* 9 (1944): 318.

38 Zelda, "Rivka Alper," *Dvar Ha-Po'eelet* 25 (1959): 169.

39 She refers here to the biblical figure of Rebecca the Matriarch.

40 Rivka Alper, *Ha-mitnahalim ba-har* (Tel Aviv: Am Oved, 1944), 194–5.

41 Ibid., 206.

42 Ibid.

43 Ibid., 207–8.

44 Ibid., 208.

45 Daniel Boyarin, *Unheroic Conduct: The Rise of Heterosexuality and the Invention of the Jewish Man* (Berkeley: University of California Press, 1997); Michael Gluzman, *Ha-guf Ha-tsiyoni: leumiyut, migdar u-miniyut ba-sifrut ha-'Ivrit ha-hadashah* (Tel Aviv: Hakibbutz Hameuchad, 2007); Tamar Mayer, "From Zero to Hero: Masculinity in Jewish Nationalism," *Gender Ironies of Nationalism: Sexing the Nation* (London: Routledge 1999), 283–307.

46 Ada Mimon, *Hamishim shana shel tnu'at ha-po'aalot* (Tel Aviv: Am Oved, 1959), 123.

47 Margalit Shilo, *Princess Or Prisoner?: Jewish Women in Jerusalem, 1840–1914* (Waltham: Brandeis University Press, 2005), 73.

48 Ibid., 74.

49 Yael Guilat, "Between Lulu and Penina: The Yemenite Woman, Her Jewelry, and Her Embroidery in the New Hebrew Culture," *Nashim: A Journal of Jewish Women's Studies & Gender Issues*, no. 11 (2006): 207–8.

50 Ibid., 207.

51 Ibid.

52 Dan Miron, "The Endless Cycle: The Poetic World of Dvora Baron," trans. Haim Watzman, in *Hebrew, Gender, and Modernity: Critical Responses to Devora Baron's Fiction*, ed. Sheila Jelen and Shachar Pinsker (Bethesda: University of Maryland Press, 2007), 17–31.

53 Shachar Pinsker, "Unraveling the Yarn: Intertextuality, Gender, and Cultural Critique in Dvora Baron's Fiction," *Nashim: A Journal of Jewish Women's Studies & Gender Issues* 11 (2006): 244–79; Orly Lubin, "Tidbits from Hehama's Kitchen: Alternative Nationalism in Dvora Baron's The Exiles," in *Hebrew, Gender, and Modernity: Critical Responses to Devora Baron's Fiction* (Bethesda: University Press of Maryland, 2007), 91–104; Seidman, *A Marriage Made in Heaven: The Sexual Politics of Hebrew and Yiddish*, 67–101. Wandy Zierler, *And Rachel Stole the Idols: The Emergence of Modern Hebrew Women's Writing*, 228–45.

54 The two sequel novellas composing the novel, "For the Time Being" ("Le-'et 'ata"; 1943), which takes place mostly in Egypt, and "Since Last Night" ("Me-emesh" 1955), which is set in Palestine, were published together as a novel only in 1970 in fulfillment of the late Baron's wishes. For an English translation of the first novella, see Dvora Baron, "For the Time Being," trans. Sheila Jelen, in *Hebrew, Gender, and Modernity: Critical Responses to Devora Baron's Fiction* (Bethesda: University of Maryland Press, 2007), 225–78. In the following pages, I use Jelen's published translation with certain revisions for quotations from the first part of the novel, and my own translation for quotations from the second part.

55 Dvora Baron, *Ha-golim* (Tel Aviv: Am Oved, 1970), 5.

56 During World War I, the Ottoman authorities displaced Jews who were not Ottoman citizens, especially residents of towns around the Mediterranean coastline for fear that they will collaborate with the British enemy. Some of these communities were deported to Egypt, which was under British rule. See also: Nurith Govrin, "Pgishatam shel goley Mitzrayim ve-ha-kehila ha-yehudit ba be-milhemet ha-'olam ha-rishona," *Pe'amim* 25 (1985): 73–101.

57 Baron, "For the Time Being," 270. Translation slightly revised.

58 The name Lulu means a pearl in Arabic and connects with the function of the Jewelry as part of the bride price system as "it is also a component in the dress (*lulwi*) worn by San'a brides until the nineteenth century." See Guilat, "Between Lulu and Penina," 208.

59 Baron, *Ha-golim*, 85.

60 Baron, "For the Time Being," 270–1.

61 Ibid., 272.
62 Ibid.
63 Ibid., 236.
64 Ibid., 237.
65 Ibid.
66 Ibid., 237–9.
67 Richard Dyer, *White: Essays on Race and Culture* (New York: Routledge, 2017), 48.
68 Ibid., 57.
69 Vron Ware, *Beyond the Pale: White Women, Racism, and History* (London: Verso, 1991), 11–18.
70 Dyer, *White*, 45–60.
71 Ibid., 41–81.
72 Baron., *Ha-Golim*, 159.
73 Baron., "For the Time Being," 271.
74 Ibid., 272.
75 Ibid.
76 Baron, *Ha-golim*, 177.
77 Otto Preminger, *Exodus* (United States: United Artists, 1960).
78 For an illuminating analysis of the politics and aesthetics of this film, see also: Yosefa Loshitzky, "National Rebirth as a Movie: Otto Preminger's Exodus," *National Identities* 4, no. 2 (2002): 119–31.
79 The Irgun, also called Etsel, was a right-wing para-military organization active during the pre-state period. It was established in 1931 by members of the Labor Movement's organization "Ha-haganah" who split from the organization because they wanted more aggressive armed resistance to the British Mandate in Palestine.
80 Loshitzky, "National Rebirth," 24.
81 Ware, *Beyond the Pale*, 4–11; Dyer, *White*, 26–30; Angela Woolacoot, *Gender and Empire* (Hampshire: Palgrave Macmillan, 2006), 38–58.
82 Baron, "For the Time Being," 251.
83 Ibid, 246.
84 Dyer, *White*, 28–9; Lynda Nead, *Myths of Sexuality: Representations of Women in Victorian Britain* (Oxford: Basil Blackwell Ltd, 1988), 95–6.
85 Baron, "For the Time Being," 270.
86 Baron, 274.
87 Dyer, *White*, 207.
88 Miron, *Imahot meyasdot*, 153–4.
89 Ibid., 154.
90 Ibid.
91 Ibid.

92 Goldberg's poem arguably refers to her Lithuanian homeland, and yet, its reception in Israeli culture construes it as a national song for "the Land," which, like Bluwstein's poem, is often performed on ceremonial national occasions.

93 Shmuel Fisher (lyrics), Henrik Gold-Zehavi (music), "Artzenu ha-ktantonet," 1943.

94 Oren Yiftachel and Batya Roded, "Lalekhet shevi aharayikh: 'al merhavey 'ha-moledet' ba-zemer u-va-nof," in *Motherland/McDonald's Trends in the Construction of Space and Culture in Israel*, ed. Oren Yiftachel, Batia Roded, and Uri Ram (Beer Sheva: The Negev Center for Regional Development 2003), 12.

95 Uri Kesari, "Shmuel Fisher hozer le-artsenu ha-ktantonet," *Maariv* (27 April 1966).

96 Dvora Gilula, *Nathan Alterman ve-va-bama ha-'Ivrit* (Tel Aviv: Hakibbutz Hameuchad, 2008), 70.

97 אַרְצֵנוּ הַקְּטַנְטֹנֶת / הוֹרִידִי הַכֻּתֹּנֶת / וְאִם אַתְּ מַזִּיעָה / הוֹרִידִי חֲזִיָּה / אַנְגְּלִים מוּכָנִים / הוֹרִידִי תַּחְתּוֹנִים / וְהֵם יָזִינוּ אוֹתָךְ עַד הָעֶצֶם. See *Radio Zemereshet*, https://www.zemereshet.co.il/song.asp?id=4337&artist=1595.

98 For example, Hayim Nahman Bialik's famous sarcastic depiction of the pogrom, in which husbands watch passively as their wives are being raped, has been aptly read as a metonym of national humiliation. The poem reads:

> Descend then, to the cellars of the town / There where the virginal daughters of thy folk were fouled / Where seven heathen flung a woman down / The daughter in the presence of her mother / The mother in the presence of her daughter / Before slaughter, during slaughter, and after slaughter! ... Crushed in their shame, they saw it all / They did not stir nor move / They did not pluck their eyes out / they Beat not their brains against the wall! / Perhaps, perhaps, each watcher had it in his heart to pray: A miracle, O Lord, – and spare my skin this day! / Those who survived this foulness / who from their blood awoke / Beheld their life polluted / the light of their world gone out – How did their menfolk bear it / how did they bear this yoke? / They crawled forth from their holes /they fled to the house of the Lord / They offered thanks to Him, the sweet benedictory word / The Cohanim sallied forth / to the Rabbi's house they flitted: Tell me, O Rabbi, tell, is my own wife permitted?

> Hayim Nahman Bialik, *Complete Poetic Works of Hayyim Nahman Bialik*, ed. Israel Efros (New York: The Histadruth Ivrith of America, 1948), 129–43. On the gendered implications of Bialik's poem, see also: Michael Gluzman, "Pogrom and Gender: On Bialik's Unheimlich," *Prooftexts: A Journal of Jewish Literary History* 25, nos 1–2 (2005): 39–59.

99 Hagai, "Ma omrim," *Lamerhav* (29 April 1956): 2.

100 Ibid.

101 A. Steinman, "Holot lohatim u-midbar ha-umot," *Davar* (7 July 1967). My emphasis.

102 Simha-Bunam Aurbach, "Maagar koakh ve-hashkafat 'olam," *Ha-Tzofe* (11 August 1967). My emphasis.

103 Shapira, *Herev ha-yona*, 179–296.

104 Yoram Teharlev (lyrics), Yigaal Bashan (music), "Artzenu ha-ktantonet," 1986.

105 Yoram Teharlev (lyrics), Rami Kleinstein (music), "'Od lot tamu kol plaayikh," 1987.

106 Yiftachel and Roded, "Lalekhet shevi aharayikh," 5.

107 Carol Bardenstein, "Trees, Forests and the Shaping of the Israeli Collective Memory," in *Acts of Memory: Cultural Recall in the Present*, ed. Mieke Bal, Jonathan Crewe, and Leo Spitzer (Hanover: University of New England Press, 1999), 149–68; Liat Berdugo, "A Situation: A Tree in Palestine," *Places*, 2020, https://placesjournal.org/article/a-situation-a-tree-in-palestine/?cn-reloaded=1.

108 Ilan Pappe, *The Ethnic Cleansing of Palestine* (Oxford: One World Publications, 2006). Notably, the verb *kavash*, used for paving a path, is the same verb used for "occupy" or "conquer" in modern Hebrew as in the word *kibush* often used to refer to the Israeli occupation.

109 Ethan Bronner, "A Road Becomes a Dividing Line in the West Bank," *New York Times*, 26 March 2008, https://www.nytimes.com/2008/03/26/world/africa/26iht-highway.4.11447813.html?pagewanted=all.

Epilogue

1 Galia Oz, *Davar she-mithapes le-ahava* (Or Yehuda: Kineret Zmora-Bitan Dvir, 2021), 1, e-vrit.

2 Yigaal Schwartz, "Interview," *Ma she-karukh* (Literary Podcast), 24 February 2021.

3 Ibid.

4 Amos Oz, *Tale of Love and Darkness*, trans. Nicolas De Lange (Orlando: Harcourt Books, 2004).

5 Yael Feldman, *Glory and Agony: Isaac's Sacrifice and National Narrative* (Stanford: Stanford University Press, 2010), 31.

6 See also Tamar Katriel, *Dialogic Moments: From Soul Talks to Talk Radio in Israeli Culture* (Detroit: Wayne State University Press, 2004), 29–134.

7 Alon Gan, "The Tanks of Tammuz and The Seventh Day: The Emergence of Opposite Poles of Israeli Identity after the Six Day War," *Journal of Israeli History* 28, no. 2 (2009): 159.

8 Galia Oz was born in 1964, and so her childhood was undoubtedly marked by the two wars. Arguably, the difficult emotions that drove Amos Oz to the *Siah Lohamim* project in the wake of 1967 also shaped his fatherhood, but this is not addressed in the book.

9 Oz, *Davar she-mithapes le-ahava*, 99.

10 Tamar Merin, *Spoiling the Stories: The Rise of Israeli Women's Fiction* (Evanston: Northwestern University Press, 2016).

11 Adi Ophir, "Identity of the Victims and the Victims of Identity: A Critique of Zionist Ideology for a Post-Zionist Age," *Mapping Jewish Identities*, ed. Laurence Jay Silberstein (New York: New York University Press, 2000), 174–200.

12 Ibid., 180.

13 Ibid., 182.

14 The term "present-absentee" is taken from the Israeli definition of Palestinians who were displaced during the 1948 War but remained within the territory of the State of Israel. The State definition of "present-absentees" in these cases allowed the State to appropriate Palestinian property. In turn, the term also came to be used metaphorically to refer to the elusive presence-absence of the Palestinian Other in Israeli culture.

15 Edward Said, "Zionism from the Standpoint of Its Victims," *Social Text* 1 (Winter 1979): 7–58; Ella Shohat, "Sephardim in Israel: Zionism from the Standpoint of Its Jewish Victims," *Social Text* 19/20 (Autumn 1988): 1–35.

16 Oz, *Davar she-mithapes le-ahava*, 13.

17 The political ramifications of the Zionist homemaking are interrogated in Hagar Kotef, *The Colonizing Self or, Home and Homelessness in Israel/Palestine* (Durham: Duke University Press, 2020).

18 On the connection between the kibbutz conceptions of childhood and parenthood and the abduction affair, see Meira Weiss, "Hi hayta rak bat shnatayim va-hetsi: hem natnu la lamut levad be-veit holim," *Haaretz* (Jerusalem), 10 September 2020. https://www.haaretz.co.il/magazine/the-edge/.premium-1.9143005. On the affair in the context of nationalist preception of children as national resource, see Esther Hertzog, "Hafk'aat horut: mi-parashat yaldey teyman ve-'ad hayom," in *Yeladim she ha-Lev: hebetim hadashim be-heker parashat yaldey teyman*, ed. Tova Gamliel and Nathan Shifriss (Tel Aviv: Restling, 2019), 163–208.

INDEX

Page numbers in *italics* denote
illustrations.

Abramowitch, S.J. (Mendele Moycher
Sfoyrim), 37, 161n74
Agnon, Shmuel Yosef, 69
Aharonowitz, Yosef, 69–70
Akhmatova, Anna, 116
Aley Kinneret / Of Kinneret
(Shoshana Bluwstein), 95–7
Ali Teyman / Ascend Yemen
(Shoshana Bluwstein), 95–6
Alliance Israélite Universelle, 158n5
Almog, Oz, 116, 178n6
Alper, Rivka, 20, 121–7
Alterman, Nathan, 140
American Zion Commonwealth, 67
Amram Association, 177n125
Anderson, Benedict, 77
androcentrism, 4, 7, 11, 17, 70
angel of the home, 42, 96, 120–1, 129
Anzaldúa, Gloria, 108
Arabs, 59, 62–4, 68–9, 73, 76, 107–8,
136, 154n14, 162n90, 167n34, 169n58.
See also colonization; Palestine;
Palestinians
Ashkenazim (European Jews):
"civilizing mission in Palestine,"
43; and division of land, 153n3;
and gender, 6; hegemony of, 4,
148; languages of, 37, 41–2; and
Mizrahim, 6, 19–20, 23, 82, 104,
109–14; and modesty, 129–30, 135;
old *yishuv*, 41, 104, 162n93; and
Sephardim, 41–2, 44, 48, 104; and
Yemenites, 89–90, 99–101, 109–14

"Ashkenazi stories" (Pohatchevsky),
84, 90
avoda (worship or labour), 63, 85,
169n61
Avrahami, Yael, 12–14

Bahar, Shirly, 50
*Ba-kfar u-ba-'avodah / In the Village
and at Work* (Pohatchevsky), 61
Barabish, Rivka-Leah, 27
Baron, Dvora, 69–77; about, 7–8, 10,
19–20, 78, 156n40
—WORKS: "Bney Kedar" / "The
Kedarites," 74, 77; *The Exiles*, 130–5;
"Metamorphoses" / "*Gilgulim*,"
72–3; "*Shavririm*" / "Fragments", 74;
"Since Last Night" / "*Me-emesh*,"
181n54; "For the Time Being" /
"*Le-'et 'ata*," 181n54
Bat-Miryam, Yocheved/Yokheved,
116, 137–8
Bedouin communities, 55–7, 154n14,
167n34, 167n35
Behar, Moshe, 62, 84
beit midrash (Jewish schoolhouse), 69
Bekhar, Fortuna, 40, 43, 163n103
Bekhar, Nissim, 23, 41, 43, 158n5,
163n103
Belkind, Israel, 167n34
Ben-Avi, Itamar, 23, 26, 34–7, 41–2
Ben-Gurion, Immanuel, 124–5
Ben-Yair, Michael, 107
Ben-Yehuda, Dvora: about, 18, 26–32,
34–6, 41–4; death of, 22, 44–8;
death of her children, 47; education
of, 160n51; and Eliezer, 163n101;

as feminine mother-martyr, 149;
and the *Sephardim,* 40–4, 128,
162n88, 163n103; *"takanat bnot
yerushalayim,"* 43
Ben-Yehuda, Eliezer (was Perlman,
Elianoff): about, 18, 31, 56, 160n45;
and Dvora, 45, 163n101, 164n125;
and his son, 36; in jail, 47–8;
"Mitsvot she-tsrikhot kavana" /
"commands in need of intention,"
47–8; quarrel with Frumkin, 158n2;
as reporter for *Havatzelet,* 158n2;
and the *Sephardim,* 41
Ben-Yehuda, Hemda, 56–61; about,
8, 10, 26, 160n51; activism of, 24;
and Dvora, 26–7, 31, 46, 159n19,
164n125; and Eliezer, 32, 46, 55; in
phallic authorial position, 60, 68;
relationship with Hebrew, 36; as
universalist, 78; writings of, 18–19,
24–5
—WORKS: "The Farm of the
Rekhabites" / *"Havat Bney
Reikhav,"* 56–61; *Kokho shel goral
/ The Power of Fate,* 26, 159n19,
164n125; "The Sin of Ephraim" /
"Hataat Ephraim," 56–7
Ben-Yisrael, Goni Kasuto, 90
Berlovitz, Yaffa/Yaffah, 62, 87, 90,
155n23
Bhabha, Homi, 50
Biale, David, 6, 37–8
Bialik, Hayim Nahman, 183n98
Bialik, Mosad, 137
birds, feeding of, 84, 173n18
"Bi-vdidut" / "In Solitude"
(Pohatchevsky), 62–4, 67
Bi-Yehudah ha- ḥadashah / In New
Judea (Pohatchevsky), 61
Bluwstein, Rachel (Rachel the Poet):
about, 20, 95, 117, 137–8, 179n12;
"On the Mark of Our Times,"
118–19; "The Mother's Bosom of

Memories," 7; "To My Land" / *"el
artzi,"* 115–17, 138, 143–4; "Phrase" /
"niv," 118–19; "A Visit" / *"Bikur,"* 122
Bluwstein, Shoshana: about, 20,
95–101, 106–7, 111–12; *Aley Kinneret
/ Of Kinneret,* 95–7; *Ali Teyman /
Ascend Yemen,* 95–6
"Bney Kedar" / "The Kedarites"
(Baron), 74, 77
Bossel, Hayuta, 7
Boyarin, Daniel, 6, 77–8, 102–3
Boyarin, Jonathan, 77–8
Brenner, Yosef Hayim, 69
bride price system, 181n58
British Mandate in Palestine, 11,
182n79
Brontë, Charlotte, 11

Capitol insurrection, US, 145
caregiving, 17, 19–20, 43, 80–114, 149.
See also contact zone
Central Zionist Archive, Jerusalem,
159n19
chess, 30–1
Chicago Dyke March, 156n36
Children of the Ghetto (Zangvil),
102, 106
Chodorow, Nancy, 17
Christianity, 77–8
civilizing mission, 20, 43–4, 68, 81, 103,
162n90
Cixous, Hélène, 17
clothing: gender differences, 13, 41;
jewellery, 43, 120, 128–30, 163n105,
181n58; of Sephardic community,
41, 163n105
Cohen, Efrat, 86, 92
Cohen, Hillel, 48
Cohen, Tova, 27, 120
colonialism, 4, 11, 17, 54–61, 165n16,
169n58
colonization: decolonization, 10,
71; of "empty land," 67, 138; and

femininity, 50, 65; of Palestine, 21; of Shimon Ha-tzadik, Jerusalem, 107. *See also* Palestinians: displacement of

"Commands in need of intention" / *"Mitsvot she-tsrikhot kavana"* (Eliezer Ben-Yehuda), 47–8

contact zone, 19–20, 81–3, 108–14. *See also* caregiving

COVID-19, 145

Crenshaw, Kimberlé, 9

daughter of Israel, 15, 120, 129, 130–5

Davar (newspaper), 141, 164n2, 179n12

"Davar she-mithapes le-ahava" / "A Thing Masquerading as Love" (Galia Oz), 145–6

Dayan, Dvora, 53, 165n14

Dayan, Moshe, 53–4, 165n14

Dayan, Zohar (Zorik), 53

decolonization, 10, 71

Dictionary of Old and New Hebrew (Ben-Yehuda), 24

diminishment: intersectionality of, 128–30; metaphors of, 116; and nationalization of women's bodies, 130–1; of Palestinian land, 138, 143; poetics of, 121–7

"Does Feminism Have Room for Zionists" (Shire), 10

Dvar ha-po'eelet (women worker's publication), 49, 53, 113, 164n2

Dyer, Richard, 17, 133

Dyke March, Chicago, 156n36

Egypt, 131–2, 136, 142, 181n56

Ein Harod (kibbutz), *14*

Eisen, Arnold, 63

elders/senior citizens *(vatikim)*, 3

Elianoff, Eliezer. *See* Ben-Yehuda, Eliezer (was Perlman, Elianoff)

enslaved people, 76

Epstein, Itzhak/Yitzhak, 68, 83

Etsel / Irgun, 135, 182n79

Evelina de Rothschild School, 40, 43–4, 128

exile, 70–1, 74, 90, 97–8, 106, 149

The Exiles, 130–5

Exodus (film, Preminger), 135

exogamy, 55, 59

Eyal, Gil, 162n90

family, 23, 30–1

"The Farm of the Rekhabites" / *"Havat Bney Reikhav"* (Hemda Ben-Yehuda), 56–61

Feldman, Yael, 146

fellahin (Palestinians peasants), 68, 167n34

Fellman, Jack, 41

femininity: and colonization, 50; as diminished, 139; *nashiyut versus ishut*, 39–40; and nationalism, 20, 69, 129; particularism and power, 77–9; production of, 12–18; and smallness, 116; and Zionism, 116, 129–30, 135, 144. *See also* caregiving

feminism: maternal, 102; and missing children, 110; and non-violent politics, 49–50; and Orthodox Judaism, 103; poststructuralist, 17; white, 11, 17; and Zionism, 10, 103

feminist scholarship, 8, 25, 81, 155n29

Fifty Years of the Women Workers' Movement (Mimon), 128

First Wave *(Aliyah Rishona)*, 85, 168n49, 169n58

Fisher, Shmuel, 140, 143

"Flora Sporto" (Pohatchevsky), 62, 83–4

"For the Time Being" / *"Le-'et 'ata"* (Baron), 181n54

Founding Mothers, Stepsisters (Miron), 7

French feminist scholarship, 8, 155n29

Frishman, David, 37–8

Frumkin, Yisrael-Dov, 22–3, 120, 158n2

"G'alut" / "Exile" (Pohatchevsky), 90–1

Gamliel, Tova, 109

Gan, Alon, 147

gender issues: Ashkenazim, 6; clothing, gender differences, 13; colonial gender dynamics, 59; division of labour, 23; and ethnicity, 128–35; and Hebrew Labor, 63; LGBTQ issues, 156n36; modesty, 41, 116, 118, 124–5, 135; myth of equality, 5; national (men's) *versus* private (women's) stories, 116–17, 178n5; and non-violent politics, 49–50; Oedipal system, 5–7, 25, 146, 147; property ownership, 68; silence of women, 18, 24, 28, 35, 41–2, 155n23; use of Hebrew, 37–9; women's bodies and sanctity of Jerusalem, 129; women's history, 18–21; working the Land/ hospitality, 64; Zionist immigration as male phenomenon, 71. *See also* femininity; feminism; masculinity; patriarchy; women

gilgul mehilot (Rabbinic myth), 74

Gilligan, Carol, 17

giving, 82, 83–5

Gluzman, Michael, 116, 119

Golan Heights, 3–4

Goldberg, Lea, 138, 183n98

Gold-Zehavi, Henrik (Tzvi), 140, 143

Gonen, Jay Y., 5

Gordon, Aharon David, 68, 117, 170n83, 179n10

Gordon, Yehuda Leib, 39

Guilat, Yael, 130

Hadassah, 110, 156n40

Hagai (journalist), 140–1

Hagar and Ishmael story, 74–7

Ha-hagana, 182n79

Ha-herut (newspaper), 62

Ha-isha (journal), 101, 104, 121

halokh ve-tafof (mincing steps), 118–20

halutzim (pioneers), 3, 67, 153n2

Ha-Melitz (journal), 65

Ha-mitnahalim ba-har / *Settlers in the Mountain* (Alper), 124–7

Hanukkah, 47–8

Hashkafa (newspaper), 56–7

Ha-shomer (para-military organization), 56, 166n26

Haskalah movement, 27, 29, 37, 159n25

Hassidic community, 158n2

Ha-tzadik, Shimon, 104–8

Hatzofe (newspaper), 141–2

Ha-tzvi (journal), 47–8, 158n2

Havatzelet (journal), 120, 158n2

Haworth, Jill, 136

Hazleton, Lesley, 5–6

Hebrew, language: *Dictionary of Old and New Hebrew* (Ben-Yehuda), 24; gendered use of, 36–9; Hemda's relationship to, 36; journals, 158n2, 65; as the national language, 6; New Jewish/Hebrew Man, 103, 116; pronunciations, 40–1; public *versus* private usage, 37–9; revival of, 23–4, 28, 34, 158n10; and silencing of women, 41–2. *See also* Modern Hebrew Culture; New Jewish/ Hebrew Man

Hebrew Labor, 63, 97, 169n58, 169n61, 179n10

Hebrew Women's Organization, 104

Hebrew Women's Union for Equal Rights, 156n40

Hertz, Henrietta, 31

Hess, Tamar, 7

He Walked through the Fields (Shamir), 147

Hirsch, Dafna, 103

Holocaust, 136, 148–9

hooks, bell, 60

Hyman, Paula, 27, 159n33

IDF (Israel Defense Forces), 153n1, 153n3
Imagined Communities (Anderson), 77
incest, 6, 28–9
indigeneity: Bedouin communities, 55–7, 154n14, 167n34, 167n35; displacement of indigenous inhabitants, 53–4; ethnic groups, 48; indigenous peoples, 55, 63, 68, 126; lands/space, 14, 19, 42, 54, 61, 73, 138; other, 17, 19, 54, 71, 74, 144. *See also* Palestinians
infant centers, 108–14
"In Solitude" (Pohatchevsky), 84
insurrection, January, US, 145
intersectionality, 9–12, 81, 137. *See also* gender issues: and ethnicity
Intifada (Palestinian uprising), 142
Irgun / Etsel, 135, 182n79
Irigaray, Luce, 17
Ishmael and Hagar story, 74–7
Israel, 8, 25, 53, 153n3, 155n29, 167n35, 184n108. *See also* colonization; Hebrew Labor; Land; Palestine
Israeli Women (Hazleton), 5

Jaffa: The Orange Clockwork (Sivan), 13
Jahsi, Shlomo, 112–13
Jane Eyre (Brontë), 11
January insurrection, US, 145
Jay, Nancy, 47
Jelen, Sheila, 70, 71, 130
Jerusalem Group, 167n34
jewellery, 43, 119–20, 128–30, 163n105, 181n58
Jewish Colonization Association (JCA), 57, 166n31
Jonas, Dvora (later Dvora Ben-Yehuda). *See* Ben-Yehuda, Dvora
Jonas, Paula (later Hemda Ben-Yehuda). *See* Ben-Yehuda, Hemda
Jonas, Shlomo Naftali-Hertz, 22, 27, 47–8
"A Journey in the Land" (Pohatchevsky), 66

Kabbani, Rana, 60
Kaplan, Marion, 101
Kati'ee, N'aama, 110
Katzanelson, Rachel, 20, 63–4, 121–3, 169n64
kavash (occupy or pave), 184n108
Ke-'esev ha-sade / Like the Grass of the Field (Tabib), 92
Khazoom, Aziza, 11
kibbutzim: about, 153n2; baby homes, 150–1; Ein Harod, *14*; Kinneret commune, 100; and land divisions, 153n3; removal of rocks for creation of, 3–4; Shamir, 4; Upper Galilee kibbutz, 3, 153n3
kibush (Israeli occupation), 184n108
Kinneret commune, 95, 100
Kleinstein, Rami, 142–3
Klorman, Bat-Zion Eraqi, 86–7
Klorman, Eraqi, 86, 92
Kokho shel goral / Power of Fate (Hemda Ben-Yehuda), 26, 159n19, 164n125
korban (victim or sacrifice), 145–52
Kotef, Hagar, 4
Kristeva, Julia, 17
kvutzah (Zionist cooperative settlement), 51

Labor Zionism, 122, 168n49
Land: appropriation of, 57, 72–3, 100; connection to, 51, 91; description of, 53, 138; "empty land," 67, 70–1, 138; as feminine, 138, 143; "To My Land" / "el artzi" (Rachel Bluwstein), 115–17, 138, 143–4; "Our Tiny Land" (Fisher and Gold-Zehavi), 138–44; ownership of, 33, 48, 66–7; and Palestinians/Arabs, 54, 169n58
Lang, Joseph, 48
language, feminization of, 37–40. *See also* Hebrew, language
Lebanon War, 142
Lermontov, Mikhail, 35

Lewis, Reina, 60
Lowe, Lisa, 60
Lubin, Orly, 62, 70, 89, 130
Luntz, Avraham Moshe, 120

Makabim, 47–8
Mandatory Palestine, 11, 182n79
masculinity: attributes of, 63, 78, 116, 118, 127; and clothing, 41; and colonization, 19; femininity as negation of, 16; the "fist" of and women's writing, 49, 54, 69; and Hebrew, 40; and power, 67–8; quests of, 59; and the symbolic family, 5–7; threatened by New Jewish Women, 38; values of, 48, 65, 71; and Western colonizer, 60; and Zionism and psychoanalysis, 102–3
maskilim, 27, 33, 37–40, 120–1, 159n25, 161n65
Meir, Golda, 5
Meisel, Hannah, 95, 175n61
melitzot, 39
Melman, Billie, 60
"Memories of One of the Women-Farmers in Eretz-Yisrael" (Pohatchevsky), 65
Mendelson, Dorothea (later Schlegel), 31
Merin, Tamar, 8, 148
"Metamorphoses" / "Gilgulim" (Baron), 72–3
metaphors of diminishment. See diminishment
#MeToo movement, 150
Meyuhas, Yosef, 41
Mimon, Ada, 128
mincing steps (halokh ve-tafof), 119–20
Minor Detail (Shibli), 60–1
Miron, Dan, 7, 116, 123, 130, 137, 178n5
missing children, 108–14
"Mitsvot she-tsrikhot kavana" / "commands in need of intention" (Eliezer Ben-Yehuda), 47–8

Mizrahim: about, 153n3, 154n14; and Ashkenazim, 6, 19–20, 82, 104, 109–14; missing children of, 109, 177n125; Pohatchevsky's story, 62; and women's bodies, 128
Modern Hebrew Culture, 16, 25, 39–41, 62, 71, 74, 116, 120
modesty, 41, 116, 118, 124–5, 135
Mohanty, Chandra Talpade, 51
molekh, 46–7
Moscow, Russia, 31, 32
moshavot (Zionist settlements/colonies), 168n49
motherhood, 7, 8, 76–7, 81–2, 92–3, 155n29
"The Mother's Bosom of Memories" (Bluwstein), 7
"mothers of Israeli feminism," 4, 7, 9–12. See also Baron, Dvora; Ben-Yehuda, Hemda; Pohatchevsky, Nehama; Thon, Hannah
"My Homeland" / "Mekhora sheli" (Goldberg), 138, 183n98

Nadav, Tzvi, 55–6
Naftali-Hertz, Shlomo. See Jonas, Shlomo Naftali-Hertz
nationalism, 30–5; and femininity, 20, 69, 129; and motherhood, 76–7; national-patriarchal home, 18, 23, 30, 37–40, 46, 124; of Palestine, 118; path to, 36; and Pohatchevsky, 62, 68, 78, 149; as threat, 48; and women's bodies, 130–1
national metonym, 116, 178n5
New Jewish/Hebrew Man, 103, 116
New Jewish Woman, 28, 30–5, 38, 56, 59, 159n33
Newman, Paul, 136
Nini, Yehuda, 90, 99
nurses, 111–13

Oedipal system, 5–7, 25, 146, 147
old yishuv, 41, 104, 162n93

"On the Mark of Our Times" (Rachel Bluwstein), 118–19

"On the Roads / ba-drakhim" (Yaffe), 49, 51–2

"Operation Jephthah," 153n3

Ophir, Adi, 148–9

Orchan, Nurit, 26

Orthodox Judaism and feminism, 103

Other/Otherness: annihilation of, 77; Arabs as, 64, 67; East as, 33–4, 59–60; feminine as, 17, 39, 143–4; feminized Jewish diaspora, 71–2; indigenous people as, 17, 19, 54, 71–2, 74, 144; Jewish people as, 64, 102; making of, 30; motherhood as, 82, 96; non-Ashkenazi Jew as, 84; Palestinians as, 185n14; women as, 6, 78–9, 117; Yemenite Jews as, 85, 94; yiddishe momme as, 8

Ottoman, 11, 47–8, 131, 162n97, 181n56

"Our Tiny Land" / "Artzenu haktantonet" (Fisher and Gold-Zehavi), 138–44

Oz, Amos, 145–52

Oz, Galia, 145–52, 184n8

Palestine: British Mandate in, 11, 182n79; decolonization of, 10; Intifada (Palestinian uprising), 142; Israeli occupation of, 144, 184n108; nationalism of, 118. See also Land

Palestinians: about, 154n14; deaths of in 2014, 77; displacement of, 4, 53–4, 67, 76, 107; fellahin, 68, 167n34; peasants (the fellahin), 68, 167n34; as present-absentees, 150, 185n14

Palmah, 3, 153n1

Pappenheim, Bertha, 102–3

Paris, France, 31

particularism, 77–9

Parush, Iris, 28, 35, 37–8, 156n43, 159n33

patriarchy: Baron on, 70; national-patriarchal home, 18, 23, 30, 37–40, 46, 124; and Zionism, 10, 62, 90

peace agreement (1979), 142

"Pe'amim" / "Steps" (Pohatchevsky), 92

Penn, Alexander, 138

Perlman, Eliezer. See Ben-Yehuda, Eliezer (was Perlman, Elianoff)

"Phrase" / "niv" (Rachel Bluwstein), 118–19

Pickman, Dora, photos of, 13

Pinsker, Shachar, 70, 71, 72–4, 130, 171n101

pioneers (halutzim), 3, 67, 153n2

Pirpurey Mahapekha / Quivers of Revolution (Alper), 123

Pohatchevsky, Nehama, 61–9, 85–94; about, 10, 19–20; as employer, 92–3; as mother, 8, 92–3; and nationalism, 62, 68, 78, 149; substitution of women, 93; and the threshold of giving, 83–5; women's association, 80

—works: "Ashkenazi stories," 90; Ba-kfar u-ba-'avodah / In the Village and at Work, 61; "Bi-vdidut" / "In Solitude," 62–4, 67; Bi-Yehudah ha-ḥadashah / In New Judea, 61; "Flora Sporto," 62, 83–4; "G'alut" / "Exile," 90–1; "A Journey in the Land," 66; "Memories of One of the Women-Farmers in Eretz-Yisrael," 65; "Pe'amim" / "Steps," 92; "Regret," 83; "Ruma," 88–90; "Sheelot gluyot / Well Known Questions," 68–9; "In Solitude," 84; "Yemenite stories," 85, 87–9

Pohatchevsky, Yhiel Michal, 61

Politically Koreet (feminist blog), 12

postcolonialism, 14, 19, 50

Power of Fate / Kokho shel goral (Hemda Ben-Yehuda), 26, 159n19, 164n25

Pratt, Mary Louise, 19–20, 50, 81

Preminger, Otto, 135–7

present-absentees, 150, 185n14

Protective Edge (military operation), 77

psychoanalysis, 5–7
"pure patient poverty," 122

Raab, Esther, 116, 138
Rabbinic myth *(gilgul mehilot)*, 74
Rabinowitz, Yaakov, 121, 123–4
Rachel the Poet (Bluwstein, Rachel).
    See Bluwstein, Rachel
Rattok, Lily, 7, 8
Raz-Krakotzkin, Amnon, 70–1
"Regret" (Pohatchevsky), 83
"Retelling the Story of O" (Boyarin),
    102–3
Rishon Le-Zion (Zionist settlement),
    61, 80, 86, 168n49
rituals, 41–2, 46–7
Roded, Batya, 139, 143
Rosh ha-'ayin transit camp, 109
Rothschild, Baron de, 57, 166n31
Rubin, Gayle, 26
"Ruma" (Pohatchevsky), 88–90
Russia, 27, 31, 32, 116, 160n45

sabra, 116, 135, 178n6
sacrifice, 44–8, 55–6, 135–7, 145–52
Said, Edward, 60
Sanbar, Elias, 13–14
Sarsour, Linda, 10
Schwartz, Yigaal, 146, 148
Second Wave *(Aliyah Shniya)*, 85,
    165n14, 169n58
Sedgwick, Eve Kosofsky, 30
Seidman, Naomi, 6, 24, 28, 34, 70, 130,
    163n101
Sephardim, 40–4, 104, 162n88, 162n90,
    162n93. See also *Mizrahim*
Sfoyrim, Mendele Moycher (also
    S.M. Abramowitch), 37, 161n74
Shabbat Shira, 84, 173n18
Shamir (kibbutz), 4
Shamir, Moshe, 147
Shapira, Anita, 118

Shavririm / Fragments (Baron), 74
"Sheelah na'alamah" / "Hidden
    Question" (Epstein), 68
"Sheelot gluyot" / "Well Known
    Questions" (Pohatchevsky), 68–9
Sheikh Jarrah (Shimon Ha-tzadik),
    Jerusalem, 104–8, 177n121
Shibli, Adania, 60–1
Shifriss, Nathan, 109
Shilo, Margalit, 128, 163n105
Shirav, Pnina, 7, 8
Shire, Emily, 10
shooting and weeping soldier, 147
Showalter, Ellaine, 46
shtetl, 70–2, 130–1
Siah Lohamim / The Seventh Day
    (Amos Oz, editor), 147, 184n8
Sibahi, Saadya, 174n32
silence of women, 18, 24, 28, 35, 41–2,
    155n23
Sinai Desert, 142
"Since Last Night" / *"Me-emesh"*
    (Baron), 181n54
"The Sin of Ephraim" / *"Hataat
    Ephraim"* (Hemda Ben-Yehuda),
    56–7
sisterhood, 25, 49. *See also* Ben-
    Yehuda, Dvora; Ben-Yehuda,
    Hemda
Sivan, Eyal, 13
Six Day War, 53, 165n14
slaves. *See* enslaved people
Smilansky, Moshe, 68
Smolenskin, Peretz, 48
soldier, shooting and weeping, 147
Spivak, Gayatri Chakravorty, 11, 59
Star of David, 156n36
Stav, Shira, 28–9
Stoler, Ann Laura, 17
substitution of women, 26–30, 44–6,
    56, 58, 64, 93, 137
Szobel, Ilana, 50

Tabib, Mordechai, 92

"*takanat bnot yerushalayim*" (Dvora Ben-Yehuda), 43

Tale of Love and Darkness (Amos Oz), 146–7

tarbush, 41, 162n97

Teharlev, Yoram, 142

"A Thing Masquerading as Love" / "Davar she-mithapes le-ahava" (Galia Oz), 145–6

Third Wave, 169n58

Thon, Hannah, 10, 20, 101–8

Three Guineas (Woolf), 49–50

Tomer, V., 124

"To My Land" / "*el artzi*" (Rachel Bluwstein), 115–17, 138, 143–4

Torah, student of *(yeshiva bocher)*, 29, 161n65

"The Traffic in Women" (Rubin), 26

Tsamir, Hamutal, 16, 46–7

Tzarum, Sarah, 110–11

United States, 8, 67, 145, 155n29

Upper Galilee kibbutz, 3, 153n3

vatikim (elders/senior citizens), 3

"A Visit" / "*Bikur*" (Rachel Bluwstein), 122

Wallach, Yona, 116

Ware, Vron, 17

wars: Lebanon War, 142; War of 1948, 4, 53, 76, 107, 153n3; War of 1967, 141; War on Gaza (2014), 151; World War I, 131, 181n56. *See also* Six Day War

white femininity, 134, 135–8

white feminism, 11, 17, 20–1

whiteness, 20–1, 132–4, 136, 137

"A Wider Bridge" (LGBTQ rights group), 156n36

Williams, Delores S., 76

Wolfe, Patrick, 55, 63

women: agents of civilizing mission, 20, 43–4, 81, 103, 162n90; characteristics of, 49–54; daughter of Israel, 15, 120, 129, 130–5; *Dvar ha-po'eelet* (women worker's publication), 49, 53, 113, 164n2; education of Jewish women, 28, 32, 160n51; Hebrew Women's Organization, 104; Hebrew Women's Union for Equal Rights, 156n40; *Israeli Women* (Hazleton), 5; as Land, 16, 60–1, 138, 139, 143; "Memories of One of the Women-Farmers in Eretz-Yisrael" (Pohatchevsky), 65; mental health of, 45–6; motherhood, 7, 8, 76–7, 81–2, 92–3, 155n29; "mothers of Israeli feminism," 4, 7, 9–12; New Jewish Woman, 28, 30–5, 38, 56, 59, 159n33; as Other/Otherness, 6, 78–9, 117; silence of, 18, 24, 28, 35, 41–2, 155n23; substitution of, 26–30, 44–6, 56, 58, 64, 93, 137; Women Workers' Movement, 49, 128, 156n40, 164n2; working, 13, 14; writing, 54, 78, 123. *See also* Baron, Dvora; Ben-Yehuda, Hemda; caregiving; femininity; feminism; gender issues; Pohatchevsky, Nehama

Woolf, Virginia, 49–50

Working Mothers Organization, 110, 156n40

World War I, 131, 181n56

Yaffe, Tova, 49, 51–2, 53–4

Yavneeli, Shmuel, 85–6

Yavneeli Aliyah, 85, 97

Yegenoglu, Maida, 60

Yemenite Community: and Shoshana Bluwstein, 95–101; disappearance of babies/children, 109–13, 177n125; expulsion from Kinnaret, 100–1; girl at agricultural school, 129; immigration to Palestine, 85–7; namelessness of, 98–9; and Pohatchevsky, 85–94

"Yemenite stories" (Pohatchevsky),
85, 87–9
Yeshayahu, Yisrael, 93–4
yeshiva bocher (student of the Torah),
29, 161n65
yiddishe momme, 8
Yiftahel, Oren, 139, 143
yishuv, 41, 61, 104, 162n93
"*Yom Geshem*" / "Rainy Day" (Thon),
104–5
"Your Wonders are not Yet Gone"
(Kleinstein), 142–3

Zakai, Orian: grandparents, 3–4,
12–15; at protest, 77; readings of
missing children, 113–14; trip to
Israel (2014), 151

Zangvil, Israel, 102, 106
Zelda (poet), 125
Zerubavel, Yael, 57
Zierler, Wendy, 70, 71, 130
Zionism: and femininity, 18–19, 116,
129–30, 135, 144; and feminism, 10,
12, 103; Labor Movement, 117, 153n2,
164n2, 179n10; Labor Zionism, 122,
168n49; and patriarchy, 62, 90;
settlements/colonies *(moshavot),*
168n49; Thon on, 101–8; waves of
immigration, 71, 85, 165n14, 168n49,
169n58. *See also* colonialism;
colonization; kibbutzim; Land;
nationalism; sacrifice